D1756758

The Agamben Dictionary

Edited by Alex Murray and Jessica Whyte

Edinburgh University Press

© editorial matter and organisation, Alex Murray and Jessica Whyte 2011
© in the individual contributions is retained by the authors

Edinburgh University Press Ltd
22 George Square, Edinburgh

www.euppublishing.com

Typeset in 11/13 Ehrhardt
by Servis Filmsetting Ltd, Stockport, Cheshire, and
printed and bound in Great Britain by
CPI Antony Rowe, Chippenham and Eastbourne

A CIP record for this book is available from the British Library

ISBN 978 0 7486 4059 1 (hardback)
ISBN 978 0 7486 4058 4 (paperback)

The right of the contributors
to be identified as author of this work
has been asserted in accordance with
the Copyright, Designs and Patents Act 1988.

Contents

Introduction: The Lexicographer and the Sovereign

Alex Murray and Jessica Whyte

Every revolutionary theory has had to invent its own terms, to destroy the dominant sense of other terms and establish new meanings in the "world of meanings" corresponding to the new embryonic reality needing to be liberated from the dominant trash heap. The same reasons that prevent our adversaries (the masters of the Dictionary) from definitively fixing language enable us to assert alternative positions that negate existing meanings. But we already know that these same reasons also prevent us from proclaiming any definitive certitudes. A definition is always open, never definitive. Ours have a historical value, they are applicable during a specific period, linked to a specific historical practice.

Mustapha Kayati 2004, "Captive Words
(Preface to a Situationist Dictionary)"

In 1755, Samuel Johnson published *A Dictionary of the English Language*, which would remain the authoritative account of the language for a century to come. Johnson's ambitious and arduous endeavour culminated in the dictionary's 43,500 definitions – Johnson's contribution to rectifying what he saw as the dire state of a language beset by impurity and disorder. In a letter to his patron, Lord Chesterfield, Johnson outlined the struggle he saw facing him, the possible futility of which he acknowledged, in distinctly biopolitical terms. "It remains", he wrote, "that we retard what we cannot repel, that we palliate what we cannot cure" (Wells 1973: 43). Michel Foucault, who used the term "biopolitics" to refer to the process by which the state becomes directly concerned with the biological life of its population, has drawn attention to the analogies between the work of medicine and that of political government that have characterised the Western political tradition since the time of the Greeks (Foucault 2002: 250). The prince, Foucault notes, must cure the ills of the city, while the doctor must give his opinion on the ills of the soul as well as the body. In Johnson's letter, the role of the lexicographer is brought into alignment with that of the doctor and the prince, as the malaise affecting the English language, in his view, is the same one that threatens the constitution. "Life", his letter continues, "may be lengthened by care, though death cannot be ultimately defeated: tongues, like governments, have a natural tendency to degeneration; we have long preserved our constitution, let us make some struggles for our language" (Wells 1973: 43). Sovereign, doctor, lexicographer – merely an analogy, perhaps, but one which, none the less, suggests that the attempt to impose order on language is not without its (bio)political significance.

Lord Chesterfield turned out not to be the benevolent patron for whom Johnson had hoped, and the latter took his revenge by exercising his prerogatives as a lexicographer: a "patron", according to Johnson's dictionary, is "a wretch who supports with indolence and is paid with flattery" (Winchester 1998: 85). None the less, the Lord shared Johnson's view that the English language was in dire need of purity and order, and, like Johnson, he relied on an analogy with statecraft to formulate the action required. The language, he bemoaned, had been neglected, and required an authority capable of "purifying, and finally fixing" it (Wells 1973: 39). In a 1754 letter to Johnson, Chesterfield wrote that the toleration and adoption of foreign words had gone far enough. "Good order and authority", he stressed, "are now necessary" (Wells 1973: 39–40). Yet, he asked, where shall we find them, and, moreover, secure the requisite obedience? Here, Chesterfield reveals the authoritarian thrust of his desires for purification and fixedness. "We must have recourse to the old Roman expedient in times of confusion and choose a dictator," he wrote (Wells 1973: 39–40). Chesterfield's letter must have convinced Johnson that the support he was desperately seeking would be forthcoming.

Upon this principle [the former wrote], I give my vote for Mr. Johnson to fill that great and arduous post. And I hereby declare, that I make a total surrender of all my rights and privileges in the English language, as a free-born British subject to the said Mr Johnson during the term of his dictatorship. (Wells 1973: 39–40)

This image of the lexicographer as sovereign, committed to restoring the order that would enable the application of a fixed body of rules, provokes us to question the wisdom of devoting a dictionary to the thought of a thinker whose work has consistently challenged the desire for purity, order and authority that underpinned the first significant attempt to systematise the English language. Giorgio Agamben is perhaps best known in the English-speaking world for his *Homo Sacer: Sovereign Power and Bare Life*, in which he traces the relation between these two figures, sovereign power and bare life, in part through a critical engagement with the German legal thinker Carl Schmitt's justification of dictatorial powers. For Schmitt, any system of legal norms presupposes a normal situation in order to apply, and any legal order rests on the non-legal production of social order. Like him, Agamben is well aware that "there is no norm that is applicable to chaos" (Schmitt 2005: 13). Unlike the conservative jurist, however, his thought does not aim at the restoration of an order to which the law could be reapplied, but, rather, gestures to the possibility of breaking free of the relation that binds all life to the legal order. Thus, his project is directly at odds with the decidedly Schmittian thrust of the early period of the development of the English dictionary, which was conceived as a project that could restore order to what Johnson called "a chaotic dialect of heterogeneous phrases" (Wells 1973: 42). Once order was produced from chaos, various thinkers of the time hoped, it might then be possible to apply a norm, or a set of rules, that would no longer be subject to major change. Jonathan Swift provided a succinct elaboration of this position in his "Proposal for Correcting, Improving, and Ascertaining the English Tongue". Once the language is sufficiently purified and "refined to a certain standard", he wrote, "perhaps there might be Ways to fix it forever" (Wells 1973: 35). Like Chesterfield, Swift saw the need for an authority capable of securing such order. In his case, however, it would not be a single dictator but an academy, modelled on the Académie Française, which would decide on proposed changes, allowing only those that were additive, and refusing to allow changes to existing words.

Along with the dream of fixing the language was a conservative commitment to the preservation of the tradition. The stability and order of the language, Swift averred, would assure the immortality of its writers, whose works would otherwise be destined to disappear, and ensure the continuity of tradition.

I have always disapproved that false Compliment to Princes, that the most lasting Monument they can have, is the Hearts of their Subjects [he writes]. It is indeed their greatest present Felicity to reign in their Subjects Hearts; but these are too perishable to preserve their Memories, which can only be done by the Pens of able and faithful Historians. And I take it to be Your Lordship's Duty, as *Prime Minister*, to give order for inspecting our Language, and rendring it fit to record the History of so great and good a Princess. (Swift, 1712)

The dream of a fixed language and a stable tradition that would be overseen by authorities capable of deciding on its limits could not be further from Agamben's own project. The stabilisation of tradition, he warns, deprives us of access not only to the past, but also to our own present. Tradition, he notes, following Martin Heidegger, covers over our access to that which it transmits. In Heidegger's words, "it takes what has come down to us and delivers it over to self-evidence" and thereby blocks our access to the sources of our concepts (*ST*, 88). "Criticism", Agamben writes, "concerns not just the ancient character of the past but above all the mode in which the past has been constructed into a tradition" (*ST*, 87). In contrast to the conservative orientation to tradition, Agamben seeks to confront the freezing of tradition in order to return anew to its sources. None the less, he shares Swift's view that the question of tradition is inescapably bound to that of language. "Every reflection on tradition", he writes, "must begin with the assertion that before transmitting anything else, human beings must first of all transmit language to themselves" (*Po*, 104). Much of what is passed on in tradition is, Agamben suggests, not accessible at the level of consciousness. In every moment of perception, something is simultaneously remembered and forgotten, leaving us to transmit a weight of unlived experience that exerts its force in the present. It is this unlived, in his view, that "gives shape and consistency to the fabric of psychic personality and historical tradition and ensures their continuity and consistency" (*ST*, 101). Language bears the traces of this unlived experience, and, in every act of transmission, it continues to exert a powerful hold on us: "whoever has not had an experience", Agamben writes, "always has the same experience" (*ST*, 102).

   For those who would seek to fix and stabilise language and tradition, and cover over other possibilities that once lurked within them, the dictionary seems to offer a privileged means with which to do so. Agamben notes that "dictionaries, in particular those that lack a historical–etymological character", tend to "divide and separate a term into a variety of meanings" (*WA*, 8). And yet, he suggests that this fragmentation "nevertheless, generally corresponds to the historical development and articulation of a unique original meaning that we should not lose sight of" (*WA*, 8). The role of the dictionary is not only to foster the forgetting of the historical development of the terms it contains, however. The dictionary also holds the potential to bring to light the historical context in which a term emerged, and the various uses that have been made of it. Concepts, as Walter J. Ong notes, "have a way of carrying their etymologies with them forever" (Ong 2004: 12). Agamben's thought is permeated by the conviction that, in Ong's words, "the elements out of which a term is originally built usually, and probably always linger somehow in subsequent meanings, perhaps obscurely but often powerfully and irreducibly" (Ong 2004: 12). By tracing the etymology of a term, it is possible to uncover the possibilities of other forms of thought and life, and reactivate the energies of the past in the present. Agamben's project, however, is not simply to bring to consciousness that which has been repressed in the course of tradition. Relying on the ambivalence of the French term *conjurer*, which means both to dispel and to evoke, Agamben suggests that a philosophical archaeology must conjure up, or evoke, an absent origin, in order to dispel it. Its orientation towards the past is thus "a matter of conjuring up its phantasm, through meticulous genealogical inquiry, in order to work on it, deconstruct it, and detail it to the point where it gradually erodes, losing its originary status" (*ST*, 102).

This dictionary seeks to trace both the philosophical lineages of Agamben's terms, and their development throughout his *œuvre*. In doing so, it aims not to stabilise terms by referring them back to the authority of an origin, but to reveal new possibilities for use deposited and forgotten beneath their currently accepted meanings. This will allow the reader to return to the sources, both the philosophical sources on the basis of which Agamben builds his conceptual edifice, and the places in his work in which a term first appears. This will enable a greater appreciation of the philosophical constellation in which his thought arose, as well an understanding of both the continuities and discontinuities between his thought and that of his philosophical sources. Such an approach has not been without its adherents in the history of English lexicography, which has been characterised by the conflict between the desire for fixedness and purification that typified Johnson's project, and the contrary view that a dictionary should testify to the historical transformations of words by providing a record of their use. In an 1857 speech that was to inspire the first stages of the production of the dictionary that would ultimately surpass the authority of Johnson's, the *Oxford English Dictionary* (*OED*), Richard Chenevix Trench argued that a dictionary was simply an inventory of a language – it could not, and should not, attempt to fix it and provide a guide to proper use. The method of providing illustrative quotations, beginning with the earliest one available, by which the *OED* proceeded, testifies to this concern with the historical transformations in the semantic field of a term.

To examine the history of the attempts to produce a dictionary of the English language, however, is to reveal that what is transformed throughout history is not simply the usage of terms but the very possibility of historical knowledge itself. In "Philosophical Archaeology", Agamben situates his own approach to tradition within the archaeological paradigm made famous by Foucault in *The Archaeology of Knowledge*. Archaeology, he writes, "cannot confront tradition without deconstructing the paradigms, techniques, and practices through which tradition regulates the forms of transmission, conditions access to sources, and in the final analysis determines the very status of the knowing subject" (*ST*, 89). Faced with the project of a dictionary, we should therefore ask not only about the status of the definitions it provides but also about the very conception of knowledge that underlies its categorisations.

In the preface to *The Order of Things*, where the term archaeology made "its discreet – though decisive – first appearance", Foucault recounts a well-known passage from Jorge Luis Borges about "a 'certain Chinese encyclopedia' in which it is written that 'animals are divided into: (a) belonging to the Emperor, (b) embalmed, (c) tame, (d) sucking pigs, (e) sirens, (f) fabulous, (g) stray dogs, (h) included in the present classification, (i) frenzied, (j) innumerable, (k) drawn with a very fine camelhair brush, (l) *et cetera*, (m) having just broken the water pitcher, (n) that from a long way off look like flies'" (Foucault 2002: xv1) What is revealed in the wonder that greets such a taxonomy, Foucault writes, is the limit of our own system of thought, "the stark impossibility of thinking *that*" (Foucault 2002: xv). It is with such wonder that we may approach some of the earliest attempts to produce dictionaries of the English language. In the second half of the sixteenth century, soon after the word "dictionary" had appeared for the first time in the title of a lexicographic work, John Withal produced a "Shorte Dictionaire for Yonge Begynner's" in English and Latin. The dictionary, which was far from a comprehensive record of the words in either language, was not arranged alphabetically, but by subjects, each of which was then subdivided in the following way: "the names of Byrdes, Byrdes of the water, Byrdes about the house, as cockes, hennes, etc."

Faced with this taxonomy, the individual terms of which are familiar to us, we should recall that, for Foucault, it was not Borges's evocation of fabulous creatures, sirens and animals drawn with a fine camelhair brush that confounds our thinking. Rather, it is the system of categorisation itself that appears to us today as impossible, reflecting as it does a "historical a priori" which conditions the very possibility of knowledge in any given period (Foucault 2002: xxvi). Archaeology, Agamben notes, is an investigation into this "historical a priori", which underlies our attempts to provide categorisations and taxonomies capable of bringing order to chaos. Faced with the early dictionary projects, we find ourselves confronted not only with meanings that have disappeared but also with a mode of thought that no longer seems possible to us. This dictionary may well itself be a source of puzzlement or wonder at some point in the future. And yet, its limits are not clear to us, as editors, nor, presumably, to those who wrote its many entries. As Heidegger remarked to students who questioned him at the conclusion of his Le Thor seminar, which Agamben attended: "You can see my limit – I can't" (*IP*, 59). This dictionary draws on the insights of scholars who have each, in their own ways, made important contributions both to understanding Agamben's thought, and to developing it in new directions. The limits of this dictionary, we feel, therefore coincide with the limits of Agamben scholarship as it currently exists. It is our hope that putting this dictionary into the world will enable those who can see its limits to transcend them.

TERMINOLOGY

If the project of any dictionary is a fraught one, its tensions take on a new importance when faced with the attempt to define the terms used by a philosopher for whom terminology itself has a decisive philosophical character. In his recently published essay, "What is an Apparatus?", Agamben notes the importance of terminological questions in philosophy. "As a philosopher for whom I have the greatest respect once said," he writes, in an oblique reference to Gilles Deleuze, "terminology is the poetic moment of thought" (*WA*, 1). In an unpublished lecture on "Movement", he extends this by stating that terminology is poetic "because productive" (Agamben 2005). The productive moment of thought is both poetical and terminological in the sense that language is always to find itself as part of a conflict, an endless battle to imbue words with meaning. Agamben's work has, arguably, been characterised by an extended series of exercises in the poetics of terminology. His etymological method is concerned with this contested terrain of terminology. More than simply revealing the constitution of meaning, however, terminology is poetical in the sense that repeated attention to it can draw attention to the enigmatic nature of language itself.

Yet, at the same moment as he praises terminology, Agamben suggests that this does not mean that a philosopher must define his central terms. Herein lies the paradox of the terminological: it is the grounds on which productive (in the Foucauldian sense) meaning is produced, but also where poetical qualities are drawn out. The power of philosophical thought, arguably, lies in its rejection of the terminologically concrete, the universal and perpetual attribution of meaning, and instead in redefining the very idea of what constitutes the terminologically "productive". Perhaps it might be valuable to look at the word "terminology" itself, which was first used in the late eighteenth century – the period in which Johnson was compiling his great dictionary. Terminology is generally understood to be not just any use of language but the doctrine or study of a system of scientific terms. It was widely used in etymological studies of the Latin language, as well as natural philosophy. The word itself is made up of *terminus*, which in medieval Latin designated a boundary stone, as well as *logos*, of course, meaning simultaneously discourse, word and reason. Yet *terminus* itself comes from the boundary stones that were engraved with the figure of Terminus, the Ancient Roman god who protected boundaries. The *gromaticus* (Roman land surveyor), Siculus Flaccus, in his *De Condicionibus Agrorum*, outlines how the remains of sacrificial offerings would be buried under the *terminus* when it was constructed. The *terminus* was an attempt to create division through the imposition of a limit for the purposes of constructing boundaries, and that boundary was anchored through the animistic figure of Terminus as the sacred object that was used to order the profane space of property. The figure of the *gromaticus* is central to Agamben's essay, "K", on Kafka, in which he traces the means by which the land surveyor in Roman law attempted to divide and separate the space of the fortress from the space of the village through the use of the *kardo*. Ultimately K. from *The Castle* works against the authority invested in the power of the law that seeks to divide, in the same way that Agamben will advocate an "absolute profanation" of the division between the sacred and the profane. As he states in "K":

K. is the "new land surveyor" who renders inoperative the boundaries and borders that separate (and keep bound together) the high and the low, the castle and the village, the temple and the house, the divine and the human. (2008a: 26)

The rendering inoperative of power that we see in "K" resembles the ways in which Agamben understands terminology. If terminology, as the terminus of language, works to impose order and division, so Agamben will work, as we discuss below, to call into question the imposition of meaning and reveal instead the potentiality of language freed from a terminological imperative.

Mustapha Kayati's words, which provide the epigraph to this introduction, draw attention to the fact that any attempt to create new political realities requires a struggle in language, one that is capable of creating new terms, and wrenching old ones from the dominant meanings that have been imposed on them. In *State of Exception*, Agamben engages in one such struggle over the political stakes of terminology. Noting that "terminological choices can never be neutral" (*SE*, 4), he challenges the terms used by Anglo-Saxon and European jurisprudence to refer to the suspension of the legal order – amongst them "martial law", "emergency powers", "emergency decrees" and "state of siege" (*SE*, 4). In each of these, he sees a terminological fiction that attempt to render law's suspension as simply another legal mechanism. This is clearest in the Anglo-Saxon use of the term "martial law", which he identifies as an attempt to cast law's suspension as simply another form of law (*SE*, 4). In the term "full powers" – favoured, amongst others, by the Swedish jurist Herbert Tingsten, for whom it referred to laws which granted the executive "an exceptionally broad regulatory power", extending to the power to abrogate existing laws by means of decree (*SE*, 7) – Agamben sees recourse to the myth of the *plenitudo potestatis*, with its implication of an originary fullness, prior to the separation of powers between the legislature, the judiciary and the executive (*SE*, 6). Despite this willingness to engage in terminological disputes, however, his primary concern is not with the re-signification of terms, nor with the attempt to free language from its dominant meanings in order to allow it to mean otherwise, in the service of another politics or another history. His concern with tradition and transmission is not a matter of "writing the history of the excluded and defeated, which would be completely homogeneous with the history of the victors, as the common and tedious paradigm of the history of the subaltern classes would have it" (*ST*, 98). Rather, his philosophy of language is oriented to the limits of language, to what must be presupposed in every dispute over terminology – the pure fact of language, the existence of speaking beings.

Jean-Claude Milner has formulated this limit that linguistics cannot cross with the term *factum loquendi*, which refers not to the existence of *languages*, which can be distinguished from non-language, grouped into classes and determined according to their properties, but to the very fact that speaking beings exist, that there is language. Linguistics, Milner suggests, does not have language as its object. Rather, "language is its axiom" (*Po*, 66). If linguistics must presuppose the simple fact of language, Agamben's concern, in contrast, is to expose it. The *factum loquendi*, prior to division into particular languages, escapes the terrain of linguistics, and can only be the object of philosophy. It is not, Milner writes, that it is impossible to consider the conditions of possibility of the fact of language: "It is only that then one finds a question of the following kind: 'Why is there language rather than no language at all?' And this is a properly metaphysical question" (*Po*, 66). All of Agamben's work on language is animated by this succinctly posed question. His concern is less with the properties of language, than with the existence of speaking beings. Thus, while he is at times prepared to engage in terminological disputes, his decisive contribution is to a philosophy of language that concerns itself with that for which there is no name. But what could such a thing be? "The linguistic term", Milner answers, "has no proper name" (*Po*, 71). The only thing for which we have no name is, in fact, not a thing, but the name itself.

It is from this anonymity of the linguistic term that Agamben draws the possibility both of a consideration of pure existence, and, in political terms, of a form of community without predicates, and so without identity, inclusion or exclusion. "Pure existence", he writes, "corresponds to the pure existence of language, and to contemplate one is to contemplate the other" (*Po*, 74). Both the construction of grammars and the constitution of political communities, however, have obscured our access to the pure existence that underlies them. Just as linguistics has presupposed the pure fact of language, politics, he argues, has presupposed the *factum pluralitatis,* the pure fact that people form communities. Modern political discourse, he argues, has been defined by the attempt to unify language and people, using one obscure concept in order to shed light on another. In the process, the unification of language and people transforms these two "contingent and indefinite cultural entities" into natural organisms, subject to necessary laws (*ME,* 66). In opposition to the presupposition of language that underlies the construction of every grammar and the pre-supposition of community that underlies the attempt to anchor a people to a state, he advances the striking claim that we "do not have, in fact, the slightest idea of what either a people or a language is" (*ME,* 65). In contrast to the desire for purity that characterised the thought of early advocates of the dictionary, he highlights the essential instability and unnatural-ness of every language. It was this instability that earned the ire of Swift, who blamed the Civil War for the "infusion of enthusiastic jargon" that the English language had received (Baugh and Cable 1993: 253). For Agamben, however, Swift's fight was lost from the beginning; "all peoples are gangs and *coquilles,*" he writes – referring to of the "gangs of evildo-ers" and dangerous classes who, it was said, spoke a secret language, which distinguished them and identified them to each other; "all languages are jargons and argot" (*ME,* 67). Any language is necessarily impure and disordered, and no great dictator will succeed in fixing it forever.

This is not to suggest, however, that language is simply anarchic, able to be used in any way a sovereign individual subject sees fit. Language, Agamben suggests, is an apparatus (*dispositif*) – a term he borrows from Foucault, and extends to refer to anything that has the capacity to capture, order and model the gestures, the behaviours, the discourses or the opin-ions of living beings. Foucault's work has accustomed us to thinking of schools, hospitals, the panopticon or disciplines as apparatuses. For Agamben, however, language is "perhaps the most ancient of apparatuses – one in which thousands and thousands of years ago a primate inadvert-ently let himself be captured, probably without realising the consequences that he was about to face" (*WA,* 14). If language is an apparatus, if it serves to order the behaviours of living beings and capture the *factum loquendi* in the net of *logos,* does this mean that we should look outside it for some ineffable meaning or sense? And if this were so, should not the very project of a dictionary be dispensed with, in favour of a mystical experience unmediated by linguistic capture?

Nothing could be further from the truth. Agamben's work consistently contests the idea of an unsayable or ineffable meaning to which language has no access. In an early book, he notes that, if every thought must take a position on the limits of language, then his own has attempted to think this limit "in a direction other than that of the vulgarly ineffable" (*IH,* 4).

To posit an unsayable sense inaccessible to language takes us, he suggests, into the realm of experience of the mystics. In his more recent *Remnants of Auschwitz*, he returns to this theme, and recounts an anecdote that provides a warning against the attempt to oppose linguistic capture with an ineffable sense; several years earlier, he tells us, after writing an article on the concentration camps for a French newspaper, he was accused in a letter to the editor of having sought to ruin the "unique and unsayable character of Auschwitz" (*RA*, 31). "I have often asked myself", he writes, "what the author of the letter could have had in mind" (*RA*, 31). No doubt, he writes, Auschwitz is unique. "But why unsayable? Why confer on Auschwitz the prestige of the mystical?" (*RA*, 32). Here, he offers a powerful argument against the view that silence is the only possible response to the horror of the exterminations. After all, he writes – with reference to John Chrysostom's 386 AD text "On the Incomprehensible Nature of God", which defended the thesis that God's being was inaccessible to human language and understanding – to designate something as "unsayable" or "unspeakable" is the best way to glorify it. We, in contrast, he writes, should stare into the face of the unsayable, and refuse to presuppose the existence of an ineffable meaning or experience divorced from language.

The consequence of the position Agamben borrows from Milner, according to which the only thing for which there are no names is the name, is that our only access to pure being is through an experience of language. We have seen that it is only through an experience of the *factum loquendi* that philosophy can approach being without properties; that "[o]nly the *experience of the pure existence of language allows thought to consider the pure existence of the world*" (*Po*, 68). Our only access to the pure existence of language, however, is through particular languages. This dictionary is in the English language, and its terms are translations, from Agamben's Italian and, at times, from the various languages of those whose thought imbues his own. The task that has faced the authors of its many entries is not without parallels to that which Walter Benjamin laid down for the translator: "to release in his own language that pure language which is under the spell of another, to liberate the language imprisoned in a work in his re-creation of that work".

In contrast to both the desire for purification and order, and the recourse to a mystical experience outside language, Agamben proposes what he terms an *experimentum linguae* – an experience, or experiment, in language – that would bring the *factum loquendi* to light. "Languages", he argues, are "the jargons that hide the pure existence of language, just as peoples are the more or less successful masks of the *factum pluralitas*. This is why our task cannot possibly be either the construction of these jargons into grammars or the recodification of peoples into state identities" (*ME*, 69). Rather, it is the common experience of being in language, which he takes as the basis for a completely new form of community that would break the "nexus between the existence of language, grammar, people, and state" (*ME*, 70). Such an experience is both political and ethical – indeed, it provides Agamben with his key insights in regard to both politics and ethics. This becomes clear in *Infancy and History*, in his response to Ludwig Wittgenstein's suggestion that the "correct expression in language for the miracle of the existence of the world, albeit as expressing nothing *within* language, is the existence of language itself" (*IH*, 10). If this is so, Agamben asks, then what is the correct expression for the existence of language? "The only possible answer to this question", he writes, "is: human life as *ethos*, as ethical way" (*IH*, 11).

The *experimentum linguae* is an ethico-political experiment because language, Agamben stresses, is the *common* itself. "The first outcome of the *experimentum linguae*," he writes, "therefore, is a radical revision of the very idea of Community" (*IH*, 10). To bring to light the potentiality of language that is presupposed by every particular language, he suggests, opens the possibility of a form of community without presuppositions – that is, without identity, and so without exclusion. The forms of such an experiment – which would break the nexus between language, people and state, allowing the pure fact of language to come to light – are manifold and diverse (*ME*, 70). Amongst the examples he proposes are "the reactivation of a jargon, *trobar clus* [of the Provençal troubadours], pure language, minoritarian practice of a grammatical language, and so on" (*ME*, 70). Given all we have said about the authoritarian aspirations underlying the early English dictionary, can the production of a dictionary really contribute to such an experiment? Or is it destined to cover over the potentiality of language and undermine the attempt to interrupt the suture of language to the state? The history of the *OED* would suggest that we should be cautious in assuming that a dictionary cannot itself be an experiment in language. Richard Chenevix Trench, whose influence on the shape of the early stages of the *OED* we have already discussed, is credited with the insight that a project as ambitious as recording and defining all the words in the English language must rely on the combined action of many. This insight was fundamental to the eventual project, which owes its existence to thousands of often anonymous volunteers, who contributed six million slips, each of which provided a quotation that would help illustrate the sense of a word (Winchester 1998: 99). Far from Lord Chesterfield's vision of a dictator who would impose order on the language by suspending the rights of all those who used it, and Swift's desire for a conservative authority that could ensure the stability of the language, the *OED* was the product of a general intellect, an anonymous community without identity or borders.

This dictionary, too, was produced by many people. Not only have we relied on numerous contributors to write the entries, but also the very possibility of writing such a dictionary draws on the thought and the writings of numerous others – not only Agamben himself, and all those who have contributed to the growing body of scholarship on his work, but all those thinkers whose proper names appear within this dictionary, many of whom will never know of the posthumous life of their own thought. Both authors and readers of the dictionary enter into a general intellect that exceeds them: "the author and the reader enter into a relation with the works only on the condition that they remain unexpressed in it" (*Pr*, 71). What remains unexpressed, however, is not for that reason insignificant, and we cannot underestimate the work and the thought that this dictionary's contributors have put into its many entries. Just as Agamben's account of tradition is oriented towards that which is unlived in each moment, his account of the author rests on the view that it is "that which is unexpressed in each expressive act" that makes expression possible. By combining the work of various authors, each of whom subsist in this text, this dictionary aims to highlight that which escapes the individual expression of any one person, drawing attention to the potentiality of language itself.

TERMINUS

The dictionary, this dictionary also, is an apparatus of capture. But, as Agamben notes, "writing (any writing, not only the writing of the chancellors of the archive of infamy) is an apparatus too, and the history of human beings is perhaps nothing other than the hand to hand confrontation with the apparatuses they have produced – above all with language" (*Pr*, 72). If all writing is an apparatus, then the task with which we are faced is not to do away with writing but to experiment with it in order to free the common from its capture by state identities, canons and academic disciplines. Such an experiment is not counter-posed to the project of the dictionary. The very idea of a language freed from the imperative to mean can only exist in relation to a dominant language. Without the dictionary there could be no *argot*, no *patois*, no minor languages and no resistance. The *experimentum linguae* is a form of linguistic disruption, but it does not seek to do without language – or without the dictionary. The "pure" language of which Agamben often writes will not be ushered in through the absence of the dictionary but through a deactivation of the power invested in the dictionary itself. The definitions provided here are endlessly contestable and unstable, each an act of recreation rather than a slavish definition for all time. A dictionary of concepts and proper names will inevitably provide a new piece of work, not to be read as conforming to Agamben's own use of the word but as developing each word anew. So in that sense we offer it to our readers as a partial document, a text unfinished – in fact, never able to be finished. Any dictionary only makes sense as a series of fragments, definitions that work to both support and disrupt each other. So in that way a dictionary, it could be argued, is the best possible means of presenting Agamben's thought. Whereas an "introduction" is designed to provide structure and control, the dictionary only works by looking at the relation between terms and encouraging its reader to discover, or create, new relations and new forms of relation. For that reason it is a task for the reader to put this dictionary to a new use, to read across and against, to see in this apparatus of capture an invitation to a critical and creative reading that would bring to light the common that underlies every linguistic act. If the dictionary is indeed an apparatus, then our task, as Agamben suggests, is "the liberation of that which remains captured and separated by means of apparatuses" (*WA*, 17). It is this task that we hope will be taken up by this dictionary's readers.

A

ABANDONMENT/BAN

Claudio Minca

These are key terms in Agamben's political philosophy, found most importantly in *Homo Sacer*. Abandonment names the position of *homo sacer*, who finds himself in a position both inside and outside the law, at the mercy of the sovereign exception. If the exception constitutes the fundamental realm of sovereign power, it is also "the originary structure in which **law** refers to life and includes it in itself by suspending it". The relation of exception is therefore a relation of ban (*HS*, 28).

Agamben's theorisation of the ban is inspired by Jean-Luc **Nancy**, who presents the ban as the capacity of the law "to maintain itself in its own privation", to apply by "(dis)applying" itself:

He who has been banned is not, in fact, simply set outside the law and made indifferent to it but is rather *abandoned* by it, that is, exposed and threatened on the threshold in which life and the law, outside and inside, become indistinguishable. It is literally not possible to say whether the one who has been banned is outside or inside the juridical order. (*HS*, 28–9)

A key **example** that Agamben adopts to describe the structure of the ban is that of the *lupo mannaro* (werewolf), a figure that inhabits a zone of indistinction between the human and the feral: "a man who is transformed into a wolf and a wolf who is transformed into a man"; a *bandito* ("he who is banned"). The life of the *lupo mannaro* constitutes a **threshold** of indistinction and a passage between the animal and the human, between *physis* and *nomos*, between exclusion and inclusion, for the werewolf is, at its origin, the figure of the man banned by his community (*HS*, 105).

This *"lupificazione dell'uomo"* (the "becoming-wolf" of man) and the concurrent "humanization" of the wolf, Agamben insists, is "at every moment possible" within the state of exception: "the transformation into a werewolf corresponds perfectly to the state of exception, during which [. . .] time the city is dissolved and men [*sic*] enter into a zone in which they are no longer distinct from beasts" (*HS*, 107; also *O*, 62). It is this very threshold, which is neither natural life nor social life but, rather, bare – or "sacred" – life that is "the always present and always operative presupposition of sovereignty" (*HS*, 107).

The *homo sacer*, for Agamben (*HS*, 83), represents the "originary figure of life taken into the sovereign ban", as far as "the sovereign sphere is the sphere in which it is permitted to kill without committing homicide and without celebrating a sacrifice, and *la vita sacra* (sacred life) – that is, life that may be killed but not sacrificed – is the life that has been captured in this sphere". The werewolf, however, does not only metaphorically inhabit this threshold of indistinction; he inhabits and moves through real spaces, spaces which, with his very presence and his hybrid nature, he contributes to creating. It is here that Agamben identifies the "survival of the state of nature at the very heart of the State" (*HS*, 106), but it is also here that the confine between bare life and a life worth living is rendered explicit – by means of an originary and thus hidden spatialisation.

Agamben's affirmation that the original juridico-political relation is the ban does not only regard the *formal* structure of sovereignty; it is also *substantial*, for "what the ban holds together is precisely bare life and sovereign power" (*HS*, 109). We must therefore abandon, he argues, all conceptualisations of the original political act as a "contract", which imagine the transition from the "state of nature" to the state as occurring in a definitive and distinct fashion. There exists, rather, a much more complex "zone of indiscernability between *nomos* and *physis*, in which the State tie, having the form of the ban, is always-already also non-State and pseudo-nature, and in which nature always already appears as *nomos* and the state of exception" (*HS*, 109).

It is precisely this (mis)understanding of the Hobbesian *mythologeme* as a (social) contract – rather than as a ban – that has "condemned [modern] democracy to impotence every time it had to confront the problem of sovereign power", and that has rendered it "constitutionally incapable of truly thinking a politics freed from the form of the State" (109). It is this structure of the ban that "we must learn to recognize in the political relations and public spaces in which we still live" for it represents, still, the sovereign *nomos* that conditions every other norm; it is "the original spatialization that governs and makes possible every localization and every territorialization" (*HS*, 111).

In a regime of exception, sovereign power manifests itself precisely in the faculty of deliberately deciding and enforcing the ban, while making it appear as the logical consequence of the norm. And if, in modernity, "life is increasingly placed at the centre of State politics (which now becomes biopolitics), [. . .] this is possible", for Agamben (*HS*, 111), "only because the relation of the ban has constituted the essential structure of sovereign power from the beginning".

ACTUALITY

Kevin Attell

One of the fundamental goals of Agamben's work is to reconfigure the traditional hierarchy that Western philosophy has established between actuality and **potentiality**. Whereas actuality (or being *as* actuality) has generally been thought of as the ultimate ground and guarantor of all that exists, Agamben programmatically argues that "[i]nstead one must think the existence of potentiality without any relation to Being in the form of actuality" (*HS*, 47). Such a heterodox privileging of potentiality over actuality is also evident in the way Agamben characterises the motivation of his thought as asking not about "what is" but about the meaning of the verb "can" (*potere*) (*Po*, 177), a questioning aimed ultimately at the development of a "new and coherent ontology of potentiality" (*HS*, 44).

To understand Agamben's view of actuality, one must first establish its meaning as the functional counterpart to potentiality in **Aristotle**'s thought. More than simply an absolute "reality" or "being", actuality or the act (*energeia*) is most precisely that into which potentiality (*dunamis*) realises itself; it is the *telos*, goal, or fulfilment of the potentiality to be or do. This being the case, any questioning of actuality must ultimately entail a questioning of the relation between act and potentiality. There are several reasons for which actuality has traditionally been granted primacy in this relation, and Aristotle outlines them in Chapter 8 of Book Theta of the *Metaphysics*. One is that since the specific act is that which defines a given potentiality (in so far as it is a potentiality *for* that act), the act is seen as determining that potentiality, which would otherwise remain unthinkable (see *Met* 1049b 12–17). Another justification for the primacy of actuality is based on the chronological priority of cause and effect. Although acts indeed arise out of the realisation of potentialities, an existing actuality is nevertheless required to bring about the change from potentiality to act; or in other words, something must already be actual to initiate motion or to cause the realisation of a potentiality. Even though he famously polemicises with the Megarians' actualism in Book Theta, Aristotle nevertheless has recourse to a prime and unmoved mover to stop the infinite regress implicit in this oscillation (see *Met* 1049b 17–27). A third reason why actuality is prior to potentiality is that, even though the actual thing (or act) appears to be posterior to the thing in potentiality, it is prior in so far as it possesses the form that is the end or *telos* for the sake of which the thing (or act) in potentiality exists (see *Met* 1050a 4–14).

Arguing, however, against most interpretations of Aristotle (and against the grain of Aristotle's apparent line of argument in Chapter 8 of Book Theta), Agamben emphasises the interdependence of the two, suggesting that "[a]ccording to Aristotle's thought, potentiality precedes actuality and conditions it, but also seems to remain essentially subordinate to it" (*HS*, 44), and that "it is never clear, to a reader freed from the prejudices of tradition, whether Book Theta of the *Metaphysics* in fact gives primacy to actuality or to potentiality" (*HS*, 47). There is, then, for Agamben, a "constitutive ambiguity [in] the Aristotelian theory of *dunamis/energeia*" (HS, 47), which has remained unresolved. This issue is largely addressed in Agamben's analysis of the necessary co-belonging of potentiality and "impotentiality" (*adunamia*) and of the precise way in which potentiality passes over into act (see **potentiality/impotentiality**), but Agamben's argument concerning the primacy of pure potentiality over actuality (and of the human as a "being of pure potentiality" (2007b: 2)) can also be understood by returning to the original Greek word *energeia*.

In the essay, "The Work of Man", Agamben notes that the term *energeia* – which is derived from the word *ergon* ("work"; Italian, *opera*) and literally means "being at work" – "was, in all probability, created by Aristotle, who uses it in functional opposition to *dunamis*" (2007b: 1). In the *Nicomachean Ethics*, Aristotle considers the way certain "works" or activities provide the criteria for defining certain types of beings. For example, the flute player is defined by playing the flute, the sculptor by making sculptures. These arguments would appear to confirm the first and third justifications of the priority of actuality noted above, wherein the *ergon* or act determines the nature of the potentiality or capacity at issue. But problems arise when we ask about the human as such. The sculptor clearly produces *agalmata*, but what is the "work of man" as man? Is there no distinct *ergon* into which the potentiality of the human realises itself? Is man as such *argos* (without work)? This quandary in the Aristotelian argument provides Agamben (via later commentators such as Averroes and Dante) with the basis for his account of the human not as a being endowed with this or that particular potentiality or capability (or any corresponding "work"), but as a being of "pure potentiality". Because of the impossibility of "identifying the *energeia*, the being-at-work of man as man, independently of and beyond the concrete social figures that he can assume" (2007b: 2), Agamben suggests that in Aristotle we can discern "the idea of an *argia*, of an essential inactivity [*inoperosità*] of man" (2007b: 2). In much the same way as the term "impotentiality" does not mean inability or impotence but rather "potentiality-not-to", here too *inoperosità* does not mean mere stasis or inertia, but rather a sort of potentiality not to pass into any *ergon* or *energeia*. *Inoperosità* (translated variously as inactivity, inoperativeness and inoperativity) is the distinctive potentiality of man in so far as what characterises the human as such is not the capacity to do or be this or that, but precisely the capacity *not* to (be or do), a potentiality that exists autonomously and indifferently to any particular actuality or "work". The essential lack of a "work of man" as such disrupts the justification of actuality's primacy, and suggests the human as a being of pure (im)potentiality. Just as actuality must be thought of not merely as the realisation of potentiality but also as the "act of impotentiality" (*Po*, 183), so the *ergon* and *energeia* of man must be thought as the work of inoperativity. This does not mean mere passivity, but rather indicates a kind of "working that in every act realizes its own *shabbat* and in every work is capable of exposing its own inactivity and its own potentiality" (2007b: 10).

ADORNO, THEODOR

Yoni Molad

If intimacy is the mother of enmity, then Agamben's relationship to the thought of Theodor Adorno (1903–1969) is a case in point. Member of the Frankfurt Institute for Social Research and, along with Max Horkheimer, the leading representative of Critical Theory, Adorno raises similar questions to Agamben in his work, which was brought forth by the same sense of urgency. The decisive influence of Walter **Benjamin**, and the commitment to articulating an *"ethica more Auschwitz demonstrata"* (*RA*, 13) are amongst the many things the two thinkers share.

In two specific cases however, Agamben identifies Adorno as a direct philosophical rival. On questions of method and epistemology (*IH*, "The Prince and the Frog"), Agamben attacks Adorno's Hegelian critique of Benjamin's "Dialectics at a Standstill". On the question of **redemption** (*TR*, 35–42), Agamben accuses Adorno of remaining caught in an idealised impotential *ressentiment*. Agamben instead wishes to overcome this through a discussion of the modal category of exigency, leading to a praxis, rather than a contemplation, of redemption. The difference between the two thinkers could be described thus: rather than rescuing the **subject** by way of remembering its loss, as Adorno would have it, Agamben would prefer to lose the subject in order to allow for its redemption.

AESTHETICS

Jason Maxwell

In his first book, *The Man Without Content*, Agamben calls for a "destruction" of aesthetics and a reinstitution of the original function of art within culture. Regarding aesthetics as overly formalistic, he claims that this discipline – inaugurated by Immanuel **Kant** in his third critique – produces a disinterested attitude toward the work of **art** that has effectively severed the once existing connection between artist and audience. The breakdown of this relationship manifests itself in the cool and passionless manner in which modern society responds to art. In the past, Agamben argues, artistic works had the power to produce "divine madness" in the audience, but this deeply emotional response to the work has since "migrated" and now resides solely in the figure of the tortured artist, a figure whose very isolation testifies to his separation from the larger community. Indeed, for Agamben, the alienation of the artist from the culture in which he lives demonstrates that while works of art still occupy a space within modern society, they lack the capacity to shape and direct that society actively like they once did. Agamben asserts that art originally occupied the central role within society, possessing "the wonderful and uncanny power of making being and the world appear, of *producing* them in the work" (*MC*, 34). In other words, rather than serving as one mere facet of culture, art can and should be a force that determines this culture itself. Without this central role within society, the creation of art becomes merely a formal exercise, one devoid of the content that would make it significant to the culture as a whole. In this respect, the artist proves to be the ominous titular figure: "[t]he artist is the man without content, who has no other identity than a perpetual emerging out of the nothingness of expression" (*MC*, 55). The most that the modern artist can do is expose this current separation between artist and audience in the artwork itself, foregrounding its own status as just another circulating **commodity**.

Taking his work on aesthetics in a different (albeit related) direction, Agamben's second book, *Stanzas*, seeks to undermine the distinctions that have long separated **poetry** from philosophy. In the introduction, Agamben claims that the division between the two discourses has assured the insufficiency of both, arguing that "philosophy has failed to elaborate a proper language" while "poetry has developed neither a method nor self-consciousness" (*S*, xvii). Arguing that criticism has long been regarded as a positivistic discipline, which dismisses the poetic from the pursuit of its object, he contends that even modern art itself has renounced its creative dimension in favour of a more critical function. To address this complete failure, Agamben calls for a creative criticism that would join together poetry and philosophy, thereby restoring the "unity of our own fragmented word" (*S*, xvii). Unlike traditional criticism, which always requires an object of inquiry for its existence and perpetuation, Agamben's proposed creative form of criticism would constitute a "science without object" that centres on potentiality itself (*S*, xvi). Several years later, Agamben reiterates many of these same concerns in *Language and Death*. Addressing once again the respective limitations of both poetry and philosophy, he writes that perhaps "only a language in which the pure prose of philosophy would intervene at a certain point to break apart the verse of the poetic word, and in which the verse of poetry would intervene to bend the prose of philosophy into a ring, would be the true human language" (*LD*, 78). For Agamben, creative criticism, combining poetic and philosophical approaches into one discourse, would be the most authentic experience of language.

In *The Idea of Prose*, Agamben enacts in practice what he proposed theoretically in *Stanzas* and *Language and Death*, effectively blending poetry and philosophy to produce a simultaneously creative and critical form of writing. Here, unlike in *The Man Without Content*, where he sustained a clear and coherent book-length argument, Agamben instead proceeds through a series of unrelated fragments that only indirectly reveal their subject matter. More specifically, none of the thirty-three brief chapters in *The Idea of Prose* directly addresses the material referred to in their respective chapter headings. For instance, the chapter entitled "The Idea of Thought" discusses punctuation marks, while "The Idea of Power" examines the relationship between potentiality and pleasure. While the form of the chapter titles alludes to the Platonic Ideas, thereby suggesting the promise of a pure and direct engagement with their topics, the chapters themselves prove anything but direct. Not only do they often fail even to mention the ostensible "idea" of the chapter, but they also deploy a wide range of literary techniques – including the aphorism, the fable and the riddle – not seen in philosophical discourse. Indeed, only through a laborious interpretive process typically reserved for poetic works can the reader make sense of the connection between the chapter heading and the writing that follows. In doing so, Agamben's writing blurs the line between poetry and philosophy, occupying the indistinct region between the two forms.

While Agamben's vocabulary and tactics concerning aesthetics shift significantly over the course of his career, he consistently maintains that a deep affinity exists between art and **potentiality**. From his perspective, humans are essentially poetical beings that continually create and refashion themselves in the world. Poetic language calls attention to itself as language, and this experience of language as language – elsewhere, Agamben refers to this as the *experimentum linguae* – serves as the foundation for grasping humankind's pure potentiality.

ANIMAL

Claire Colebrook

Agamben's arguments regarding animality are articulated extensively in his short book, *The Open*. The title of this book is significant, for it situates the problem of animality in terms not of what a being is (the essence of humans versus the essence or specific biology of animals), but in terms of relations, in terms of how beings comport themselves to a domain of potential actions. Further, animals and humans are not only distinguished by the ways in which they relate to what is not themselves. Rather, the primary mode of relating is towards the "opening" – not what is simply given as present, but what is offered in terms of potential action, creation and world production. Humans, after all, do not simply have an environment but are altered or defined according to the degree to which their world is open. (There is, in modernity, an increasing contraction of such an opening, for the world is less and less presented as a domain of potentiality and creation, and more and more as so much fully actualised life that is simply to be managed.) Enquiring into the precarious distinction between human (or world-creative) and animal (or world-responsive) life will not only enable us to confront the fragile status of human speech and potentiality in late modernity; it will also prompt us to question the degree to which we take the animal's seemingly lesser being as self-evident. Agamben is not, though, seeking to destroy the distinction between humans and animals (as some animal rights philosophers might seek to do), nor asserting the self-evident and rational distinction of the human. Rather, he enquires into what he refers to as the "anthropological machine", or the ways in which man must continually (or ought continually to) create a speaking and world-creative comportment that would divide him from his own animality. We (we humans) are fascinated by animality not because it is radically other, nor because there is a simple continuum or kinship, but because we become the speaking, political, ethical and deciding beings that we are by constantly creating ourselves as not merely or not solely animalistic. There have been historical and aesthetic moments when this labour breaks down: when man's speaking and creative powers fail, or when art's meditation on animality brings us close to that aspect of our being from which we distance ourselves. These thresholds bring us, according to Agamben, into close contact with an animality that is at once intimate and extrinsic, at once the ground of our being and that which we must externalise in order to experience ourselves as human, as speaking political beings.

According to Martin Heidegger, objects such as stones are "worldless", while the animal is "poor in world". Heidegger was, despite being insistent on the distinction between animal being and what he referred to as "*Da-sein*", highly critical of simply accepting the difference of humans as rational animals. Like Agamben after him, Heidegger questions the difference between animals and humans, but not because he wants to assert a continuum. Rather than accept that there are simply two types of being – animals and rational humans – both Heidegger and Agamben theorise the ways in which humans as speaking beings orient themselves towards the world (which is not simply the physical object of planet earth). Both Agamben and Heidegger refer to the work of the biologist Jakob von Uexküll (1864–1944), who argued that an animal's *Umwelt*, or specific world, was defined not by what it represented to itself, but by its mode of life or comportment; a tick's world, for example, is defined by its responses to the smell of skin and blood, which will prompt the tick to act in a certain way. The world is not an object that we encounter and then represent but is given through the potential actions and modes of life that create a milieu or range of perceptions and encounters. Agamben focuses on the animal's quite specific production of its own unique worlds to extend insights and criticisms that are important in his corpus as a whole. First, "man" is not a self-evident distinct being or type of animal whose life can be an object of social-scientific knowledge. Man is produced through the relations and actions he bears in relation to beings that are always given as part of an entire world, never as simple, self-present and distinct objects. Second, man does not simply encounter animals as objects among others within his world. He constantly works to distinguish his own speaking being from animal silence. It is, then, in man's moments of silence – when he is deprived of his potentiality to speak – that he at once draws close to animality at the same time as he offers the opportunity to think human potentiality, precisely when that potentiality is not actualised.

APPARATUS – see *'Dispositif'*

APPROPRIATION

Mathew Abbott

Agamben's understanding of appropriation is exemplary not only of the decisive influence of **Heidegger** on his work, but also of his attempts to think beyond the German philosopher. In the essay "*Se: Hegel's Absolute and Heidegger's *Ereignis*" (*Po*, 116–37), Agamben gives the Hegelian (see **Hegel**) motif of the end of **history** a Heideggerian inflection, such that post-history is understood in terms of what comes after the epochal sending of being. More in line with the late Heidegger of *Time and Being* than the Heidegger of the *Contributions to Philosophy (From Enowning)*, Agamben reads *Ereignis* not just as an event of "enowning" or "making proper", but also in terms of the owning of a poverty, of the **human**'s appropriation of its "ungroundedness" (*Po*, 134). This represents the exhaustion of every figure of destiny, understood as that which consigns the human to its role in the history of being; it is what emerges at the end of history as the end of philosophy. For Agamben, post-historical humanity must find its ethos in this poverty.

In "The Passion of Facticity" (*Po*, 184–204), Agamben reads *Being and Time* as a text in which Heidegger, perhaps despite himself, grants priority to impropriety, or the "essentially falling" character of *Dasein* (quoted in *Po*, 197), as constitutive of **facticity** and indeed of authenticity (*Eigentlichkeit*). Here appropriation emerges as "the apprehension of the improper" (*Po*, 197), or the appropriation of the impossibility of appropriation. In *The Time That Remains*, appropriation gives way to a Pauline/ Marxist (see **Paul** and **Marx**) concept of **use** (*TR*, 34).

ARCHAEOLOGY

Alex Murray

The term archaeology has only recently assumed prominence in Agamben's work with the publication of "Philosophical Archaeology" in *The Signature of All Things: On Method*. Yet arguably archaeology, as it describes a particular method, names the entire practice of Agamben's work. Agamben outlines the temporal and ontological structure of an approach to **history** that sees its goal not as uncovering an **origin** but as transforming the present through an approach to the past. Agamben begins his essay with a discussion of Kant, who mused on the difficulty of a "philosophical history of philosophy", the writing of philosophy that would be able to understand the past but without attempting to impose on it the logic of its own method. This problem is Agamben's: how can one understand the structure of a particular "**apparatus**" of power and capture that functions in the present without simply repeating that logic? The goal, then, is to look not at an origin but at emergence, process rather than essence. Archaeology names a "practice which in any historical investigation has to do not with origins but with the moments of phenomenon's arising and must therefore engage anew the sources and tradition" (*ST*, 89). The result of this practice is that we are not returning to the past but transforming the present by seeing in the past the manifest expressions of both our own present and the numerous presents we have never grasped. This temporal structure is clearly related to the work of Walter **Benjamin** and should be understood in relation to Agamben's work on the messianic (see **messianism**) and inoperativity (see **inoperative**), similar technical terms that name both the method and goal of Agamben's critical project.

ARCHĒ – see 'Origin'

ARENDT, HANNAH

Andrew Schaap

Together with Michel **Foucault**, Hannah Arendt (1906–75) is a key reference point for Agamben in *Homo Sacer*. Agamben takes Arendt's discussion of "The Perplexities of the Rights of Man" in *The Origins of Totalitarianism* as a starting point for his analysis of *homo sacer*. For Arendt, herself a Jewish refugee from Nazi Germany, the plight of stateless people revealed human rights to be illusory since the world "found nothing sacred in the abstract nakedness of being human". Arendt describes the rightlessness experienced by stateless people in terms of the loss of a place in the world in which one's opinions might be significant and one's actions effective. This deprivation corresponds to the two traits in terms of which Aristotle defines what it is to be human: a *polis*-dwelling animal (that could realise its nature only by participating in political community) and a speaking animal (capable of distinguishing between right and wrong by virtue of possessing language). Deprived of access to a public realm and thrown back on the givenness of their mere biological existence, stateless people were barely recognisable as human since they were indistinct, suffering *en masse*.

While Agamben admires Arendt's work, he thinks that "a biopolitical analysis is altogether lacking" in her discussion of the perplexities of the rights of man (*HS*, 4). Indeed, Arendt suggests that when people lose their artificial persona as rights-holders they are left in a state of nature. In contrast, Agamben argues that, rather than simply being reduced to their biological existence, the withdrawal of rights in fact functions to politicise life; it *produces* **bare life**, a subjectivity that is not natural but is a form of life. It was Arendt's insight that the Nazis were only able to send certain categories of people to the death camps by first destroying the "juridical" person and thereby leaving them vulnerable to arbitrary arrest and indefinite detention. However, Agamben radicalises this insight by insisting that the politicisation of natural life is paradigmatic of modern politics.

In *The Human Condition*, Arendt critically describes how life itself has become the object of politics in modernity. However, she differs fundamentally from Agamben in wanting to recuperate from Greek thought an idealised image of the citizen as world-constituting actor, which is the counter-point to her analysis of the world-poor refugee. By participating in action, citizens reveal their singularity and thereby distinguish themselves as human. This existential achievement of action is denatured when politics becomes preoccupied with the concerns of the life process itself; hence, the need to revive a conception of politics as an end in itself, through which humans invest the world with meaning and actualise their freedom. For Agamben, in contrast, there can be "no return from the camps to classical politics" (*HS*, 188). For in the camps the fundamental distinction between *zoē* and the *bios polikos* that Arendt wants to revitalise was "taken from us forever" (*HS*, 188). Rather, political reflection must begin from the clear recognition that our biology and politics are irremediably bound together. We thus need to imagine and invent an entirely new form of politics in which the (in)distinction between *zoē* and *bios* would be overcome.

ARISTOTLE

Daniel McLoughlin

Aristotle (384–322 BC) is, along with **Plato**, the most influential of the Ancient Philosophers. Aristotle entered Plato's Academy at the age of eighteen, and studied there for some two decades, leaving after Plato's death in 347. After a period spent as tutor to Alexander the Great, he went on to found his own school of philosophy in Athens, the Lyceum, in

335. When Alexander died in 323, anti-Macedonian sentiment flared in Athens, and Aristotle was denounced for impiety. Infamously saying, in a reference to the execution of Socrates, that he would "not allow the Athenians to sin against philosophy twice", Aristotle withdrew to his mother's estate in Chalcis, and died a year later of natural causes.

A substantial portion of his work has been lost; only fragments of his popularly published works and dialogues survive, and the treatises that we do have are thought to be notes for his lecture courses. The work that survives covers an incredibly broad array of subjects, including metaphysics, logic, theatre, biology, rhetoric, politics, poetry, ethics and physics. Aristotle's thought was profoundly influential for the Western philosophical tradition, with Thomas Aquinas referring to him simply as "the Philosopher". His manuscripts were received into the medieval West from the Islamic world in the twelfth century, playing a key role in the flowering of intellectual life in this period. His analyses of physics and biology dominated the physical sciences until the development of modern science. Christian scholastic thought was deeply shaped by its engagement with Aristotle, bringing together elements of his metaphysics and Christian theology. Martin **Heidegger**'s *Being and Time* (1927) revived and reworked Aristotle's thought for the twentieth century. Heidegger's *magnum opus* was developed through a confrontation with Aristotle's thought in a series of lecture courses in the years leading up to its publication, the aim of the text being to destroy the metaphysical tradition that had been built upon this Aristotelian foundation, and which, he argued, had foreclosed the question of Being that was still alive in Aristotle.

Aristotle is one of the philosophical figures with whom Agamben most consistently and explicitly engages. He first appears in Agamben's work in *The Man Without Content*, in a discussion of the distinction between *poiesis* and *praxis* that leans heavily on Heidegger. Subsequently, innovative readings of Aristotle provide Agamben with many of his crucial philosophical insights. Central to Agamben's critique of the negativity of Western metaphysics is an engagement with Aristotle's analysis of first substance (*prote ousia*) and its relation to language in "The Thing Itself". According to Aristotle's canonical account of the propositional statement, speech is always "saying something on something". That is, a sentence is always composed of a being about one speaks, which corresponds to first substance (*prote ousia*), and qualitative determinations that one makes abut that entity. First substance is, then, "not said on the basis of a presupposition: it does not have presuppositions, because it is itself the absolute presupposition on which all discourse and knowledge are founded" (*Po*, 37). As the foundation of predication, however, first substance cannot itself be predicated, and remains in itself ineffable. Agamben links this account of linguistic presupposition to his analysis of the **Voice** and his critique of Jacques **Derrida**, arguing that the *gramma* (letter) in Aristotle's *De Interpretatione* corresponds to first substance, as the ineffable foundation of the interpretation of language. In this limited sense, Agamben argues that it is Aristotle who is the founder of Western mysticism, rather than Plato. Where Aristotle presupposes an ineffable thing outside of language, through an esoteric reading of his Seventh Letter, Agamben states that Plato argues that knowledge presupposes only the **communicability** of the thing, its being in language. While this cannot be said in language, neither is it an ungraspable thing outside of language.

Where Agamben's critique of linguistic presupposition plays Aristotle off against an esoteric reading of Plato, two of the most important themes of Agamben's work involve an unorthodox reading of Aristotle himself. The theme of **potentiality** and its relation, actuality, which is central to his ontological and linguistic work of the mid-1980s and shapes his analysis of **sovereignty**, is read out of Book Theta of Aristotle's *Metaphysics*. Aristotle also provides Agamben with his most potent image of the potentiality for thought: the writing tablet on which nothing is yet written (see *IP*, 34; *Po*, 215, 244–51).

When Agamben turns to the problem of politics, Aristotle once again plays a key role. In *Homo Sacer* and later essays, Agamben critically engages the distinction between *zoē* and *bios* in Aristotle's thought, his definition of man as rational animal, and his account of politics as the "work of man". In these analyses, Agamben undermines a reading of Aristotle that attempts to prioritise one term of the opposition, focusing on the mechanism that divides the two terms from one another. Thus, in his analysis of potentiality, Agamben argues that it is impotentiality that makes potentiality possible, by preventing it from passing immediately into actuality. In his analysis of politics in *Homo Sacer* and "The Work of Man", Agamben argues that the originary moment of politics is not *zoē* as a pre-political natural life, but, rather, the conceptual caesurae through which Aristotle divides the continuum of life, separating out *zoē*, as the most general mode in which life appears, as a ground for other, more specific forms of life.

ART

Clare Colebrook

Agamben's conceptualisation of the work of art – and art is always a *work* or outcome of the bringing into being of a positivity and not just a copying or representation of a prior content – is not a theory of **aes-thetics**. On the contrary, it is the modern notion of aesthetic theory or art criticism, and its delimitation of the work of art from other social, political, ethical and productive domains, that Agamben's work seeks to displace. He achieves this overcoming of "the aesthetic" by a philological retrieval of pre-modern experiences of the work of art, and by a consideration of a (possibly ideal) post-aesthetic future. Agamben defines the work of art through two crucial oppositions: between *poiesis* and *techne*, and between **human** and **animal**. These concepts open a thought of art's past and future respectively. First, Agamben argues that there was once a time when *poiesis* and *techne*, or the production of works and formalised practices and skills, were not divorced from a broader and political creation of a shared world of expression. Artists were not privileged subjects whose intentions were uniquely embodied in signed works of art; nor were works of art pure objects in themselves, critically set apart from all interest, social activity and communication. For Agamben, the fact that today we can value an object because it as "a" Warhol, is a sign that art is no longer one expression among others in a collective domain of world formation and political-social dynamism and communication. Duchamp's "ready-mades" both diagnose and intensify the separation of the art object (as *poiesis* or detached form); the ready-made is no longer the putting into production, or creative expression, of the potentiality of a shared world. Rather, it is the act of the artist, and its critical relation to the separateness of the art object, that is now placed into view. What has been lost, then, is art as a practice capable of bringing **potentiality** into **actuality**; this has been replaced by simply taking actual objects and regarding them with a new attitude, the attitude of the spectator. Second, Agamben's critical relation to aesthetics is tied directly to his broader investigation into the (today) seemingly self-evident notion of man as an animal whose politics can be managed by considering his material life. Man is, for Agamben, not simply an actual being whose life can be investigated and then charted in order to make correct political decisions (regarding, say, the health of populations). On the contrary, it is through an ongoing production of himself as a speaking, expressing, poetic and creative being that man distinguishes himself from mere life. All living beings have a world and natural life, but it is through artworks that man constantly brings his natural life before himself, considering himself as never coinciding with, but never fully divorced from, a **bare life** that will never be fully transparent.

B

BAN – see 'Abandonment'

BARE LIFE

Arne De Boever

Agamben's later work, and especially the volumes published in the *Homo Sacer* series, is structured by the distinction between *zoē* and *bios* that Agamben uncovers in Ancient times, specifically in the works of **Aristotle**. To these two terms for life, Agamben adds a third: "bare life". Agamben adapts this term from Walter **Benjamin**'s essay, "Critique of Violence", in which it figures as "the bearer of the link between violence and **law**" (*HS*, 65). In Agamben's analysis, bare life forms a couple with **sovereignty**, whose "fundamental activity" is "the production of bare life" (*HS*, 181). For Agamben, bare life is "the originary political element" (*HS*, 90) (see **politics**).

Bare life – "nuda vita", also translated as "naked life" and "mere life" (*ME*, 143 n1) – is neither *zoē* nor *bios*. Rather, it is **life** that is produced whenever *zoē* is separated from *bios*, and *bios* (ethical (see **ethics**) and political life) calls *zoē* (biological life) into question. Following Michel **Foucault** and Hannah **Arendt**'s analyses, Agamben argues that modern times progressively reduce **human** beings to bare life: a life that is neither human nor **animal**, but rather an inhuman kind of life that exists at the limits of ethical and political categories. The "werewolf" (*HS*, 107), who exists in a zone of **indistinction** between the animal and the human, is one of the examples of bare life that Agamben cites. Agamben's most important figure of bare life is *homo sacer*. In *Remnants of Auschwitz*, he analyses bare life through a study of the *Muselmann*, who, in the words of Jean Améry, "was a staggering corpse, a bundle of physical functions in its last convulsions" (*RA*, 41). Neither human nor animal, neither *zoē* nor *bios*, bare life is a life stripped of its form of life. At the end of *Homo Sacer*, Agamben offers what, as he himself acknowledges, may seem like an "extreme, if not arbitrary" (*HS*, 186) list of other figures of bare life: "the *Flamen Diale*, one of the greatest priests of classical Rome"; "the bandit"; "the Führer in the Third Reich"; "Wilson, the biochemist who decided to make his own body and life into a research and experimentation laboratory"; and the over-comatose person, Karen Quinlan (*HS*, 182–6).

Although bare life is central to Agamben's later, political work, the questions that this work raises are closely related to those about **language** that are central to his earlier writings. In the introduction to *Homo Sacer*, Agamben writes that "[t]he question 'In what way does the living being have language?' corresponds exactly to the question 'In what way does bare life dwell in the *polis*?'" (*HS*, 8). Agamben's later essay, "What Is an Apparatus?", restates this connection when it discusses a primate's entry into language as an example of life's progressive becoming caught up in biopolitical (see **biopolitics**) *dispositifs* (*WA*, 14). This does not mean that Agamben's project goes against language. A future beyond bare life is opened up in his work through the notion of a **form-of-life**, which can be glimpsed in one's **experience** of language as such.

BARTLEBY

Arne De Boever

In 1993, Agamben published an essay entitled "Bartleby, or On **Contingency**", in a book that also included Gilles **Deleuze**'s essay "Bartleby, or The Formula". Both essays are about Herman **Melville**'s "Bartleby, the Scrivener", a story that was originally published in *Putnam's Monthly Magazine* in 1853, and republished as part of *The Piazza Tales* in 1856. The story revolves around a scrivener who takes up a position as a law-copyist in the offices of its anonymous narrator. On his third day in the job, when his employer asks him to compare the copy of a document to its original, Bartleby replies that he "would prefer not to". Bartleby will ultimately give up writing altogether. The disorientation that his formula "I would prefer not to" produces is so radical that his employer will decide to move his offices in order to rid himself of the scrivener.

In his essay, Agamben situates Bartleby in a philosophical constellation of figures who, like Avicenna, are "in full possession of the art of writing in the moment in which [they] do not write" (*Po*, 247). Bartleby thus represents a **potentiality** that, instead of passing into **actuality**, remains a pure potentiality, as theorised by **Aristotle**. Drawing on the messianic (see **messianism**) references in the story, the essay concludes by associating Bartleby's renunciation of copying to an abolition of the **law**. Bartleby becomes a second Messiah, who, unlike Jesus, does not come to save what was, "but to save what was not" (*Po*, 270). In *Homo Sacer*, Bartleby thus comes to carry the promise of a liberation from sovereign (see **sovereignty**) violence (*HS*, 48). Agamben's essay, "Beyond Human Rights", may also include a reference to Bartleby when the position of the refugee is theorised as that of "non-citizens . . . who prefer not to benefit from their own states' protection" (*ME*, 23). Before this, Bartleby had already appeared in the section of *The Coming Community* entitled "Bartleby", where Agamben theorises Bartleby as "the extreme image of this angel that writes nothing but its potentiality to not-write" (*CC*, 37); and in *The Idea of Prose*, in which Bartleby is placed in a literary constellation including Franz **Kafka** and Robert **Walser**, and is theorised as the figure of a potentiality that "does not precede but follow its act, has left it behind forever" (*IP*, 65).

BATAILLE, GEORGES

Alex Murray

Agamben has, usually fleetingly, referred to the work of the French novelist and philosopher George Bataille (1897–1962) on a number of occasions, beginning with *Language and Death* (*LD*, 49) and more decisively in *Homo Sacer* and *The Open*. Here Agamben's discussions of Bataille are always within a presentation of the debate between Bataille and Alexandre **Kojève**. Crucial to that debate, as Agamben presents it, was the broader question of experience or life beyond the Hegelian (see **Hegel**) dialectic. For Bataille, as Agamben suggests, life beyond the dialectic would be "a sovereign and useless form of negativity" (*HS*, 62), whereas for Kojève, the end of history saw the end of the very idea of Man and the struggles that constituted its being. In short, Bataille wants to retain the negative, to think what man will do with the negative once the work of man is over (in Kojève's Marxist-inflected (see **Marx**) reading of Hegel).

In that particular discussion between Bataille and Kojève, the meaning of the term *désœuvrement* (inoperativity; see **inoperative**) is crucial. For Kojève it was being without work after the end of history, and for Bataille the idleness of the negative. For Agamben, however, the term designates the "generic mode of potentiality that is not exhausted in a *transistus de potentia ad actum*" (*HS*, 62). This movement from **potentiality** to **actuality** is one which Agamben rejects. For Agamben, Bataille's thought, as Kojève's, sees the overcoming of work and negativity as the product of the Hegelian dialectic, whereas Agamben sees within the function of the dialectic itself a series of slippages and inconsistencies, and therefore the possibility for rendering the logic and division of separation itself inoperative. Ultimately, Agamben's reading of Bataille is of a thinker concerned with the **sacred** as a negativity that disrupts. Agamben, too, sees the disruptive potentiality of the negative basis of Hegel's dialectic. Yet, unlike Bataille, he sees its overcoming through the transformation of the sacred, rather than through its continuation, and, unlike Kojève, he sees its negativity as essential to its overcoming rather than completion.

BENJAMIN, WALTER

Anton Schütz

Two German-speaking philosophers of the twentieth century, Martin **Heidegger** (1889–1976) and Walter Benjamin (1892–1940), are given Agamben's constant and privileged attention. They make an unequal couple on many counts. For one remarkable contrast, Heidegger's fame had been firmly established in Germany since the publication of *Being and Time* (1927) at least, and after than world-wide, while Benjamin's repeated bids for academic recognition were unsuccessful, and his work reached a wider public only with the publication of his collected works, starting in the 1970s, more than thirty years after his death. Another, even more striking difference is Heidegger's undeniable and passionate, if short-lived, endorsement of National Socialism; in contrast, Benjamin put an end to his life in a moment of despair over the success of an adventurous attempt to escape anti-Jewish persecution, on the French–Spanish border, in 1940.

During his early years Agamben repeatedly encountered Heidegger, whose writing has clearly played a decisive role in his philosophical evolution. Throughout his life he will sympathise with Heidegger's thinking without scruple or hesitation, if always in an alert and often outspokenly critical way. Agamben's connection to Walter Benjamin, on the other hand, has its roots in entirely different, more subtle and yet incomparably more powerful areas. Title and topic of the article, "Benjamin and the Demonic" (*Po*; 291–3), bear witness to both the unfathomable candour and the potency, inexorable yet unspectacular, of the unique influence exerted on Agamben by Benjamin – an influence certainly at odds with the philosophical canon properly speaking, the study of whose tenets from **Aristotle** to **Hegel** constitutes the more structured axis of Agamben's work.

During the 1980s, Agamben, who was at the time participating in the the publication of Walter Benjamin's works in Italian, came across a collection of hitherto unidentified manuscripts in the Bibliothèque Nationale, which he recognised as part of Benjamin's work from his Paris period. Of the numerous and heteroclite topics on which Benjamin had written, Agamben has studied a large percentage. It is tempting to diagnose that the choice of topics in itself constitutes the point of greatest proximity between both authors, yet at least two chapters should be treated in particular. There is, on the one hand, the aesthetic encounter; Agamben is interested in Benjamin's unusual and in-depth knowledge of matters of style and the written form. Second, there are Benjamin's interests in Jewish **messianism**, echoed by Agamben.

In the 1960s and 1970s, the idea that Jewish messianism somehow coincides with a utopian political commitment was prevalent amongst European, and especially German, intellectuals, as a category of description of forms of political *praxis*. Like Benjamin earlier on, Agamben takes issue with this idea. The coming of the Messiah, understood in the way in which Agamben (reading Benjamin reading **Kafka**) approaches it, has nothing to do with the long and ever-postponed arrival of a remedial agent expected at the end of time, or with the hope of righting of what had gone wrong before. The coming of the Messiah is not a programme-generating promise, but an unexpected incident. The attention it nourishes results in a vast literary landscape of reflection and meditation. Unencumbered by the burden of teleology and the duty of final restitution or restoration, the Messiah stands in for an experience and for the claim this experience has on the messianist's mind; the Messiah's coming, far from marking the final point in a pre-established series or programme of historical unfolding, interrupts or brings to a halt the unwinding of history's series of increasingly catastrophical events. The Messiah, it is said, operates unspectacularly. If he changes the world, this will be by means of what Benjamin calls a "small adjustment"; the world's redemption by the Messiah is a world not of a stunningly re-established integrity, but of "integral actuality" (Benjamin 1972–, vol. I, 3: 1238). In other words, the Messiah "will come only when he is no longer necessary, not on the last day but on the day after the last" (Kafka). Agamben's ethico-political stance is located, like Benjamin's and Kafka's own, at the diametrically opposed end of the "progressive", social-democratic, political party-related reading of messianism or messianist utopianism; it is the clear antithesis to any employments of the messianic message that would suppose its "tapping" as a resource or argument or rational utility in the service of political action or management of progress. For both thinkers, what counts infinitely more than any historical realisation is the emphatic uninstrumentalisability of messianism.

This uninstrumentalisability is at stake when we read that messianic time, the time that is left, cannot be understood as the last fragment of time in a sequence of times following each other. It is what is at stake when

Agamben suggests we replace the notion of an *end of time* – the time also known, in the language of theology, as eschatological time – with that of the *time of the end*, and suggests the unplugging of a direct chronological linkage. The opposition is not between messianic time, coming forcibly at the end, and all other times that would precede it. It is between the programmable time of organisation, especially legal organisation, on the one hand, and a time dispossessed of goals, ends and purposes, on the other. "The fallacy lies in changing operational time into a supplementary time added to chronological time, in order to infinitely postpone the end." Following Benjamin's explanations of why the Kingdom of God cannot be understood as the *telos* of the historical dynamics (Benjamin 1972–, vol. 2, I: 203), Agamben shows that what **Paul** calls "the moment right now" (*ho nyn kairos*) refers not to a quantity of a different time yet to come, but to any time whatsoever, if abducted from its status within the chronological *dispositif* (*TR*).

BENVENISTE, EMILE

Paolo Bartoloni

French structural linguist (1902–76) and author of the seminal work, *Problems in General Linguistics*, published in two volumes between 1966 and 1974, Benveniste was influenced by the work of the Swiss linguist, Ferdinand de **Saussure**. He developed it further by refining Saussure's distinction between *langue* and *parole* through the discussion of the differences and relations between the spheres of the semantic and the semiotic, or that of **language** and discourse. While Saussure posited a general language that is common to everybody but spoken to no one (*langue*), and a particular language that is unique to the subject (*parole*), Benveniste located the opposition between two modalities of language not so much in the general versus individual as in the relation between the sign (language, semantic) and the sign in context (semiotic, discourse). Agamben employs the work of Benveniste in the Preface to *Infancy and History* to illustrate his conceptualisation of the **voice**. Following Benveniste, Agamben claims that language is an inherent property of humans, characterised by stages of development passing through the elemental emission of sounds, to the construction of single words, and the elaboration of complex meanings through grammar and syntax. The latter stage is that of discourse, and it is brought about by the exposure to culture and education. If, on the one hand, language merely shows, on the other discourse denotes, and this passage and relation are mediated by the **potentiality** of humans who are naturally able to progress, as well as individually capable of manipulating language. The voice, which Agamben identifies as a stage of indetermination between language and discourse, allows him to expand not only on the categories of **actuality** and potentiality but also on that of the potentiality not-to-be. This is also the very human trait of volition and will which can bring about action both in its subordinate and insubordinate meanings of "working" and "worklessness". "Worklessness", a term that in Agamben is much indebted to the Blanchotian notion of *désœuvrement*, plays a fundamental role in *The Open* and its discussion of the indetermination between human and animals.

BIOPOLITICS

Nicholas Heron

The concept of "biopolitics" remains one of the most celebrated and contested notions of the philosophical legacy of Michel **Foucault**. From its first, discreet appearance in his lexicon in the context of a discussion about social medicine, through to its highly condensed theoretical elaboration in a few dazzling pages of the first volume of his *History of Sexuality* and beyond, Foucault's concept has assumed such contemporary purchase that it has even been suggested that the entire framework of political philosophy has emerged profoundly modified in its wake.

What did Foucault intend by this term? On a simple, diagnostic level, he sought to account for the process by which, starting from the advent of modernity, the very natural life of the living individual (and, by extension, the biological existence of the human species) began to be integrated, with ever-increasing urgency, into the techniques and strategies of a political power bent on optimising the productive forces of life itself. Reflected in this process, however, for Foucault, was a profound mutation in the "nature" of power itself. This would no longer be exercised over legal subjects in so far as they belonged to a certain jurisdiction, but over living beings in so far as they formed part of the species; its principle, accordingly, would no longer be that, juridical, of territorial sovereignty, but that, biological, of the living population. As is well known, Foucault would seek to articulate the sense of this shift by means of an exemplary formula – a formula which would give the clearest expression to what ultimately was at stake in it for him: nothing less than an unprecedented transformation of the very paradigm of classical politics. "For millennia," he writes, "man remained what he was for Aristotle: a living animal with the additional capacity for a political existence; modern man is an animal whose politics places his existence as a living being in question" (Foucault 1978: 143).

It is this last aspect, in particular, the distinctly "epochal" dimension of Foucault's presentation, which is especially determining for Giorgio Agamben's own unique deployment of this concept. For Agamben, too, the admission of natural life as such into the political sphere constitutes "the decisive event of modernity and signals a radical transformation of the political-philosophical categories of classical thought" (*HS*, 4). Yet he brings to it a decisive new inflection, one that sharply distinguishes his own approach from that of Foucault. What in Foucault's account, predicated on the model of radical historical discontinuity, is registered at the level of unprecedented and yet irreversible novelty (the "birth of biopolitics", precisely) appears in Agamben, instead, as the extreme outcome of an extended historical process determinately still in course. For him, that is to say, the birth of biopolitics represents nothing less than the coming to light of the hidden foundation upon which the entire Western political tradition rests. In this sense, the defining political experience of modernity becomes something like an Archimedean point from which to redescribe the history of politics in the West – a history which is, in its essence and from its very beginning, eminently biopolitical.

For Agamben, the originary biopolitical fracture is, indeed, already present, in paradigmatic form, in that very definition, canonical for Western politics, whose singular inversion alone, in Foucault, served as the marker for a society's "threshold of biological modernity" (Foucault 1978: 143; translation modified). The fundamental opposition, internal to the Greek language itself, between simple natural life (*zoē*), on the one hand, and politically qualified life (*bios*), on the other, provides the interpretative matrix for Agamben's renewed approach to Aristotle's foundational text. If the *polis* is, indeed, in Aristotle's definition, "born with regard to life, but exists essentially with regard to the good life" (*Politics* 1252b 30), it is the sense of precisely this strategic opposition that underpins it, he suggests, which must be reconsidered anew. Foundational in the most precise sense, the opposition itself, Agamben suggests, is first constituted through the "inclusive exclusion" of one of its terms within the other. Articulated in its very separateness – that is to say, according to that principle of ground which, elsewhere, Agamben has termed the "strategic *dispositif* par excellence of Aristotle's thought" (*O*, 14; translation modified), simple natural life appears here as that which must be experienced as removed in order to allow for the attribution of that "supplement of politicity" (*HS*, 3) which alone defines the "good life" of the perfect human community. What Agamben seeks to underscore, by means of his interrogation of this opposition, is thus not just– as, indeed, should be perfectly evident

– that simple *zoē* as such in the classical world was strictly excluded from
the *polis* (this, to be sure, was by contrast the great animating gesture of
Hannah **Arendt**'s essentially anti-modern project), but rather that its
exclusion in fact furnishes the very ground for the articulation of the political sphere in the positivity that is proper to it. What is politics, he asks,
if its essential articulation rests upon the fundamental exclusion (which is
also, and at the same time, an inclusion) of **bare life**? And, as a corollary,
what is politics if, as Foucault has suggested, this excluded element is now
consubstantial with the space of the *polis* itself? With this second question
Agamben's articulation of biopolitics in its modern form receives its most
distinct formulation. What specifically characterises modern biopolitics,
for him, is not simply the inclusion of natural life in the political sphere
but, more precisely, the inclusion of that very excluded element – that
element which is included through its exclusion – whose exclusion alone
first secured the constitution of the political sphere.

With respect to Foucault's conception of biopolitics, Agamben thus
proposes three substantive corrections (corresponding to the three distinct
sections of his *Homo Sacer*). The first concerns the specific form that law
assumes in the age of "biological modernity". For Agamben, the birth
of biopolitics does not mark the decline of the sovereign function but an
unparalleled extension of it. Indeed, one of the principal achievements
of his study is precisely to have demonstrated the essential contiguity
between the juridical and the biopolitical models of power. In the **state of
exception** become the rule, the very content of law coincides with what
it succeeds in casting outside itself. The outside of the law is the inside
of the law; this paradox confronts us with a figure of life whose absolute
externality with respect to the law constitutes its sole legal status. The
second correction concerns the specificity of sovereign power's referent:
the very "life" which, according to Foucault's diagnosis, has become the
"stakes" in modern politics. This is neither a natural life nor a politically
qualified life (according to the classical distinction); nor is it even a natural
life become political (in Foucault's sense). It is, rather, what results from
the constitutive separation of these two categories – which is to say, from
the "inclusive exclusion" of the one within the other: a life absolutely
"separated and excluded from itself" (*O*, 38), to which no concrete form
corresponds; what Agamben, following **Benjamin**, terms "bare life" and
whose distinct paradigm he discerns in the archaic Roman legal figure of
the *homo sacer*. The third correction, finally, concerns the distinct space
that opens up when the state of exception and the bare life that is separated in it are granted a "permanent and visible localisation" (*HS*, 20). For
Agamben, it is the birth of the **camp** (and not that of the prison) which
characterises the political space of modernity. This is what Foucault's

analyses were not in a position to intuit. "The inquiry that began with a reconstruction of the *grand enfermement* in hospitals and prisons did not end with an analysis of the concentration camp" (*HS*, 119).

BIOS

Arne De Boever

Agamben begins *Homo Sacer* by observing that "[t]he Greeks had no single term to express what we mean by the word '**life**'" (*HS*, 1). Instead, they used two terms: *zoē* and *bios*. Unlike *zoē*, which expresses "the simple fact of living common to all living beings" (*HS*, 1) and tends to coincide in Agamben's work with biology, *bios* expresses "the form or way of living proper to an individual or group" (*HS*, 1) and relates to **ethics** and **politics**. It is from the distinction between *zoē* and *bios* that Agamben develops the notion of **bare life**, which is Agamben's name for politicised *zoē*.

Although Agamben uncovers the distinction between *bios* and *zoē* in the Greeks – specifically in **Aristotle** – in the introduction to *Homo Sacer*, he also refers to Hannah **Arendt** and Michel **Foucault** as two modern interpreters of the distinction. Arendt's *The Human Condition* is cited there as a book that "analyzed the process that brings *homo laborans*, and with it, biological life as such – gradually to occupy the centre of the political scene of modernity" (*HS*, 3); Foucault's *The History of Sexuality* "summarizes the process by which, at the **threshold** of the modern era, natural life begins to be included in the mechanisms and calculations of State power, and politics turn into biopolitics" (*HS*, 3). These two citations suggest that the problem with the relation between *zoē* and *bios* lies in *zoē*'s progressive inclusion in *bios*. But this is only one side of the problem. As Agamben reveals in *Means Without End*, the problem of inclusion is actually preceded by one of exclusion: namely, the separation or "isolation" (*ME*, 3) of life – *zoē* – from its form – *bios*. This separation is operated by **sovereignty** and produces bare life. Combining both arguments, *Homo Sacer* argues that bare life exists in an excluded position within the political sphere; it is life that is internally excluded or excepted. In response to this, Agamben calls for a **form-of-life**, "a life that can never be separated from its form, a life in which it is never possible to isolate something such as naked life" (*ME*, 3–4). Such a form-of-life would deactivate (see **deactivation**) the sovereign logic of the exception. One can glimpse this form-of-life in one's **experience** of language as such.

Although *bios* is most central to the *Homo Sacer* series, especially *Homo*

Sacer and *Remnants of Auschwitz*, it is also relevant for Agamben's analysis of the production of the difference between **human** and **animal** life in *The Open*. At stake here is the separation of animal life from human life: in other words, a process of internal exclusion that is similar to the separation of *zoē* from *bios* and bare life's excepted position within the political sphere. Messianic (see **messianism**), "concluded humanity" would be depicted, Agamben suggests, as human beings "with animal heads" (*O*, 2) – a depiction that needs to be related to his call for a form-of-life. The distinction between *zoē* and *bios* is not uncontested; it has been challenged most powerfully by Jacques **Derrida** in the first volume of his lectures on *The Beast and the Sovereign*.

BLANCHOT, MAURICE

Carlo Salzani

A passing reference to Maurice Blanchot (1907–2003), a French writer and philosopher, can already be found in Agamben's first book, *The Man Without Content* (*MC*, 11). The references to this author, however, revolve around three themes: the question of community in "Tradition of the Immemorial" (1985) (*Po*, 113) and *The Coming Community* (*CC*, 85); the theme of inoperativity (see **inoperative**) in *Homo Sacer* (*HS*, 61); and the meaning of the **human** – for Blanchot's comment on Robert Antelme's *L'Espèce humaine* [1947], "Man is the indestructible that can be infinitely destroyed" – in *Remnants of Auschwitz* (*RA*, 134–5) and *The Time That Remains* (*TR*, 53).

CAESURA

William Watkin

Agamben's first full engagement with the term "caesura" is to be found in the essay "Idea of Caesura" (*IP*, 43–4), where he presents an example from the verse of Penna to show how the pause in a line of **poetry** has come to be seen within European prosody as a pause for thought. Thus the "breaking action of the caesura" (*IP*, 43) allows Agamben to note that "for the poet, the element that arrests the metrical impetus of the voice, the caesura of verse, is thought" (*IP*, 43). Here the relation between the ongoing flow of the **semiotic** in the form of **enjambment**, and the arresting motion of the **semantic** within the semiotic in the form of a caesura, directly relates *poiesis* to the thing of thought as such: namely, **language** as immediate medium and gestural (see **gesture**) support for thought.

In *The Open* Agamben uses caesura in a different sense to describe the crucial history of the development of the term **life** in terms of an obsessive division of life into **human** and **animal**. He defines life as "*what cannot be defined, yet, precisely for this reason, must be ceaselessly articulated and divided*" (*O*, 13), a process he comes to see as the rule of caesura. Agamben's most recent use of the term caesura is a means of describing messianic (see **messianism**) time "as a caesura which, in its dividing the division between two times, introduces a remainder [*resto*] into it that exceeds the division" (*TR*, 64). Caesura here is another name for the activity of kairotic time which intercedes between *chronos* and *eschaton*, resulting in a "zone of indiscernibility, in which the past is dislocated into the present and the present is extended into the past" (*TR*, 74).

CAMP

Claudio Minca

As part of his critique of the foundations of modern political structures, Agamben has outlined a spatialisation of sovereign power and the production of **bare life** through the construction of the camp, which has appeared most importantly in *Homo Sacer*, *Remnants of Auschwitz* and *Means Without End*. The camp here is both a literal camp – the concentration camps of National Socialism, the refugee detention centres of our own period and most infamously America's Camp Delta at Guantánamo Bay – and also a theoretical understanding of the way in which the "state of exception" manifests itself in space.

The camp-as-a-space-of-exception is a portion of territory that lies outside of the juridical order – but is not simply *external* to that order: It is a "hybrid of law and fact in which the two terms have become indistinguishable. [. . .] Only because the camps constitute a space of exception [. . .] in which not only is law completely suspended but fact and law are completely confused – is everything in the camps truly possible" (*HS*, 169–70).

The "political" therefore no longer orders forms of **life** and juridical rules in a determinate place but, instead, contains at its very centre what

Agamben terms a "dislocating localisation" that exceeds it and into which every form of life and every norm can be virtually taken. The camp, as dislocating localisation, is the hidden matrix of modern politics. He argues:

> the birth of the camp in our time appears as an event that decisively signals the political space of modernity itself. It is produced at the point at which the political system of the modern nation-state, which was founded on the functional nexus between a determinate localization (the territory) and a determinate political-juridical order (the State) and mediated by automatic rules of the inscription of life, enters in a lasting crisis, and the State decides to assume directly the care of the nation's biological life as one of its tasks. (*HS*, 174–5)

For Agamben, the camp is thus the spatialisation that precedes the normalisation of a permanent **state of exception** and constitutes a potential fourth element within the old state–nation–territory triad of power, with its (dis)locating localisation as the new "global biopolitical nomos" (*ME*, 41).

In the camp lies the spatio-political *arcanum* that all contemporary theories of the sovereign exception must consider: "the nexus between localization and ordering that constitute the '*nomos* of the Earth' for Carl **Schmitt** contains within it a fundamental ambiguity, an unlocalisable zone of indistinction or exception that [. . .] acts against it as a principle of its infinite dislocation" (*HS*, 19–20). When our age tried to grant this unlocalisable a permanent and visible localisation, "the result was the concentration camp" (*HS*, 19–20). The camp is the space that appears when the state of exception becomes the rule and gains a permanent spatial form (*ME*, 37).

For this reason, according to Agamben, the concentration camp represented the extreme and absolute realisation of the National Socialist project (*SE*, 71), a "direct effect" of the National Socialist revolution (*HS*, 169). It was the product of a permanent state of exception, a "preventative police measure" (as it was sometimes described by Nazi legal theorists), an unfortunate necessity in order to protect the security of the state; the camp allowed individuals to be "taken into custody" (*HS*, 167) in order to assure the well-being and reproduction of the biological corpus of the nation. Agamben argues that the Nazi camp is the place within which "an unprecedented absolutization of the biopower *di far vivere* ['to make live'] intersects with an equally absolute generalisation of the sovereign power *di far morire* ['to make die'], such that biopolitics coincides immediately with thanatopolitics" (*RA*, 83).

It is in this sense that the camp becomes the very "**paradigm**" of modern political space – and that politics becomes biopolitics. The ultimate aim of the camp is that of producing an "absolute biopolitical substance that, in its isolation, allows for the attribution of [every and all] demographic, ethnic, national and political identity". This is why, in the Nazi camp, the **Muselmann** "not only shows the efficacy of biopower, but also reveals its secret cipher, [. . .] its *arcanum*" (*RA*, 156). This *arcanum imperii*, embodied by the *Muselmann*, is "invisible in its very exposure", hidden and un-revealable; it is "nothing other than the *volkloser Raum*, the space empty of people at the centre of the camp that, in separating all life from itself, marks the point in which the citizen passes into [. . .] the Muselmann", step after step, in a series of biopolitical **caesurae**; passes into "a bare, unassignable and unwitnessable life" (ibid.).

If the camp is, indeed, not simply an "event" that indelibly marks the political space of modernity but also its true "hidden matrix" – that is, the *nomos* of the political space in which we still live – it also represents a concrete space of exception whose juridical-political structure must be interrogated:

inasmuch as its inhabitants have been stripped of any political status and reduced completely to bare life, the camp is also the most absolute biopolitical space that has ever been realized – a space in which power confronts nothing other than pure biological life without any mediation. (*ME*, 40)

What is at stake in the camp is the definition of the threshold between life and death: a threshold that must somehow be "traced on the ground" to materialise, to allow violence to be effective; to allow for the exercise of a power with no referent or need for persuasion. In the camp, "not only is necessity reduced, in the end, to a decision, but that which necessity decides is, in truth, an 'undecidable' *de facto* and *de jure*"; it is the exercise of true *potenza*, with no before or after. The camp, for Agamben, is not only an extra-territorial space where particular individuals are "banned"; it is a constitutive part of the new geographies of terror, which speak directly to all of us, inside and outside of the camp.

CAPRONI, GIORGIO

Paolo Bartoloni

Giorgio Caproni (1912–90) is an Italian poet whose writing is criss-crossed by philosophical preoccupations centring on the relation between language and things, presence and absence, authenticity and inauthenticity. Agamben collected, edited and introduced Caproni's posthumous collection of poetry, *Res Amissa* (1991). His introduction later appeared in the book, *The End of the Poem*, under the title "Expropriated Manner". In Agamben's reading, Caproni comes to represent a contemporary example of poetry and language as the guardian of the thing – see also Agamben's discussion of **Hegel** and poetry in *Language and Death*. The "amissed thing" (*res amissa*) is, therefore, the quintessential figure of the disappearance of the thing under the custody and protection of language, which by removing the thing safeguards its secrecy.

COMING COMMUNITY

Carlo Salzani

"Coming community" is the pivotal concept of the book of the same name published in Italian in 1990. The book was written in the aftermath of the fall of the Berlin Wall, the Tiananmen protests and the dissolution of Eastern Europe socialism, but, more than a reflection on geopolitical changes, it was a response to the philosophical debate about the idea of community which originated in France with the publication in 1983 of Jean-Luc **Nancy**'s essay, "La Communauté désœuvrée" ("The Inoperative Community"), followed the same year by Maurice **Blanchot**'s response, "La Communauté inavouable" ("The Unavowable Community"), and again, three years later, by Nancy's expansion of the earlier ideas in book form. At the centre of the debate stood the notion of belonging and the question of an idea of community immune to exclusion, isolation and violence. Whereas both Nancy and Blanchot approach the question by way of Martin **Heidegger**'s *Mitsein* (being-together), Agamben takes a surprising route that leads to the disavowal of the very logic of belonging, identity and representation.

At the core of the problem lies the fact that every idea of community sets criteria of inclusion, which are at the same time also criteria of exclusion; every politics of identity transforms belonging, the "being-in", into standards of identification and differentiation which necessarily become the subject of violent dispute. Agamben's proposal is to reject the very notions of belonging and identity, and to centre the idea of community on the notion of **"whatever singularity"**. Whatever singularity, as pure singularity, has no identity and thus severs any obligation to belonging; it eludes the antinomy of the relation between universal and particular by becoming an **example**, which is neither singular nor universal, and allows the disappropriation of all proprieties as the possibility for the **appropriation** of **impropriety** as such; pure singularities "are expropriated of all identity, so as to appropriate belonging itself" (*CC*, 11). In this sense, Agamben provocatively proposes to take on the very impropriety and **inauthenticity** of the world's petty bourgeoisie, because they constitute a possibility. Having no identity and no belonging, the whatever singularities cannot possibly build a *societas*, and as such they disavow the logic and workings of **sovereignty**; therefore, the "whatever singularity [. . .] is the principal enemy of the state" (*CC*, 87).

The meaning of the "coming" (*che viene*) of the coming community is manyfold. As the "most **common**", as pure exposition, the whatever singularity subsists only in its approach, its exposition, its "coming". It is thus a "potential" being, and its **potentiality** is the hinge around which the whole construction revolves. The coming community is a community which has no being proper to it except for its bordering on all its possibilities; it has no destiny to fulfil and no essence, no historical or spiritual **vocation** to attain. Always expropriated (see **expropriation**), it is as such inhabited by the impossibility of exclusion. "Coming" thus means never present in the first place, the pure possibility of any relation whatever. As such, it is an "absolutely unrepresentable community" (*CC*, 25); it cannot be tied to classifying concepts since no terms, concepts and representational axioms could claim to represent it.

"Coming" also establishes a relation with awaiting and desire. Whatever singularity, Agamben states, is not that being which does not matter, which is indifferent, but rather "that being such that it always matters"; it is "lovable" (*amabile*) (*CC*, 1). **Love** is, in fact, one of the pivots of the coming **politics**: a love that has little to do with a psychological or emotional state, but rather constitutes an ontological mode, an ontological openness and relation to the world and its irreparability. The possibility of a coming community, which entails the possibility of **redemption**, must be construed on the acceptance of the **irreparable facticity** and **contingency** of the world. This "passion of facticity", which Agamben explores in the homonymous essay on Heidegger (cf. *Po*, 185–204), does not mean indifference and **passivity**; it constitutes, on the contrary, the necessary precondition for attending to the most present needs.

"Coming" thus presents also a temporal valence. The 2001 Italian re-edition of the book contains an apostille, which re-orients its scope in the direction taken by Agamben's project from the publication of *Homo Sacer* (1995), and confers on it the more accentuated messianic (see **messianism**) overtones of the later work. A small clarification, confined to the suspension of two parentheses, states: "*coming* does not mean *future*"

(Agamben 2001: 92). The "coming" of the coming community is devoid of the tension towards something that lies ahead, in the future. It is devoid of a linear understanding of time which sees it as a cumulative progression. Its temporality is that contraction of past, present and future which, in *The Time that Remains* (2000), Agamben will call "*the time of the end*": that is, the messianic "now", "the present as the exigency of fulfilment" (*TR*, 62, 76). The "coming" of the coming community is thus an "always coming", and its politics find its place neither in the romanticism of the past nor in the yearning for an utopian future, but rather in a messianic presentness, in the realisation that within the present lies the possibility of change and transformation.

The coming community is therefore not a future one that we have to "produce"; rather, it is one that, in the 2001 apostille, Agamben defines as **"inoperative"**. As "potentiality", the coming community already exists, here and now; we just need to take a little break from the world and let it "come". This implies rendering inoperative all historical and present projects; redemption is not *opera*, work, but rather "a peculiar sort of sabbatical vacation" (Agamben 2001: 92) from all the communities of the present and the future, from everything that demands a production. Its figure is **Melville's Bartleby**, who opposes his "I'd prefer not to" to all the demands of the world and thus restores the world to its potentiality.

COMMODITY

Jessica Whyte

Karl **Marx** begins volume one of *Capital* by examining the structure of the commodity form, and outlining his theory of "commodity fetishism", which, Agamben argues, was "foolishly abandoned" in the Marxist milieu of the 1960s (*ME*, 76). Like Marx, Agamben views the world of the commodity as an enchanted world, in which the commodity itself "stands on its head, and evolves out of its wooden brain grotesque ideas, far more wonderful than if it were to begin dancing of its own free will" (Marx 1990: 164–5). What was grotesque and wonderful, in Marx's view, was not a sensuous property inherent in the object but the way in which the commodity form masks the human labour of which it is a product, giving the human relation of exchange the appearance of a relation between things. The correspondence between "the misty realm of religion" and commodification, which is particularly important to Agamben, finds its origin here; in both cases, Marx writes, "the products of the human brain appear as autonomous figures endowed with a life of their own" (Marx 1990: 165). For Marx, capitalism, like religion, is thus a structure of separation, in which humans are faced with their own powers as though by something purely external.

In *Stanzas,* in the course of his earliest engagement with Marx's commodity fetishism, Agamben writes, "the transfiguration of the commodity into *enchanted object* is the sign that the exchange value is already beginning to eclipse the use value of the commodity" (*S*, 38). Discussing the world exhibitions, which Walter **Benjamin** describes, in a beautiful phrase, as "pilgrimage sites of the commodity fetish" (*S*, 38), Agamben argues that today we no longer need to visit a world exhibition to make our own pilgrimage, as what was once novelty is now banality. What was celebrated for the first time at the universal exhibitions "has now become familiar to anyone who has entered a supermarket or been exposed to the manipulation of an advertisement"; all of life has taken on a phantasmagoric quality, subjected to the domination of the commodity form (*S*, 38). Agamben is within a lineage of Marxian thinkers – which includes Guy **Debord**, Walter Benjamin and Theodor **Adorno** – who believe that the extension of commodification ultimately empties out what Marx termed the "use value" of commodities, leaving in place empty forms, freed from the need to be useful and thus available for a new, non-utilitarian, use. Putting such empty forms to a new use and returning them from the enchanted realm to which they are separated by commodification are the tasks of **profanation**.

COMMON

Alysia Garrison

Throughout his work, but notably in *Potentialities*, *The Coming Community* and *Means Without End*, Agamben utilises the word common to indicate the positive possibility of **politics**: the taking place of intellectual and linguistic potential (see **potentiality**) – within a sphere of free use and pure means – that has survived and overcome **nihilism** and the **spectacle**. If, at the current conjuncture, politics is stuck in a dialectic between the improper and the proper, where the improper "extends its rule everywhere", as it does in industrialised democracies, and the proper "demands the exclusion of any impropriety", as it does in totalitarian states, for Agamben we must overcome this dialectic, "at the point of indifference between the proper and the improper", through "free use" of the common (*ME*, 117). But how, he asks, following **Heidegger**, does one "use" a common? The answer is through the appropriation of an **expropriation** (*ME*, 117): that is to say, the very nihilism of the "Unparticipated principle" we share in common at the basis of community is, in its presupposition of nothing, "our only hope" (*Po*, 113). It is at this zero point, between the expropriation of the community into which we are thrown and appropriation of this expropriation by the free **use** of the common, that the political thought Agamben proposes – as "inoperative community, compearance, equality, loyalty, mass intellectuality, the coming people, [or] whatever singularity" – can take place (*ME*, 117–18).

In contradistinction to the notion of community, separated into parts and parties (as critiqued by **Nancy** and **Blanchot**), the common is not premised on any condition of belonging or claim of identity, by "being red, being French, being Muslim", but by belonging itself, by "being such" (*CC*, 2). This social power, common to thought, in affinity with the Marxian (see **Marx**) General Intellect, signals the coming of whatever being: being such as it is, the singular being that breaks free from the false dichotomy between "the ineffability of the individual" on the one hand, and "the intelligibility of the universal" on the other (*CC*, 2). As such, Agamben's understanding of the common bears a stronger affinity to **communicability** than to community. Existing in the gap in which the shifter moves around freely, what is common is the taking place of **language**. Agamben's philosophy of the common begins with **Dante**'s reading of Averroism, strongly steeped in the Aristotelian (see **Aristotle**) categories of **potentiality** and **actuality**, the multitude of thought common to the human intellect that prevents life from being separated from its form. Intellectuality and thought introduce a buffer: the power of praxis, or the materiality of corporeal processes, to constitute the "multiple forms of life as form-of-life", to reunite life to its form, rendering them inseparable (*ME*, 11). Agamben's account of the "multitude of thought" in its critique of the ban structure of sovereignty differs from Hardt and Negri's familiar account of multitude, the "common surplus" that leaves this foundational structure hidden.

COMMUNICABILITY

Daniel McLoughlin

Communicability first appears in the 1983 essay, "Language and History: Linguistic and Historical Categories in Benjamin's Thought", in the context of a discussion of the "communication of communicability" in Walter Benjamin's essay, "On Language as Such and the Language of

Man". It returns in Agamben's political thought most often in *Means Without End*, a work whose very title draws on the Benjaminian vision of pure language, and in particular, its analysis of **gesture**, as the exhibition of a means (*ME*, 58).

Benjamin's essay criticises the "bourgeois notion of language", which conceives language as a means of communication between subjects. Against this, Benjamin argues for the existence of "pure language" that does not communicate anything except its own existence: "there is no such thing as a content of language; as communication, language communicates a spiritual entity, that is, a communicability pure and simple" (*Po*, 52). This distinction between the content of communication and the communicability of language reflects Agamben's fundamental philosophical concern, the originarily divided structure of human language. On the one hand, discourse speaks about things, representing real or mental entities that are external to or presupposed by language. However, representation also presupposes the existence of language, as the system of rules and signs through which we are able to speak about things. Communication, saying something about something, thus presupposes communicability: that language exists. Communicability is then linked to a number of Agamben's other formulations for the existence of language prior to what is said in it, including "language as such", the **potentiality** for language, the Idea of language, and the *factum loquendi*.

The Benjaminian formulation of communicability is crucial to Agamben's attempt to rethink the experience of language as such beyond the horizon of metaphysics and the experience of the ineffable that is also characteristic of the **Voice**. If communication is understood only as the representation of an entity, language itself cannot be communicated, for language is not a thing but the medium through which one speaks about things. The only way to communicate the level of the name would be to have access to a meta-language, a transcendent order that would allow one to name the name, objectifying language in order to speak about it. Such a move, however, simply reproduces the structure of presupposition, and as Agamben argues in "Philosophy and Linguistics", all attempts to construct such a meta-language have failed. Language is not an object of communication but the medium of communication, the ontological opening in and through which it takes place. As Agamben argues, this medium, which mediates all things and all knowledge, is the only immediate thing that can be reached by speaking beings. To communicate communicability, which is, for Agamben, the task of philosophy, does not mean to try and speak about it as a thing, to turn it into an object that can be mediated; it is instead "to expose the word in its own mediality, in its own being a means" (*ME*, 58).

CONTEMPORARY

Connal Parsley

Beginning from a discussion of Friedrich **Nietzsche**'s notion of the "untimely", in which Agamben highlights Nietzsche's rejection of a subjective identity wholly syncretic with its historical epoch, Agamben defines the contemporary as "that relationship with time that adheres to it through a disjunction and an anachronism" (*WA*, 41). For Agamben, contemporariness is a paradoxical structure; those who are contemporary see and grasp their own time more clearly than others, by the virtue of their very disjunction with it. This clarity means perceiving not simply the "lights" of an epoch, but also the darkness and obscurity which are inseparable from them. Agamben does not characterise the darkness of a time as a simple absence, but, in a confounding of the enlightenment paradigm, as a positive "beam" of darkness, which travels toward us but cannot reach us.

The fact that one who is contemporary remains attentive to this untimely aspect of their chronological epoch is significant for two main reasons. First, Agamben expressly connects this "darkness" to an "immemorial" or prehistoric **origin**/*archē* (*WA*, 50), which constitutes an "unliveable" but nevertheless indispensable element of the present (similarly to his notion of the para-ontological (*Pr*, 50); and see **archaeology**). The contemporary's attention thus constitutes a "return to a present where we have never been" (*WA*, 52), a clear reference to Agamben's characterisation of human ethos (see *LD*, 93–8). Second, the contemporary (particularly in Agamben's key example of the poet), who "interpolat[es] the present into the inert homogeneity of linear time" (*WA*, 52–4), has an overtly messianic (see **messianism**) character. Repurposing the disjuncture constitutive of its identity, it introduces the possibility of a special relationship between different times (*WA*, 53), thus continuing Agamben's attempt to overcome a Hegelian diagnosis of subjectivity in relation to **history** (see *IH*, 107–9) by means of Pauline (see **Paul**) messianics.

CONTINGENCY

Anton Schütz

Faithful to his determination to gain access to the past, not with the project of identifying in it the historical sources of the present, but rather in the mode of *advancing backward* into it beyond history's starting point and right into the territory of the *Urgeschichte* (proto-history) in which history has its historico-transcendental moorings, Agamben finds in history the site of a contingent experience, rather than the narrative of an origin that would be able to neutralise contingency with necessity. Unfolding the Benjaminian (see **Benjamin**) idea of an access to the past predicated on the idea of the surprise or "tiger's leap", by means of which an experienceable historical element suddenly surfaces within a given here and now, subjecting the present to the force of the past's fulgurating intervention and breaking up the inertia and self-sufficiency of its continuity to the point of irreversibly dislocating it, Agamben considers the unbounded (if always punctiform) elective affinity prevailing between past and present in Benjamin's assessment of the historical ingredient of historical materialism, and launches a series of inquiries into comparable historico-transcendental approaches, both before and after Benjamin.

This notion of proto-history refers to a distinction developed by Franz Overbeck, the late nineteenth-century theologian and Friedrich Nietzsche's friend, between history mediated by tradition (or "canonized" history) and history that springs from a direct self-exposure to the sources. If what is stressed in the differentiation between tradition-anchored and source-anchored modes of approaching past events must clearly be recognised as an applied mode of asking the question of contingency, it is evident that the methodological understanding of the modality of contingency (thus also of contingency in particular and modalities in general), in *The Signature of All Things*, offers only one side of Agamben's discussion of the problem. The other connection of Agamben's thought with the theme of contingency is related less to an issue of method than to a pivotal category of philosophy – more exactly to the modality's incomparable prominence in the context of the history of Western metaphysics and its transmission. Contingency is often construed as a combination of two negations. To assert that something is contingent is to say that it is both non-impossible and non-necessary.

It is clear that – in the context of medieval metaphysics and its noteworthy oscillation between, on the one hand, the logical philosophy of pagan origin, especially Aristotle's *organon*, and on the other hand the doctrines pertaining to diverse shades and models of Islam and Christianism – the very category under which the issue of the "equally otherwise possible" must have represented an intellectual lever with which especially explosive consequences could have been achieved when it was chosen as an issue of debate. Contingent, Agamben reports, is what a being is called that can both be and not be (*Po*, 261). The anecdote taken from Duns

Scotus, even if it might go back to some much earlier thinker of logical modalities, possibly Avicenna, records the ferociously humorous argument which recommends that "those who doubt contingency should be tortured, until they admit that they could as well have not been tortured" (*Po*, 263). The emphasis laid on will by Duns significantly boasts the appearance of a potential encounter with the problem of contingency. According to the *doctor subtilis* ("the subtle teacher", the name by which Duns was known in his lifetime), not only does the actual fact of willing a thing make one experience the possibility of not willing it; it is also the singular privilege of the will to involve an indifference to contraries that can be true at the same time. It is therefore possible to argue that, knowing full well that they cannot both exist at once, God can none the less will contraries. Another important issue relevant to this discussion is, of course, the one built into the older notion of future contingents which, in the form it takes in the medieval debate, is directly related to divine prescience, with the dramatic implication of either questioning the freedom of human will or destroying the very possibility of the revelation of divine will.

Contingency, in the tradition of Western thought, is a theme which carries an inexhaustible potential. It provides Agamben – especially in a work dedicated to that most philosophical creation of that most philosophical of American writers, Herman Melville's *Bartleby the Scrivener, A Wall Street History* (1853) – with an occasion to test the linkage between a timeless ingredient of occidental philosophical history on the one hand, and, on the other hand, the evolution of a number of particularly consequential discussions within the proto-history of modern Western society: specifically, the debate about God's power, and the distinction of two distinct powers ascribed to God, *potentia dei ordinata* and *potentia dei absoluta*, God's ordered potentiality and God's absolute potentiality (cf. Zartaloudis 2010: 273ff.) The double conceptualisation has acquired its historical salience through some of the more noteworthy and controversial Franciscan thinkers of the late thirteenth and early to mid-fourteenth centuries; it draws a line of distinction between God's power as subject to an order (which in the case of God can only be the order already willed by himself) and God's power as exempted from any subjection – in such a way that God's way of acting either remains in accordance, as it were, with the order foreseen and adopted (thus, willed) by his own choice, or, on the contrary, considering his all-powerfulness, remains forever unbound by any bond. "By contingent", Agamben quotes from the Scot, "I mean not something that is not necessary or eternal, but something whose opposite could have happened in the very moment in which it has happened" (*Po*, 262). It is at the crossroad of this unlimited contingency with the notion of an equally unlimited divine power that Agamben locates the genesis of Western modernity.

DANTE

Paolo Bartoloni

References to the Italian poet, Dante (1265–1321), in Agamben's work are many and varied. The most noticeable are those in *The End of the Poem* relating to the notion of guilt and redemption in the chapter entitled "Comedy" and to the double experience of language in the chapter entitled "The Dream of Language", and those in *Stanzas* relating to the possession of love through poetry. In "Comedy" Agamben proposes an innovative interpretation of the title of Dante's most famous book, *The Comedy*, claiming that Dante's decision to align himself with the comic genre rather than the tragic one, as in the case of his model Virgil, is postulated upon Dante's belief that humans are naturally innocent and personally guilty of sin, and that their earthly journey is thus marked by a process of redemption from guilt to innocence. Dante is also an example of bilingualism, in which the language of poetry and love, the vernacular, confronts the grammatical language of politics and power, Latin.

DEACTIVATE – see 'Inoperative'

DEBORD, GUY

Yoni Molad

Guy Debord (1931–94) was a Marxist writer and film-maker, and a member of the Situationist International, which he led from its foundation to its demise in 1972. It is Debord's thought that arguably provides Agamben with his social theory of modern society and capitalism, and with the idea that philosophy is strategy and its concepts weapons – an apt description of Agamben's entire work. Agamben adopts Debord's socio-political analysis to such an extent that it features as one of the only direct sociological observations in the *Homo Sacer* series (*HS*, 10), and it is to Debord that Agamben dedicates the collection of his most directly political writings, *Means Without End*. Agamben seeks to develop Debord's concept of the **spectacle** – which the latter described not as a collection of images but as "a social relation between people that is mediated by images" (Debord 1995: 12) – by extending its reach to the very linguistic nature of human beings. If, for Debord, the spectacle was "capital accumulated to such a degree that it becomes images" (Debord 1995: 24), then for Agamben this spectacle is now **language** itself – the very linguistic nature of human beings.

Agamben's extension of Debord's thought is first developed through a series of criticisms. In *The Man Without Content*, where Agamben critiques Western aesthetics as a "metaphysics of the will, that is of life understood as energy and creative impulse" (*MC*, 72), the Situationists are taken to task for maintaining a vitalist anthropology. In a later critique, found in *Stanzas*, Agamben notes that in modern **aesthetics** the eclipse of the notion of the "work" always results in a fetishisation of the process of artistic creation, regardless of its content, and argues that the Situationists, in their attempt to realise art by abolishing it, extend art to the entirety of **life** and thus reify the very thing they desperately sought to save from alienation (*S*, 54).

Read together, these critiques make it necessary for Agamben to deepen the critique of **commodity** fetishism to encompass not only labour and imagination, but also language itself. The idea that language itself is the spectacle is expressed in almost identical fashion in two pieces published in 1990 (*The Coming Community* and *Means Without End*). More recently, in *Profanations*, Agamben adapts Debord's ideas on the museification of the world, through a reading of **Benjamin**, in order to elaborate his political strategy of profaning that which has been separated and returning it to free human **use** (*Pr*). **Profanation** is rendered possible because the total expropriation of language by the spectacle also reveals to us our linguistic nature inverted, providing an *experimentum linguae* that reveals the fact of language itself, and thus allowing for a site of human community and belonging beyond identity and presupposition.

This possibility is developed by likening the famous Situationist strategies of *détournement* and plagiarism to Benjamin's insistence on the destructive power of citation and also through an analysis of Debord's cinema. In the essay, "Difference and Repetition: On Guy Debord's Films", Agamben focuses on the concepts of repetition and stoppage, taken up from another perspective in "Notes on Gesture"(ME), in order to formulate a messianic theory of cinema.

DEGREE ZERO

Sergei Prozorov

The idea of degree zero is central to Agamben's reconstitution of the logic of messianic (see **messianism**) **deactivation** (*katargesis*) in his analysis of St **Paul**'s epistles (*TR*, 99–101). This concept has been developed in the phonology of Nikolai Trubetzkoy (1890–1937), a Russian linguist and a co-founder of the Prague School of structural linguistics. For Trubetzkoy, in a privative phonetic opposition only one of the terms is positively marked in some manner, while the other remains unmarked. Yet, this unmarked status is not equivalent to the absence of a mark, but rather to what Trubetzkoy calls a zero-degree presence, a "sign of lacking a sign" (*TR*, 101). The zero phoneme, a concept developed by Trubetzkoy's colleague, Roman Jakobson, is thus opposed simultaneously to every other phoneme by virtue of its unmarked status and to the mere absence of a phoneme by virtue of its minimal presence.

This logic also characterises **Lévi-Strauss**'s concept of a floating signifier and **Derrida**'s concept of the trace, which simultaneously presuppose the neutralisation of the signified and the maintenance of signification. For Agamben, the perpetuation of signification in its zero-degree status is ultimately equivalent to the existence of the law in force without significance in the **state of exception** (*HS*, 51). In both cases, the positive content of a process is neutralised but the process itself goes running on empty without attaining fulfilment. The specificity of Agamben's messianic politics consists in his attempt to go beyond this infinite deferral of fulfilment by rendering the **apparatuses** of zero-degree signification **inoperative**.

DELEUZE, GILLES

Claire Colebrook

Deleuze's philosophy is marked by four concepts that are also crucial for Agamben, though in modified form: difference, immanence, potentiality and life. For both Agamben and Deleuze difference cannot be reduced to the linguistic systems that would (supposedly) be imposed on an otherwise undifferentiated reality. For Deleuze, difference is positive and productive; there are linguistic and social systems of difference because there is a more profound (pre-linguistic and inhuman) power of living difference that is creative (Deleuze 1994). While Agamben is also, like Deleuze, radically opposed to the idea that one cannot think outside, beyond or before the systems of difference that are already actualised, he focuses more on the human being's peculiar relation (or non-relation) to difference and the power of language. The speaking human being has the capacity not only to be differentiated from the world and others but also to experience the event of difference, especially through the experience of **language**. Although Deleuze's work is manifestly opposed to privileging either humanity or human language (for, with Guattari (1987), he regards signifying systems to be one among many modes of difference and semiosis), he also grants a certain significance to the late modern experience of human language (Deleuze 2006: 109).

For Agamben, at certain moments we can be exposed to the event of speaking as such: not stating this or that specified content, but simply *that there is speaking*. Although Agamben probably forms this notion from his reading of Walter **Benjamin** (who is not significant for Deleuze's thought), it does remain close to Deleuze's notion that certain late modern styles of language (such as **poetry**) are not communicative or functional but are released from organic or life-serving modes to be "deterritorialised" – capable of being thought or experienced as language, and not as signs of some other grounding content. For both philosophers, then, this allows a new thought of difference. It is not the case that the world or life is undifferentiated and requires language to be rendered distinct and formed; there is language because life just is this power of differentiation.

With poetic, literary or deterritorialised language we see this power of difference that characterises all life. Language and difference therefore allow us to think a mode of **potentiality** that cannot be reduced to the possible. The possible is commonly considered to be less than the real world; some things are merely possible, while other things possess full reality. Potentiality, by contrast, exceeds **actuality** and is, for Agamben and Deleuze, thoroughly positive and real. The actual world – of, say, humans and animals, social systems and transgressions, artworks and industrial production – is the outcome of a contraction of potentiality. For Deleuze, this means that genuine thinking should not accept the actual world as it is but ought to consider the fruitful potentiality of life from which differentiated actuality has emerged. For Agamben, potentiality and productive difference require us to go beyond already given distinctions and consider the zone of indistinction from which divisions and systems emerge. Whereas Deleuze's method tends to be ontological – he uses science and the problems of the physical world to consider life and difference – Agamben's method is genealogical and philological. It is by asking about current linguistic distinctions (such as the difference between poetry and technology, *poiesis* and *techne*) that we can chart the genesis of concepts from earlier (usually Greek) usages where the distinction was not so clear-cut.

The most important example of this mode of inquiry is Agamben's criticism of biopolitics; the once significant distinction between *zoē*, or natural life as such, and *bios*, or formed political life, is at once problematic (for we need to ask about the processes that distinguish these two), and also threatened in a modernity that can *only* consider life in its purely physical, biological and never decided political sense. For Deleuze, however, there is not only a methodological resistance to going back to terminology and already defined terms; there is also a positive value to considering *life itself*, beyond its human, linguistic and even organic forms. So, whereas Agamben seeks to describe the genesis of humanity, polity and lived worlds from the prior domain of potentiality, Deleuze (especially with Guattari) aims to create a philosophy of becoming, or "higher deterritorialisation", that goes far beyond Agamben's suggestion of "returning thought to its practical calling" (*HS*, 5).

For both, though, problems of life, difference and potentiality entail and require a philosophy of immanence. In Deleuze (and Deleuze and Guattari's) philosophy, immanence is a constant struggle. Because life produces relatively stable forms and "strata" (such as systems of language, of animal territories, of social orders, of political hierarchies and technological apparatuses), one stratum can appear to be the ground of others; we think of language as organising reality, or human practice as forming "the" world. One mode of difference is taken to be the privileged, governing or transcendent ground of difference in general. The "subject" as it was theorised in the twentieth century was, for Deleuze and Guattari, just one more way of taking a life of immanence – a life with no single governing or transcendent form – and reducing life's creativity to one of its creations. Agamben, too, is generally committed to immanence, for he will refuse to explain distinctions by referring them back to a single origin (such as man, law, language or God), but he is also less explicit about the value of achieving a "becoming-imperceptible" that would liberate thought from its rigidified concepts and systems into a post-human, post-organic future.

DERRIDA, JACQUES

Alysia Garrison

Since the early *Stanzas*, written during the height of post-structuralism on the continent, Agamben's work has engaged in a complex critical interrogation of deconstruction through marginal commentaries and esoteric representations of debates with Derridean interlocutors (such as **Saussure**, **Heidegger**, **Hegel**, **Benjamin** and **Nancy**). This interrogation provides a strong basis for evaluating Agamben's position on Derrida's core works, such as *Of Grammatology*, but perhaps less material that enables us to understand Agamben's position on the late, "political" Derrida. Further exchanges between Agamben and Derrida never took place, ones that promised to develop the quarrel to which each alludes in their texts *Homo Sacer* (Agamben) and *Rogues* (Derrida). In general, philosophy's task is more radical for Agamben than it is for Derrida; while the former wishes to push the slumber of metaphysics to awakening, the latter is content to track the infinite deferrals of the dreamer. Agamben is consistently critical of the project of deconstruction, suggesting that by positing "undecideables", by being unable, for example, to see the challenge to metaphysics in **Kafka**'s famous parable, "Before the Law", deconstruction does not overcome language's sovereign claim (*HS*, 25, 54). Derrida's only explicit critique of Agamben was put forth in 2002 in *The Beast and the Sovereign* lectures, where Derrida suggests that in repeatedly declaring that he is the "first" to illuminate something unseen, Agamben fails to overcome the very sovereignty he wishes to surpass.

Ostensibly, Agamben and Derrida share much in common. Both work from a metaphysical tradition grounded in the language philosophies of Heidegger, Benjamin and Nancy. For both, concerns of language are tied to questions of the political. But their ontological foundations differ; where Derridean deconstruction sets out to unravel the metaphysics of presence by exposing the aporias that riddle a text, the unconditional condition of *différance*, the free play of language, Agamben sets out to overcome such free play, to restore the indivisibility of presence – not the presence of "the thing itself", but the presence of what Agamben calls the immediate mediation of language (*Po*, 47). Here Agamben invokes **Wittgenstein**'s image of the fly trapped under the glass that has forgotten the presupposition of the glass: that the glass mediates what it sees. What is left out is the possibility that the fly might escape, and this is the task of the coming philosophy, a task that can only take place in and through **language** (*Po*, 46).

Language, for Agamben, exposes a fundamental division at the core of Western metaphysics, one that separates *zoē* from *bios*, **voice** from language, **infancy** from **experience**. Agamben illustrates this division in *Stanzas* by suggesting that the relation between signifier and signified be reduced simply to the "barrier" (/) between them: the original fracture of presence forgotten by modern semiology, and guarded by the Sphinx as the originary problem of signification (*S*, 137–9). The coming thought must idle this division, prepare it for an end and seize it, shattering the "machine" of language. Such idling takes place at a point of zero-degree presence that Agamben calls simply "degree zero"; this non-presence amounts not to an absence of signification, but a gap at which free-floating signifiers of "zero symbolic value" mark the constitutive excess of signifiers in relation to signifieds (*TR*, 102). For Derrida, in the play between sign and signifier, speech and writing, presence is never fully present to itself, identity is never wholly identical to itself, and the contemporary is never contemporaneous with itself, resigned as they are to infinite deferral. For Agamben, presence, identity and the contemporary, riven by a presupposed divide, are continually under pressure, being urged, on the verge of being overcome by the idea of language, by its own communicability (*Po*, 39–47; *IP*, 115–17). Perhaps Agamben dedicates "The Thing Itself" in *Potentialities* to Derrida because, in deconstruction's very desire to tarry with the negative foundation that Agamben's thought urges philosophy to abandon, a "pure" experience of language, which would amount to language's overcoming, is precisely what it forecloses.

Agamben and Derrida differ also in their approach to temporality. For Derrida, the messianic (see **messianism**) promise of concepts such as the gift, hospitality and democracy "to come" is reliant on the trace structure: the spacing of time between what is passing away and what will come to pass. The future messianic promise "presses" but does not ultimately disrupt the spacing of time; as Agamben puts it, deconstruction is a "thwarted messianism, a suspension of the messianic" (*TR*, 102). For Agamben, messianic time is contemporaneous with chronological time, using it, contracting it, hollowing and nullifying it in order to prepare its end (*TR*, 68). Chronological time is always on the verge of being seized by messianic time to open the possibility for harmony and redemption profaned of their religious fittings. For deconstruction no such end is in sight, just more of the same dreary capture in the function box of metaphysics' trace structure. Agamben describes the preparation for the end of time with the image of an animal that "gathers itself before lunging" (*TR*, 68). Perhaps this animal, with its resemblance to the wolf, brings together Agamben and Derrida's reflections on the beast and the sovereign, a conversation that never took place, but is for the teleopoietic future of a coming philosophy (*HS*, 104–11).

DISPOSITIF/APPARATUS

Nicholas Heron

"What is a *dispositif*?", the question first posed by Gilles **Deleuze** in the context of an international colloquium devoted to the life and work of

Michel **Foucault** (Deleuze 1992), received a marked echo, more than twenty years later, in the title of a recent essay by Giorgio Agamben. For Agamben, too, the word *dispositif* constitutes "a decisive technical term in Foucault's strategy of thought" (*WA*, 5). Yet what is central to his account is the attempt to locate its distinct deployment within the broader horizon of Foucault's contemporaneous inquiries into the history of what he termed "governmentality".

Indeed, Agamben's intervention takes place against the backdrop of his own research into precisely the same theme. In a recent book (Agamben 2007), he has explicitly sought to deepen and extend Foucault's genealogy, an undertaking which has carried his own investigations well beyond the strict chronological limits initially envisaged by Foucault himself. And, as is often the case in his work, the specific tenor of his inquiry has been, in the first instance, terminological in nature. If the *locus classicus* of the governmental paradigm is, once again, to be sought in **Aristotle** – in his attempt, through the mobilisation of the term *oikonomia*, to consolidate a non-epistemic framework for the effective management of the house-hold – an event of unparalleled importance in its extensive subsequent history, Agamben suggests, was its decisive assumption in the lexicon of the early Church Fathers. According to Agamben's account, in the course of the process that would lead to the assumption of the orthodox dogma of the Trinity, the Fathers found themselves confronted with a singular exigency: that of defending its elaboration against charges of polytheism. Their argument, as Agamben represents it, went as follows: "In his being and his substance, God is certainly one; but in his *oikonomia* – that is to say, the manner in which he administers his house, his life and the world he has created – he is, instead, triple" (*WA*, 16). There is no fracture in the edifice of monotheism, the divine substance itself is not split, they argued, because the triplicity of which they speak refers, not to God's being, but to his *oikonomia* (Agamben 2007: 69).

According to Agamben, the unexpected consequences of this resolution have none the less been singularly far-reaching. What began as an attempt to secure the unity of divine substance, he argues, ended up, through the elaboration of the doctrine of *oikonomia* –which the Latin Fathers, sig-nificantly, rendered with *dispositio* – by introducing an irreducible split, in God, between his nature and his economy, his being and his action. Action has no foundation in being: this, according to Agamben, is "the schizo-phrenia which the theological doctrine of *oikonomia* leaves as a legacy to Western culture" (*WA*, 18).

Foucault's terminological choice of *dispositif* – this is the striking thesis that Agamben ultimately advances – is in some way caught up in this enduring theological legacy. In his own distinct adoption of this term, it thus names that *"in which* and *through which* a pure activity of governance without any foundation in being is realised" (*WA*, 19; emphasis mine).

ENIGMA

Justin Clemens

"Enigma" may not initially seem to be a key term in Agamben's work. The term none the less serves an integral function, and its apparently inconsistent use and marginal status are themselves noteworthy features. Indeed, as soon as one starts looking for "enigma", it turns up everywhere. If one looks to Agamben's own references, the word "enigma" and its cognates can already be seen to be operative in, for instance, **Benjamin, Heidegger,** Lacan and **Foucault.** The term works in at least six interconnected ways:

1. An enigma *induces* thought, including philosophical investigation.
2. It *marks* the limit of any specific philosophical investigation.
3. It *characterises* this limit as essentially uncharacterisable in and for that philosophy.
4. This limit is uncharacterisable because it cannot be *said*, only *shown*, in and by that philosophy.
5. This limit *designates* the extra-rational **"origin"** of the philosophy in question.
6. As such, it proposes the *task* to its interlocutors of transforming this limit into a **threshold**.

The enigma is therefore also a site of contestation *between* philosophies; one philosophy targets the enigma embodied by another and, in doing so, transforms the enigma into yet another. The enigma is one term in a philosophy which at once grounds and ungrounds all the other terms of that philosophy, that place at which they are all imbricated yet cannot be further elaborated.

Agamben therefore determines his own research project as an approach to enigmas, the "unsaid" (see the Preface to *Pr*, 8). As Agamben relates:

What the Sphinx proposed was not simply something whose signified is hidden and veiled under an "enigmatic" signifier, but a mode of speech in which the original fracture of presence was alluded to in the paradox of a word that approaches its object while keeping it indefinitely at a distance. The *ainos* (story, fable) of the *ainigma* is not only obscurity, but a more original mode of speaking. (*S*, 138)

An example would be the division in Foucault between sovereignty and biopower, which is never fully explained by Foucault himself, yet has significant consequences for his thought; for example, why does he never properly deal with the concentration camp, the signature biopolitical technique of the twentieth century? Agamben seeks, however, not to resolve specific enigmas, nor just to bring them into the light of day, but rather, through radical philological analyses, to reconstruct the emergence, development and import of enigmatic terms, and their unexpected articulation with sets of other, apparently unrelated experiences. In doing so, he seeks to strip the mystery from the enigma, as he shows the impossibility of turning the enigma into a proposition.

ENJAMBMENT

William Watkin

Agamben first delineates the centrality of enjambment to his thought in the essay, "Idea of Prose", where he explains how enjambment constitutes a "mismatch, a disconnection between the metrical and syntactic elements" (*IP*, 40). His definition of **poetry** as based on the tension between sound and sense rather than their coincidence is further clarified in the later essay, "The End of the Poem", which begins with the definition that "poetry lives only in the tension and difference (and hence also the virtual interference) between sound and sense, between the semiotic and the semantic sphere" (*EP*, 109).

Poetry is definable as a tensile zone of undecidability between the two historic modes of presentative thought, philosophy (sense) and poetry (sound). The balance in the poetic line between sound overwhelming sense, enjambment, and sense interrupting sound, **caesura**, results in a tensile standoff between supersensuous and sensuous modalities of thought which he calls, after **Benjamin**, "dialectic at a standstill" (*O*, 83).

This tension is perpetually under threat from its own structural necessities. Agamben wonders what happens at the point at which the poem ends: "If poetry is defined precisely by the possibility of enjambment, it follows that the last verse of a poem is not a verse. Does this mean that the last verse trespasses into prose?" (*EP*, 112). This final proposition is an essential observation for poetics but also has significant implications for the understanding of the messianic (see **messianism**) thought as a stilled, tensile dialectic between the **semantic** and the **semiotic**.

ETHICS

Jason Maxwell

If **potentiality** constitutes the linchpin of Agamben's entire philosophy, it should be no surprise that his notion of ethics is thoroughly grounded in this concept. Indeed, for Agamben, any proper ethical system must first acknowledge that human nature is merely a potential. Rather than conforming to a fixed set of characteristics that would pre-emptively govern behaviour or thought, the human being is nothing more than a potential being. As Agamben writes in *The Coming Community*, "the point of departure for any discourse on ethics is that there is no essence, no historical or spiritual vocation, no biological destiny that humans must enact or realize" (*CC*, 43). Explaining that ethics as such could not exist without potentiality, he asserts that evil consists of nothing more than the decision to "regard potentiality itself, which is the most proper mode of human existence, as a fault that must always be repressed" (*CC*, 44).

For Agamben, this potentiality of the **human** cannot be separated from the potentiality inherent in **language** itself. The realisation that language communicates its own **communicability** illustrates that there is not some hidden essence that would reveal humanity's true calling. As he declares near the conclusion of *Language and Death*, "*ethos*, humanity's own, is not something unspeakable or *sacer* that must remain unsaid in all praxis and human speech . . . Rather, it is social praxis itself, human speech itself" (*LD*, 106). Simply put, an authentic experience of language as language should demonstrate that nothing exists outside of humanity's capacity for self-creation. This does not mean, however, that Agamben subscribes to the nihilistic view of language which he sees underwriting deconstruction. In his essay on Jacques **Derrida**, he declares that the *experimentum linguae* does not "authorize an interpretive practice directed toward the infinite deconstruction of a text, nor does it inaugurate a new formalism. Rather, it marks the decisive event of matter, and in doing so it opens onto an ethics" (*Po*, 218–19). This "decisive event of matter" is nothing more than the recognition of language's pure potentiality and the foundation it creates for ethics.

Agamben's critique of the endless deferral of action in Derrida's deconstructive approach parallels his critique of the dialectic in *Infancy and*

History, revealing that his ethics emphasises the importance of seizing the present moment for actualising human potential. Borrowing from the work of Walter **Benjamin**, he charges that the dialectical operation conceives of every moment in history as working toward some universally desirable endpoint that will retroactively justify each of the points in history leading to this result, writing that "each single moment of the process is real only as 'pure negativity' which the magic wand of dialectical mediation will transform – in the end – into the positive" (*IH*, 118). Given Agamben's suspicion of the claim that humanity has definitive characteristics that could be discovered and put into action, the dialectic's conceptualisation of the present moment as a mere means to an end obviously presents a problem. To combat this, Agamben's ethics seek the radical potential in every moment, most evident in his neologism "kairology". Based on the rhetorical concept, *kairos,* roughly meaning "the opportune moment for intervention", kairology aims to transform every moment in history into an opportune moment. Since Agamben's conception of potentiality is one rooted in impotentiality, then his ethics understandably necessitates that one acknowledge that the human might *not* actualise its potential. Since human progress is far from guaranteed, it remains ethically imperative to bring about this progress continually in every moment. In doing so, messianism becomes something incredibly profane (see **profanation**).

Clearly, Agamben hopes to create a community that would not be rooted in exclusionary violence. From his perspective, this violence is the inevitable result of a political process that seeks to create clear distinctions between who should be included within humanity and who should not (hence, his supreme reluctance to assign a proper nature to the human, as this would only perpetuate the cycle of violence). Particularly troubling for Agamben is how the **law** has contaminated ethics, imposing its rigid categories on the field in a way that limits its relationship to potentiality. In other words, because law consists of prescriptive norms, it necessarily restricts humankind's potentiality. As he laments in *Means Without End*, nothing is more regrettable "than this unconditional being-in-force of juridical categories in a world in which they no longer mirror any comprehensible ethical content" (*ME*, 134).

His *Remnants of Auschwitz* explores this process more closely, examining the figure of the *Muselmann* as a means of explaining the limitations of legal and juridical concepts as a foundation for ethics. Early on, Agamben writes that ethics has always been infiltrated by the legal sphere, which has supplied it with illegitimate criteria: "it has taken almost half a century to understand that law did not exhaust the problem [of Auschwitz], but rather that the very problem was so enormous as to call into question law itself" (*RA*, 20). Throughout the remainder of the book, he describes how all of the legal categories that have been used to assess the concentration camps, including dignity and respect, fail to come to terms adequately with what really occurred there, concluding that "Auschwitz marks the end and the ruin of every ethics of dignity and conformity to a norm" (*RA*, 69). The *Muselmann*, occupying a zone of indistinction between the human and the inhuman, troubles the very notion of an ethics that ascribes any concrete positive characteristics to the human being and therefore suggests that what constitutes humanity as such must remain continually open if the violent outcome of Auschwitz is to be avoided in the future.

EXAMPLE – see 'Paradigm'

EXPERIENCE

Daniel McLoughlin

Experience is the subject of the eponymous essay in Agamben's 1982 book, *Infancy and History: The Destruction of Experience*. The essay begins by asserting that modern man has had his experience expropriated. Here, Agamben takes up a theme from Benjamin's essay, "The Storyteller", in which Benjamin diagnosed the "poverty of experience" arising from the mechanised destruction of the First World War, from which men returned "grown silent – not richer, but poorer in communicable experience" (quoted in *IH*, 15). For Agamben, however, the poverty of experience that Benjamin diagnoses has today been pushed to the limit of its destruction, and the void of experience has overflowed from the battlefield to the everyday: "Today, however, we know that the destruction of experience no longer necessitates a catastrophe, and that humdrum daily life in any city will suffice" (*IH*, 15).

Experience is related to authority – "that is to say, the power of words and narration" (*IH*, 16). What confronts modern man in his daily life, for Agamben, is a jumble of meaningful events. Agamben asserts, however, that these events cannot be translated into experience, because the authority of experience relies upon its reproducibility. Prior to modernity, in an age when storytelling was a locus of authority, it was believed that "the unusual could not in any way give rise to experience" (*IH*, 16). This is what is at stake in the expropriation or deprivation of experience that Benjamin identifies as occurring on the battlefields of World War One, in which any authority that had been handed down, and any personal experience of the generation that went to the front, was rendered mean-ingless by the event of mechanised, industrial warfare: "A generation that had gone to school on horse-drawn streetcar now stood under the open sky in which nothing remained unchanged but the clouds, and beneath these clouds, in a force field of destructive torrents and explosions, was the tiny, fragile human body" (quoted in *IH*, 15).

Agamben traces the genealogy of experience in its relation with the subject in modern science and philosophy. He argues that both are characterised by an epistemological uncertainty as to the status of expe-rience, perhaps best expressed by Descartes's experiment in radical doubt. Modern science attempts to verify experience through experiment, thereby producing certain knowledge. This does not, however, restore the authority of experience, but, rather, displaces it on to numbers and instruments. The void of experience is also at the heart of the modern philosophy of the subject, particularly in Hegel, who characterises it nega-tively as "something one can undergo but never have" (*IH*, 38). While we have been expropriated of the possibility of turning sensory impres-sions into experience, Agamben argues that this destruction opens up the possibility of a new form of experience, that of **infancy**, in which what is experienced is not this or that thing, but the limit of or potential (see **potentiality**) for language. It is in the context of such a limit experience that the word "experience" most often appears in Agamben's subsequent works, including *The Coming Community* and *Potentialities*.

EXPROPRIATION

Yoni Molad

Expropriation, the gradual loss of control by human beings over the fruits of their labour, and the nullification of the powers and faculties that make them human, is a term often used in Marxist criticism to describe the process occurring as a consequence of the development of capitalism. On one hand, Agamben identifies this process as the entire history of Western politics and social organisation which is crystallised in the history of **sov-ereignty**, the process by which **life** is expropriated by the sovereign ban, through the removal of the **voice**, and the separation of *zoē* and *bios*. On the other, Agamben identifies our epoch, the society of the spectacle, as the culmination of this process, in which the expropriation of **experience** and of **language** reaches an unprecedented intensity. It is for this reason, however, that Agamben thinks that the history of sovereignty is reaching its close and that through a process of re-expropriation, or what he terms

profanation, contemporary nihilism can be overcome and a new form-of-life can emerge.

The expropriation of experience – which began with the development of modern science, and Descartes's reduction of the subject to the empty place of a functional linguistic utterance (an appendage to the verb: I think), and was carried out forcefully through the process of capitalist accumulation and subsumption of labour – did not leave our relationship to language unchanged. Modern poetry, from Baudelaire onwards, is a series of meditations on the poverty and lack of experience, on the shock and inaccessibility of life under modern social arrangements. Language, through the development of nation-states, became alienated as an objective and separate sphere in the form of national languages and literature, and thus served as a presupposition or common foundation for peoples. Today, under conditions of spectacular capitalism dominated by media, journalism and virtual communication, language no longer reveals any foundation, but only the nothingness of things (*ME*). Expropriation reaches its zenith in the society of the **spectacle**. In this society, it is language itself that becomes an object of capitalist development; language becomes spectacle. Language as spectacle expropriates all common foundations and empties all historical forms-of-life of meaning, leading to a condition of generalised **nihilism**: the form-of-life of a global petty bourgeoisie.

Agamben, however, sees in this an unprecedented opportunity to grasp the nature of human language in a more fundamental sense. By following Hamman's critique of Kant and its development by **Benveniste**, Agamben affirms the dependence of the *I think* on an *I speak*; that is, "it is in and through language that the individual is constituted as a subject" (*IH*, 45). If the truth of the society of the spectacle is that contemporary nihilism is a consequence of the expropriation of language, the solution to this problem can only be taken up from within this experience of language – the *experimentum linguae*.

In modern poetry the expropriation of language that begins with Baudelaire is reinhabited in a new way in **Caproni** and Pessoa, amongst others, who face up to the destruction of experience and inhabit the dispersal and emptiness of desubjectivation in a way that does not cover it over with a new identity or presupposition but equates the experience of the transcendental nature of language with life itself. It is this experience of expropriation, which occurs through a profanation of nihilism, that Agamben wants to see generalised in politics, economy and society in order to bring about the **community** of **whatever singularities**. This is why the figures of the *Muselmann* and the *homo sacer* become paradigms of critique. If it is true that the state of exception is the condition of global

humanity today, then for Agamben, it is those who experience expropriation in its purest form – the refugee, the poet – who are also able to serve
as paradigms for profaning that state of exception and assisting humanity
in its struggle against the sovereign ban.

$$\boxed{\text{F}}$$

(THE) FACE

Connal Parsley

In an essay entitled "The Face", appearing in *Means Without End*,
Agamben remarks that **language** is the means by which **human** beings
– unlike other living beings – attempt to "seize hold of" their own appearance in the **open**. Agamben proposes that nature, caught in this appropriative (see **appropriation**) attempt, is transformed "into *face*" (*ME*,
91). This sense of the word "face" is broader than the literal human face
or visage; as Agamben writes, "there is a face wherever something reaches
the level of exposition and tries to grasp its own being exposed" (*ME*, 92,
97).

   Thus, whilst "The Face" does not mention Martin **Heidegger** by
name, it bears the legacy of Agamben's analysis of *Dasein*'s dualities from
the same period (see *Po*, 185–204; *ME*, 98), and also his earlier reading of
Heideggerian negativity (see *LD*). Specifically, Agamben's characterisation of the face relates to his attempt to overcome the presuppositional
ban-structure of **signification**, moving instead towards one of exposition
or revelation. What is exposed in the face? According to Agamben, what
is revealed is "not *something*" signifiable or pertaining to signification,
but rather "language itself", the very fact of openness and **communicability**. As he corroborates in *The Idea of Prose*, the beautiful human
face is the mute or silent "becoming visible of the word", the "Idea of
Language" (*IP*, 113); and more recently he confirms the face as the
place of the coming to appearance not of some *thing*, but of appearance
itself (2009: 122). This suggests, Agamben explains, why man is truly
"at home" in the silence of the face, and he attributes to this exposure
of human linguisticality a location for **politics** – a human ethos – more
originary than a negatively grounded identitarian politics based on signifiable properties or attributes: thus, his imperative to "be only your face"
(*ME*, 100).

FACTICITY

Mathew Abbott

In his most sustained treatment of facticity (*Po*, 184–204), Agamben reads Heidegger as using the term to signify the thrownness of *Dasein* into the world, and the impossibility for *Dasein* of ever getting behind that thrownness in order to seize hold of it (see **appropriation**). For Agamben, facticity represents the "constitutive non-originarity" of *Dasein*, and entails its **irreparable** consignment to its singular *Seinscharakter* ("character of being") or *Weise* (guise, fashion) (*Po*, 189).

This is why Agamben links facticity to **love**, and argues in this essay for a reconsideration of love's place in *Being and Time*. Factical life is life exposed to the improper (see **impropriety**), and this exposure presents itself in the other through its idiosyncrasies: its manner, **gestures** and characteristic comportments. This is to say that a **human** being's facticity – its inability to take hold of itself – is exactly what makes it lovable, that to fall in love is to "*fall properly in love with the improper*" (*Po*, 204).

The concept has been transformed in more recent work, reappearing in a normative and political (see **politics**) register as **form-of-life**, or a **life** that "can never be separated from its form" (*ME*, 3), whatever being (see **whatever singularity**), or a being that has to be taken (and loved) "*with all of its predicates*" (*CC*, 2), or the **face**, as the site of the "*passion of revelation*" (*ME*, 92). In *The Time That Remains*, this reading of facticity remains at work when Agamben defines faith as "an experience of being beyond existence and essence", and works to think through the "interwoven" nature of faith and love in **Paul** (*TR*, 128).

In *Homo Sacer*, Agamben devotes an extended footnote to the concept, arguing that Heidegger's philosophy and Nazism were both "rooted in the same experience of facticity" (*HS*, 152). The crucial difference, however, is that Nazism "transformed the experience of factical life into a biological 'value'" (*HS*, 152), thus breaking the "unity of Being and ways of being" that characterises *Dasein* (*HS*, 153). After this division, the **bare life** of the human became "the site of an incessant decision" and **biopolitics** turned into thanatopolitics (*HS*, 153).

FACTUM LOQUENDI

Jason Maxwell

Similar to the *experimentum linguae*, the *factum loquendi* refers to "the existence of language, the fact that there are speaking beings" (*Po*, 66).

Although this point may seem painfully obvious at first glance, it has enormous implications for Agamben. From his perspective, most attempts to understand language are only able to identify particular features of language, as "linguists can construct a grammar – that is, a unitary system with describable characteristics that could be called language – only by taking the *factum-loquendi* for granted" (*ME*, 66). What these efforts fail to take into account is the existence of language as such and its general capacity to signify. That is, beyond particular statements made within a given language, the *factum loquendi* reveals language's fundamental **communicability**. Not insignificantly, Agamben pairs the *factum loquendi* with a similar concept, the *factum pluralitatis* (the simple fact that human beings form a community). Indeed, Agamben regards language and community as inextricably linked and destined to a common fate. Just as language can only be properly grasped through its potential to communicate outside of any specific content, the human community itself must be regarded as a pure potentiality that exists beyond any fixed characteristics. Because humanity is defined by its possession of language, the potentiality of language in its pure communicability underscores the openness and potentiality inherent in the human as such.

FETISH

Justin Clemens

The fetish is a concept that Agamben develops from the Marxist (see **Marx**) notion of "**commodity** fetishism" and from Sigmund **Freud**. The standard Marxist interpretation of the fetish is as a fabricated good that, if seeming to bear a certain value in and of itself, in fact dissimulates the traces of the alienated labour that went into its production. As Marx writes in a famous passage from *Capital*, vol. 1: "A commodity appears at first sight, a very trivial thing, and easily understood. Its analysis shows that it is, in reality, a very queer thing, abounding in metaphysical subtleties and theological niceties" (Marx 1990: 163). As one commentator has underlined:

The magical moment of fetish formation in this process is the transition of the general form into a universal form, its modal shift from existence and possibility to necessity – the mysterious transubstantiation of common social practices into custom or law sanctioned by the community as a whole. (Pietz 1993: 146–7)

Capitalism entails the unrestricted reign of such fetishism, precisely because the merchandising and circulation of commodities cannot function without such a dissimulation of labour by a regime of apparently object(ive) relations.

For Freud, by contrast, "fetishism" has a primarily psychological significance. In *Three Essays on Sexuality* (1905), Freud defines fetishism as follows:

What is substituted for the sexual object is some part of the body (such as the foot or hair) which is in general very inappropriate for sexual purposes, or some inanimate object which bears an assignable relation to the person whom it replaces and preferably to that person's sexuality (e.g., a piece of clothing or underlinen). Such substitutes are with some justice likened to the fetishes in which savages believe that their gods are embodied. (2001: 153)

In a much later essay, "Fetishism" (1927), Freud further specifies the characteristic operation of the fetishist as a "disavowal", as simultaneously a recognition and denial of maternal castration. Not only a simple substitute for the "real thing", then, the fetish is the outcome of a particular process sparked by an experience of impossible lack. Drawing on both Marxian and Freudian accounts, Agamben aims to exacerbate the deleterious logics of the fetish in order to offer the possibility of another mode. *Stanzas* is the key text for such an attempt, but it is also legible elsewhere, as in his comments on advertising and **pornography** in *The Coming Community*.

FORM-OF-LIFE

Alex Murray

Among the vocabulary of Agamben's critical project "Form-of-Life" remains a central if often enigmatic term. It is primarily associated with the *Homo Sacer* project and provides a horizon to Agamben's critique of the capture of life under the sovereign (see **sovereignty**) exception. One of the clearest formulations of the term comes in a short essay in *Means Without End* in which Agamben defines it as a "life that can never be separated from its form, a life in which it is never possible to isolate something such as naked life" (*ME*, 3–4). Therefore the term can only be understood in its relation to the capture of life that, for Agamben, dominates the juridico-political tradition of the West.

In Agamben's formulation, politics was, in Ancient Greece, based upon the division between *zoē* and *bios*. The former was the term for life, the substance shared between man, animal and the gods. *Bios* was then qualified life and the realm of politics, in which life was qualified through the attribution of certain qualities. But this division between life and political life is responsible for producing **bare life**, the capturing and politicisation of *zoē* as it enters into the political.

So form-of-life is in opposition to those forms of life that work to capture *zoē*. It is worth noting here the linguistic differences between the forms and form, and the importance of the hyphens in the term under discussion. Forms of life describe the various ways in which the **apparatuses** of power work to define and control life. The plurality is important as it identifies the ways in which life is fractured and controlled by sovereign power. Form-of-life is, then, a singular life that will emerge once the fracturing of life has been rendered inoperative. It is important that Agamben only identifies this form-of-life in opposition to the capturing of naked life and therefore without it being given any presupposed qualities. As Agamben states:

Only if I am not always already and solely enacted, but rather delivered to a possibility and a power, only if living and intending and apprehending themselves are at stake each time in what I live and intend and apprehend – only if, in other words, there is thought – only then can a form of life become, in its own factness and thingness, form-of-life, in which it is never possible to isolate something like naked life. (*ME*, 9)

This idea of a life, indivisible from its forms, is also referred to by Agamben as "simply human life" (*CC*, 7). Like the **coming community**, form-of-life cannot be given any attributes or qualities, existing in opposition to the biopolitical (see **biopolitics**) capture of life. To give it attributes would be to isolate forms, splitting life from itself as one attempted to capture it. Agamben suggests that the form-of-life may be connected to the Marxian "general intellect" in that it names "*the unitary power that constitutes the multiple forms of life as form-of-life*" (*ME*, 11; italics in original). This "thought" that unifies is, for Agamben, the starting point for a new politics. In this sense we can read form-of-life as analogous to **happy life**, an "absolutely profane 'sufficient life' that has reached the perfection of its own power and of its own communicability" (*ME*, 115). Communicability is important here, as the form-of-life will also be a shift in the separation of language from itself. All of Agamben's work rests on the negative condition of language as always already estranged from the human. Language then becomes a mechanism for capture, the "jargons that hide the pure experience of language" (*ME*, 70).

Form-of-life should be read as having a crucial relation to both **potentiality** and the messianic (see **messianism**). Like them it names both a critique of a particular structure (ontological, temporal) and opens up to a condition beyond those structures where the separation upon which they are based will no longer exist, and a new life will have emerged. **Life,** beyond the capture and control of the biopolitical and anthropological machines, remains the abiding concern of Agamben's work.

FOUCAULT, MICHEL

Anton Schütz

Agamben's closest encounter with and dependence on Foucault relates to the notion of **biopolitics** and includes a cluster of further life-related developments. While taking on board Foucault's main relevant tenets, including the idea that racism plays a key role in the historical articulation or overlapping of the two *régimes* of sovereign power and modern bio-power (although in his case based on the assertion, *contra* Foucault, of the fundamental identity of both; cf. Geulen 2005: 146), Agamben identifies a subterranean continuity between the politics of those times immemorial which recognised themselves perfectly in the metaphysical tradition, and the politics of the following and current age. Unbinding the biopolitical from its strict Foucauldian moorings in modern governmentality and in the genealogy of "liberalism", Agamben effectively holds that biopolitics, more exactly the production of the biopolitical body, has been the under-lying structure, indeed the original activity, of sovereign power since its beginning. Biopolitics is thus, for Agamben, not a special condition that Western mankind has imposed upon itself as a consequence of the specific dynamics unleashed during the past two or three centuries alone; it is this inseparability from the vexed question of **bare life** – of a life deprived of any status, dignity, *officium* or identity (a notion which as such is absent from Foucault's dealing with the subject) – that warrants Agamben's step of extending its lifespan to the entirety of what is conventionally understood as Western history.

To the issue of biopolitics, which is crucial to *Homo Sacer: Sovereign Power and Bare Life*, one needs to add an equally decisive encounter in relation to an issue of historical methodology (although Foucault never treated it as such). This is an issue that shows Agamben at odds with what is often believed to be one of Foucault's most categorical and unam-biguous claims: namely, the vow, frequent and effectively respected in the work of the younger Foucault, according to which the discontinuity which presides over the emergence of any historical configuration and object whatsoever, that stipulates, on the side of the historian, perfect abstinence from any perspective that would grant the possibility of transgressing the strictly *contemporaneous* condition and frame of reference of all historical happening. The fact that there is, as French historian Paul Veyne had pointed out long ago, no such thing for Foucault as a "transhistorical entity" also means that there is no place in Foucault's view of history for historical subjects, identities or evolutions whose lifespan would transcend the present tense of discursive actuality. This understanding applies, more than to any other topic, to modernity. The history of modernity must be investigated as an independent unit, no longer remote-controlled by an earlier past or plugged into a history-transcending timelessness; for many Foucauldians, and especially for numerous Foucault-inspired historians today, the main point of the discipline at work in Foucault's writing lies in the methodic exclusion, for any single one of the features his painstaking historical and conceptual efforts have isolated as constitutive of the past two or, in some cases, three centuries, of any form of determination by modernity-external, pre-modern factors. Agamben, on the contrary, robbing modernity of its Foucauldian status of coherence and singularity, sees Foucault's claims about historical discontinuity and the datedness of every feature as much less decisive than the arguments Foucault makes about topics such as the archive and archaeology, the notion of paradigm and the theme of government – points which Agamben takes up to their full extent, often radicalising them. If, today, one thing appears obvious to an observer, it is that any interpretation of Foucault that would, as does Agamben's, downgrade or take its distance from the essential modernistic closure presiding over Foucault's inquiries of the 1960s and 1970s would have very limited chances of acceptance in the absence of the apparently distinct layer of writing and teaching on selected topics of the history of antiquity that stems from Foucault's last years. Even if it is the earlier Foucault that Agamben is most interested in, the fact that Foucault's last years witness a transfer of the historical focus from the last four centuries to the Hellenistic and Roman ages makes an important difference. It is undeniable that the late, antiquity-related production throws a different light on Foucault's earlier, modernity-related work. Yet, the distance Agamben takes with respect to the discontinuity argument in its application to modernity has elicited a rich harvest of objections from more "orthodox" Foucauldian scholars.

Agamben's recent discussion of methodological concepts starts by subjecting the notion of a paradigm, as it appears explicitly in Thomas S. Kuhn and implicitly, under various different names, in Foucault's *Archaeology of Knowledge* (first published in French in 1966) and *Order of Things* (1969), to a differential analysis that insists on the contrasts between the thought of both authors (*ST*, "Philosophical Archaeology").

Agamben contextualises Foucault's notion of archaeology by staging a conversation between Foucault – the Foucault of "Nietzsche, Genealogy, History" (1971) – and a panel of authors equally involved in the exploration of what Agamben calls the "essential dishomogeneity present in every genuine historical praxis" (*ST*, 82–3; trans. modified). Among the discussants are – apart from Heidegger – Gernet, Dumézil, Mauss, Melandri, Ricœur, Freud, and Nietzsche's close friend, the theologian, Franz Overbeck, whose distinction between pre-history and history is echoed by the sharp opposition voiced by Foucault between an origin-related take on history, and the proceeding he vows to put to test in his own work and which he defines using the Nietzschean term "genealogy". "Genealogy is not in opposition to history," Foucault explains, "it is in opposition to the meta-historical unfolding of ideal meaning and indefinite teleologies. It is in opposition to the quest of 'origin'."

FREUD, SIGMUND

Justin Clemens

Despite his hostility to many aspects of psychoanalytic theory, including its psychologism and its therapeutic pretensions, Sigmund Freud (1856–1939) is key to Agamben's own early work, in regard to two concepts in particular: melancholia and **fetishism**. The first receives its canonical determination in "Mourning and Melancholia" (1917), in which Freud makes the notorious claim that melancholia constitutes "a failure to mourn", and that, in melancholia, "the shadow of the object falls on the ego." Freud outlines the following features of melancholy: dejection, dereliction of the world, erotic destitution, physical debilitation, expressions of self-loathing and delusional guilt. In *Stanzas*, Agamben draws on this sense of the concept, in order to demonstrate long-term continuities in the theorisation of melancholy from the Middle Ages to Freud himself; Freud thereby becomes the unknowing inheritor of a deep historical formation.

Regarding fetishism (see **fetish**), Agamben picks up and redeploys the operations that Freud sees as peculiar to the fetishist, above all "disavowal". If neurotics *repress* (that is, flee an unbearable affect) and psychotics *foreclose* (that is, absolutely repudiate the fact of castration), the pervert *disavows* (that is, simultaneously acknowledges and denies the fact of castration). In doing so, the fetishist finds his or her desire in materials which designate the absence of the ultimate Object. A fetish is, under this description, at once absolutely material and absolutely ideal at the same time – a kind of phantasmagoric multiplicity. Agamben links the operations of the melancholic with those of the fetishist: the dissimulating production of the good as lost, rather than simply lacking. As such, Freud proves both a crucial conceptual resource for Agamben and an object of critique.

GENIUS

Thanos Zartaloudis

In the first chapter of *Profanations* (2007), Agamben shows, through an etymological investigation, that the understanding of the notion of genius lies in the bipolar intimacy between the demonic (in Greek: *daimon* and in Latin: *genio*) and the underlying sense of genesis or generation (*generare*) (*Pr*, 9). Etymologically, genius was not only the personification of sexual energy, birth and genesis but also the personal divination of every human being, its origin and the expression of a human being's whole existence. The name, genius, used to describe the guardian and the origination that continually co-exists within each human being from the moment of birth, provides the milieu for a further attempt in Agamben's thought decisively to dislocate the prevalent discourses on individual human subjectivity.

Agamben writes of the human individual against both the Romantic model of the genius, as either an indeterminate imagination or as an eccentric agony or madness, and the Enlightenment understanding of subjectivity as transparent under the spell of reason. Finally, he revisits the notion of genius against the psychologisation of subjectivity in late modern discourse. Agamben's thinking of genius does not conceive the subject as a mere individual, an enlightened rationality or a psychological substance. Rather, it is oriented toward a conception of subjectivity as the *ethos,* or way of being, of a **form-of-life**. Revisiting his earlier consideration of human gestures in *Potentialities* (*Po*, 77–85), Agamben writes in *Profanations*:

A subjectivity is produced where the living being, encountering language and putting itself into play in language without reserve, exhibits in a gesture the impossibility of its being reduced to this gesture. All the rest is psychology, and nowhere in psychology do we encounter anything like an ethical subject, a form of life. (*Pr*, 72)

In Agamben's analysis, genius must be considered as a contingent (see **contingency**), continuous tension within and beyond the corporeality and rational intellect of a human being. Thus, he proposes the following approach: "We must therefore consider the subject as a force field of tension whose antithetical poles are Genius and Ego. This field is traversed by two conjoined but opposed forces: one that moves from the individual to the impersonal and another that moves from the impersonal to the individual" (*Pr*, 13). Agamben uses the example of someone who wants to write not this or that particular work but generally. The desire of the Ego to write generally means that one feels that there is an impersonal power that drives one toward writing. Hence, Agamben writes:

One writes in order to become impersonal, to become genial, and yet, in writing, we individuate ourselves as authors of this or that work; we move away from Genius, who can never have the form of an ego, much less that of an author. (*Pr*, 13)

The genius is not given a power or origin by the individual, but on the contrary, it is the impersonal power (or potentiality) of a human being that gives not an origin but a force of poetic generation.

The encounter of each person with his or her genius (the impersonal) is anything but simple. It is not a mere question of identity but an encounter that generates an ethics of different types of relation with one's genius. Some – and, for Agamben, they are the worst – consider their genius as their personal magician, muse or creative demonic force; others flee from it in terror and panic or attempt "hypocritically to reduce it to their own miniscule [sic] stature" (*Pr*, 14). Agamben explains emphatically:

That is why the encounter with Genius is terrible. The life that maintains the tension between the personal and the impersonal, between Ego and Genius, is called poetic. But the feeling that occurs when Genius exceeds us on every side is called panic – panic at something that comes over us and is infinitely greater than what we believe ourselves able to bear. [. . .] What is rejected as impersonal, then, can reappear in the form of symptoms and tics that are even more impersonal, or grimaces that are even more excessive. But more laughable and fatuous than this is someone who experiences the encounter with Genius as a privilege, the Poet who strikes a pose and puts on airs or, worse, feigns humility and gives thanks for the grace received. In the face of Genius, no one is great; we are all equally small. But some let themselves be shaken and traversed by Genius to the point of falling apart. Others, more serious but less happy, refuse to impersonate the impersonal, to lend their lips to a voice that does not belong to them. (*Pr*, 14)

Key examples of writers or thinkers who Agamben believes showed creative unmitigated humility in their creativity are Robert **Walser** and Walter **Benjamin**.

The contingency of genius needs to be emphasised since the individual subject is never fully individual (as one is near-continuously traversed by the impersonal forces of his or her genius), as well as never fully in common with a collective genus (since the modality of genial being is one of potentiality, rather than one of identity and recognition). Thus, the individual is always being generated and is ever incomplete. Our genius is single but changeable, sometimes luminous, sometimes dark, "sometimes wise and sometimes depraved" (*Pr*, 16). What changes, for Agamben, is not one's genius as such but one's relationship to genius, and this relationship is one of an inessential encounter with a field of tensions, an ethical relationship in the threshold and fragile existence of one's **form-of-life**. The **origin** given by genius to the individual is not a fixed origin that belongs to a substantial determination or merely to the past. Instead, this origination is sustained as a potentiality (not a matter of fact) in the present moment where the present is conceived as a futural-past. The split futurality of this generative past (potentiality) is experienced in a non-integrative sense:

man is thus a single being with two phases; he is a being that results from the complex dialectic between a part that has yet to be individuated (*individuata*) and lived and another part that is marked by fate and individual experience. But the impersonal, non-individual part is not a past we have left behind once and for all and that we may eventually recall in memory; it is still present in us, still with us, near to us and inseparable from us, for both good and ill. (*Pr*, 11)

Genius is what is each time personalised and which yet survives this personalisation, surpasses and exceeds ourselves. In this sense, we are shown by genius to be more and less than ourselves (*Pr*, 11). Agamben's analysis of genius can be related to his earlier treatment of genus (*MC*, 80) and his recent account of genealogy in *Signatures*. This analysis of genius forms an element in Agamben's long-standing strategic assault on the apparatus (*dispositif*) of fulfilled capitalism, and should be understood in terms of **profanation**. The particular apparatuses of the religious cult of nihilistic capitalism efface personal desire into joyless consumption at the very same time as they posit the presupposed (and excluded) bare life of human beings as sacred. What is posited as the unprofanable (sacred being, bare life, the impersonal) is precisely, for Agamben, what mostly requires profanation, so that the sacred can be turned back to profane use and enjoyment against both ascetic sacrifice and the modern cult of consumption: "The transformation of the species into a principle of identity and classification is the original sin of our culture, its most implacable apparatus. Something is personalized – is referred to as an identity – at the cost of sacrificing its specialness" (*Pr*, 59).

GESTURE

Deborah Levitt

Many of Agamben's words are spent on diagnosing the catastrophic situation of a biopolitical modernity that, in its states of exception-become-rule, exposes the **bare life** of its most vulnerable subjects to extreme forms of dispossession and violence. Gesture is an extremely important figure in Agamben's work because it, along with **use** and **profanation**, is as close as he comes to elaborating a process or set of operations – even a poetics or pragmatics – which might work to counteract the disintegrative tendencies of the age. But the *modus operandi* of these terms – or, at least, of gesture – is never to counteract disintegration in the conventional sense, but rather to extend and crystallise it: to find what, from within it, might bring about a new world as a non-statist, non-teleological, non-identitarian community-to-come.

Gesture, for Agamben, is what takes place when all definitive locations – **life** and **art**, text and execution, reality and virtuality, power and act, personal biography and impersonal event – are suspended. In this opening, what appears – or plays – is gesture. According to Agamben, gesture is a special kind of action, neither a means nor an end. He distinguishes it from Aristotle's conceptions of a making that would produce something (from or by means of itself), and an action that would enact something (existing before it). Gesture pertains to a third kind of action that Agamben, following Varro, characterises as carrying, enduring, supporting. It is "pure **praxis**" freed from any pre-existing determination (such as life or art) and freed of any *telos*, including any **aesthetic** one (such as art for art's sake).

"Gesture" appears in relation to a constellation of other recurrent *topoi* in Agamben's *œuvre*: most prominently, cinema, **language** and authorship, but also including advertising, **pornography**, mime and the *commedia dell'arte*. Given Agamben's recourse to Aristotelian and Varronian categories in his definition of gesture, and of the very wide variety of reference points he provides for it, one might at first assume it is a purely a-historical or at least trans-historical category for him. In fact, however, "Notes on Gesture", his most exhaustive treatment of the topic, involves a very precise historical account of the concept. Gesture is the pivotal term in Agamben's historical account of the society of the spectacle, in which he shows the mutual imbrication of a biopolitical ratio and modern media technologies and practices in producing the contemporary cultural and political scene. And, even where Agamben frames gesture as the site of subjectivity itself, it is only in a kind of "hand-to-hand combat" with apparatuses of power and knowledge at a given moment and at a given time – and with the always historical apparatus of language itself, most especially – that the **subject** can put into play its own never-ceasing-to-disappear.

In "Notes on Gesture", Agamben proclaims, "by the end of the nineteenth century, the Western bourgeoisie had definitively lost its gestures" (*ME*, 49). While people, of course, still waved hello and goodbye, or gestured for others to approach or draw back, these gestures were no longer their own. They had been expropriated by a set of medico-industrial-legal analytics which Agamben links to Gilles de la Tourette's analysis of the gait, and Muybridge and Marey's photographic analyses of human and animal movement. All of these involved using new technological means of visualisation to break the body's movements down into hitherto imperceptible instants, and then re-assemble these instants into series of images. These gestures thus had a continued existence, but in a spectacular sphere now alienated from everyday experience.

It is precisely gesture's alienation in and as this spectacular sphere – along with the special "kind of eye" cinema will bring to gesture – that makes the "element of cinema", as Agamben will argue, the gesture and not the image (*ME*, 55), and that thus places cinema "in the sphere of ethics and politics (and not simply in that of aesthetics)" (*ME*, 56). Two forces thus meet in Agamben's conception of a gestural cinema. The first is, as described above, the alienation of human experience – and the human body – as spectacle. The other pertains to the properties of the cinematic image itself. On this second front, Agamben follows Gilles **Deleuze** in positing that the cinematic image is not most essentially a still image mechanically moved; it is a movement-image. The image is no longer bound to the *pose éternelle* and its static ontology. It is, rather, freed into a process where, without end or destiny, it follows the path of its movement and may enter into constellation with other images.

The realm of **ethics**, for Agamben, is the sphere of gesture: that is, it is that realm in which the third kind of action – as means without end – unfolds. In an essay entitled "Ethics" in *The Coming Community*, Agamben states, "the fact that must constitute the point of departure for any discourse on ethics is that there is no essence, no historical or spiritual vocation, no biological destiny that humans must realize." If humans "were or had to be this or that substance", he continues, "no ethical experience would be possible – there would be only tasks to be done" (*CC*, 43). The gesture, as we have seen, is precisely that element, that process that plays, unfolds, endures in the sphere of pure means that Agamben calls "the absolute gesturality of human beings" and also calls "**politics**". Ethics emerges precisely because of the absence of ontological ground or *telos*; gesture names an a-ontological figure that traverses this open space and catalyses events, differences and constellations within it. The "positive possibility" of the contemporary moment emerges precisely from the "experimentum linguae that disarticulates and empties, all over the planet, traditions and beliefs, ideologies and religions, identities and communities" (*ME*, 85). Where gesture was once contained by the content of propositions or by the eternal poses of the **image** sphere, the emptying out of language and the putting-into-movement of the image exposes the becoming-gesture of image, language and subject. It makes it into an experience which itself becomes a platform for experimentation.

Agamben has a kind of formula for gesture that unifies its otherwise diverse sites of appearance: "The gesture", he writes, "is the exhibition of a mediality, it is the process of making a means visible as such" (*ME*, 58). This formula holds for both the porn star whose gaze at the camera reveals that her exhibition takes precedence over her engagement with her partner, and for the mime who, estranging gestures from their normal ends, exhibits them in their pure mediality – that is, shows them in their pure being-in-a-medium. In an essential sense, all of these appearances of gesture come back to language, or more generally to communicability. The gesture, which Agamben relates to the gag – as both something put in the mouth to prevent speech and the recourse of the actor when speech fails – is a kind of silent condition of possibility for speech. Its exhibition – a showing which "cannot be said in sentences" – reveals the being-in-language of humans. Agamben moves quite easily back and forth between image and language as modes of humans being-in-a-medium in his discussions of gesture.

In "The Author as Gesture", Agamben begins with a reading of Michel Foucault's "What is an Author?" and ends with a theory of subjectivity-as-gesture. He writes, "what is in question in writing, Foucault suggested, is not so much the expression of a subject, as the opening of a space in which the writing subject does not cease to disappear" (*Pr*, 61). We can already see Agamben's own gesture in play here. This is his gloss of Foucault's statement, "the trace of the writer is found only in the singularity of his absence" (*Pr*, 61). The "singularity of his absence" describes an essentially static moment; Agamben puts it into motion. The ontological determinant (however negatively construed) of the singular absence becomes the endless motion of a not-ceasing-to-disappear. The author

becomes author as she puts herself into play in the text; she is the gesture
that opens the conditions of possibility for expression in the work but
is never thus expressed within it. She is the catalyst, the opener, of the
space of the text but not as who or what – not as a pre-existent ontological
ground – but as a how, as a style and a movement that sets its potentials in
motion: that is, as gesture.

The author becomes, for Agamben, the model for the subject as such.

A subjectivity [he writes] is produced where the living being, encountering language and putting itself into play in language without reserve, exhibits in a gesture
the impossibility of its being reduced to this gesture. All the rest is psychology,
and nowhere in psychology do we encounter anything like an ethical subject, a
form of life. (*Pr*, 72)

This style-in-movement, entering into a kind of hand-to-hand combat
with a particular *dispositif* of power at a particular moment, becomes
an ethical subject, a form of life, but only in so far as this gesture is not
exhausted, but never ceases to appear and disappear in the text or situation it has provoked. The gesture puts-into-play in so far as it catalyses
an always-developing situation through engagement with an apparatus;
what comes to pass can never be reduced to this opening gesture, as what
it opens is always in excess of and different from itself. It produces a situation that is never reducible to its opening gambit; nor is this gambit ever
exhausted in the situation. This gesture, style, movement – as it passes
into an apparatus and opens a situation – is the subject.

GLORY

Thanos Zartaloudis

In one of the most crucial passages of *Idea of Prose*, "The Idea of Glory",
Agamben situates glory in relation to the understanding of appearance,
in the Greek sense of a phenomenon, locating its threshold of meaning
between semblance or likeness (*videtur*) and a pure visibility, a shining
(*lucet*) (*IP*, 125). This significantly affects the understanding of the
appearance of things, the appearance of the human face before another
face and the meaning of the glory of God (*Kabod, doxa*). Glory (*kabod,
doxa*) signifies God's attribute of manifestation, appearance or semblance
(*IP*, 126). This is a key concern in Agamben's thought that continues to be
developed in later works like *The Coming Community*, *Means Without End*,
Profanations and *Il Regno e la gloria*. It could not be otherwise, as glory is,

in a certain sense, of central concern to human beings in particular: "only man is concerned with images as images; only man knows appearance as appearance" (*IP*, 127). Only for human beings does appearance or semblance separate itself from the thing that shines: "at the point of innervation at which the image reflected in the retina becomes sight, the eye is necessarily blind" (*IP*, 127). It is for human beings alone that things actually are in this manner: in the threshold between their independence from our relation with them and our glimpse of them as appearances. It could be said that Agamben's whole project is to think the implications of the vision of this blindness, this taking place, for our understanding of human action and being. Agamben explores this again and again: for instance, in relation to being and appearance (*CC*), the face (*ME*), language and communicability (*Po*), animality and humanity (*O*), and divine being and power (in, among others, *Il Regno e la gloria*).

The most significant and detailed analysis of glory to date appears in *Il Regno e la gloria*, half of which is devoted to rethinking glory, in order to overcome its predominant aestheticisation. For Agamben the place of glory is properly that of politics and this, he is convinced, is the case even in the early scriptural uses of the terms *kabod* and *doxa*. Through a long genealogy of the theological-historical uses of glory, Agamben takes the reader from Maimonides and Paul to Origen and back to the modern theologians, and highlights the separation of glory (supposedly as something that God either has or creates) from glorification (as what creation gives to the Divine being, as praise). The question of priority between these two understandings is crucial for Agamben's genealogy of glory in the Christian and the Judaic traditions (and elements of the Hindu tradition, via Marcel Mauss).

Most subsequent interpreters of Maimonides ground glorification on a precedent glory. In contrast, Agamben examines the dialectical relationship of *doxa* with *oikonomia* in Christianity in order to demonstrate that the economy of the trinity is constitutively an economy of glory as such. Through a crucial analysis of Origen's commentary on John, the mutual glorification of God and Christ is revealed as God's self-knowledge. This self-knowledge is itself revealed to be an empty void when the Trinitarian economy is completed and absorbed into the immanent trinity after the Last Judgment. Glory, for Agamben, points towards the messianic (see **messianism**) time of the end, the time of the perfect completion of the Trinitarian economy, and of the machine of mutual glorification whose central vacuity has been concealed by the apparatuses of power and glory in both the sacred and the so-called secular spheres. In this manner, glorification is not owned by glory because it somehow derives from it, but rather because glorification as an act creates and presupposes glory as such. For example, Agamben shows that in Judaism, God needs praise, despite of his fullness, in order to maintain his strength.

This paradoxical formation of glorious power also appears throughout Agamben's *Homo Sacer* project. Yet, this does not point to a mere instrumental dialectic between power and glory. Glory (and necessarily glorification also) is intimately linked to the constitutive inoperativity of humanity as such, its inessential being. It is this, above all, that power in its governmental apparatus captures, in order to prevent its unbinding. It is in its orientation towards the destruction of this knot, this capture, that Agamben's thought finds its rigour and strength.

GOVERNMENT/*OIKONOMIA*

Thanos Zartaloudis

The historical-philosophical genealogy of government (and, by implication, *oikonomia*) in Agamben's later writings (2007–) finds its key problem in the long-established negative relation between political authority and political activity or *praxis*. *Oikonomia* is conceived in the early Greek and later Christian theological sense as a paradigm of management. Though this conception should not be confused with modern economics, neither does it exclude the theological roots of certain aspects of economic government and management. In *Il Regno e la gloria*, Agamben investigates the reasons and modes through which Western power took the form of an *oikonomia* (economy): that is, of an administrative government of "men and things". In other words he traces the "roots" of the problem of modern government, as a form and a praxis, to the Christian paradigms of political theology and *oikonomia*, and, more specifically, to the presupposition of their necessary functional relation.

Political theology grounds the transcendence of sovereign (see **sovereignty**) power in its juridical (or juridico-political) form in the doctrine of the one God. *Oikonomic* theology bases itself on the notion of an *oikonomia*: that is, an economy conceived as an immanent and non-political order of both human and divine life. (*Oikos*, in Aristotle for instance, refers to the management of the home and not of the *polis*.) It is this *oikonomic* or managerial paradigm that leads, according to Agamben, to modern biopolitics and the current domination of economic and managerial logics over all aspects of social life. Government is in a sense a question of two polarities, one juridico-political and the other praxiological and managerial, and, crucially, of their particular functional relation.

Agamben traces the genealogy of the *oikonomic* paradigm to the second century of the Christian era, around the time of the formation of the doctrine of the Trinity. Those Church Fathers who elaborated the Trinitarian doctrine had opposed to them the monarchists (or monarchians) who held that God was one and that the introduction of the triune divinity risked the return to polytheism. Thus, the problem was how to reconcile two equally unrenounceable doctrines: the trinity and monarchism or monotheism. *Oikonomia* was the key concept, the functional instrument that rendered possible this reconciliation. The reasoning of the doctrine can be rendered simply in the following manner: God is one in his essence and his nature (*ousia*), but in the management of his *oikonomia* God can divide his power and himself in three. For the Christian theologians, *oikonomia* was an economy of government, rather than politics. In a philosophical sense, Agamben elaborates the larger question of the separation of being and praxis in relation to Aristotle's theory of being and power.

The economy as an *oikonomia* becomes, for Agamben, the central apparatus that establishes the mystery of the divine economy (as opposed to the mystery being that of God's being or substance, which was reversed by theologians such as Irenaeus and Tertullian). It is here that Agamben locates the functional distinction between ontology and praxis that defines, with devastating consequences, Western theological, philosophical, political and juridical discourse. While *oikonomia*, the heart of the Trinitarian doctrine, was later to become a metaphysical doctrine, it was first introduced as a managerial **apparatus**. In this sense, *oikonomia*, for Agamben, is the hidden ontological paradigm of modern governance, and of the negative functional relation between being and praxis more generally. Political theology can affirm itself only by suspending economic theology. Furthermore, for Agamben, there is a secret solidarity between government and anarchy; to risk a simplification, there is government only because the elements that constitute it are groundless (without origin).

The detailed illustration of the *oikonomic* paradigm of divine governance of the world takes a further form in the name of providence (of Stoic origin), which from the time of Clement of Alexandria in the late second century to the seventeenth century acquires many forms and describes government as a divine *oikonomia*. In each case, Agamben's genealogical study reveals the coordination of two aspects in a bipolar machine of governmental power: *ordinatio* and *executio*, general and particular providence, being and *praxis*, *potentia absoluta* and *potentia ordinata*, general law and execution, general will and particular will, and so forth. In the tradition of political philosophy this functional structure of bipolarity is well expressed in the old formula, "the king reigns, but he doesn't govern," already found in the sixteenth century and linked to the figure of the *Roi mehaignié*: that is, the do-nothing king, found primarily in Arthurian legends.

In terms of modern democracy, which follows the *oikonomic* paradigm, we come to think of government in terms of the division between legislative or sovereign power, which acts through universal laws and principles, and executive power, which carries out in praxis the general principle. The vocabulary and structure of government are, thus, first linked to the paradigm of *oikonomia* before political and legal theory employs the terms of public administration and order. For Agamben, the history of Western politics is thus the history of the numerous shifting articulations of the functional bipolarity of governmental power: reign and government; sovereignty and economy; law and order; law and police.

Finally, for Agamben, the way in which divine government (and today democratic government) becomes effective and realises itself is through collateral effects. The governmental machine becomes operative only as a side-effect, through collateral effects, while it oscillates constantly between two separate spheres of general and particular power. This proposition, coupled with the essential character of providential power as a power that reigns but does not govern (that is, with a power that governs not through an act of force but through the free will of the governed), renders governmental power as an essentially vicarious power that derives its supposed essence from an empty throne. God or power governs as if it were absent from the world and it does so, following the Trinitarian paradigm, in an intrinsically vicarious manner, through which there is no way to assign to one person the original, and absent, foundation of power. In modern governmental power, this can be seen clearly in the oscillation between constitutive and constituted power, sovereignty and execution, legislation and police, which makes it increasingly impossible to place the onus of real responsibility on anyone in particular. The secret core of politics is, therefore, neither sovereignty nor law, but government: ministerial power, vicariousness, policing control and the enabling (through the *oikonomic* paradigm of a fragile democratic rule) of the **state of exception**.

HALOS

Paolo Bartoloni

In Agamben's work, a halo is a luminous radiance which, hovering over things and beings, evokes their potentialities and their **glory**. It signals the existence of the idea of the thing as that which, although irreparably (see **irreparable**) other, is always already inscribed in the thing: a "paradigmatic existence", as Agamben writes in *The Coming Community*, "the manifesting beside itself of each thing (*paradeigma*). But this showing beside itself is a limit – or rather, it is the unraveling, the indetermination of a limit: a halo" (*CC*, 100). The halo is therefore the cipher of a relation predicated upon presence and absence, and the indication of an alienated entirety in which the shining of the idea is also the entrance into the inherent incompleteness of the thing. It is in this sense that Agamben's interpretation of the halo reconnects not only with **Benjamin**'s discussion of the aura of art, but most importantly with his conceptualisation of the work of art as "the death mask of its conception" (Benjamin 1986: 81). It appears that, for Benjamin, and Agamben after him, the origin of the work – what Agamben also calls *ergon* – can only be summoned through its effacement. In the Introduction to *Infancy and History*, Agamben returns to this point when he states that: "every written work can be regarded as the prologue (or rather, the broken cast) of a work never penned." (*IH*, 3) The work before us is simultaneously a testimony to (an *imago*) and a reminder of a liminal existence, which is calling like an echo and radiating like a halo.

HAPPINESS/HAPPY LIFE

Catherine Mills

In attempting to find a path through the aporias of biopolitics, Agamben indicates at times that a new conception of life based on happiness or beatitude is required in order to found a new "coming politics". The necessity of such a conception of life is occasionally gestured toward in *Homo Sacer*, but receives no real elaboration there. Elsewhere though, Agamben refers to this as "happy life" or "form-of-life". As he writes in *Means Without End*:

The "happy life" on which political philosophy should be founded thus cannot be either the naked life that sovereignty posits as a presupposition so as to turn it into its own subject or the impenetrable extraneity of science and of modern biopolitics that everybody tries in vain to sacralize. This "happy life" should be rather, an absolutely profane "sufficient life" that has reached the perfection of its own power and its own communicability – a life over which sovereignty and right no longer have any hold. (*ME*, 114–15)

Provocative as this suggestion is, one of the immediate difficulties with the notion of happy life is that Agamben himself provides no real explanation of what he means by this idea. Instead, there are occasional glimpses of what the notion may mean, as well as a number of theorisations that throw light on the idea without necessarily explicitly addressing it. We can be sure, though, that it does not refer to any kind of psychological or emotive state since, for one, Agamben tends to reject recourse to psychological substance in his theory of the subject. Instead, his description of a form-of-life or happy life relates to the question of **potentiality** and its preservation; moreover, the idea of a "happy life" draws on and extends various other elements of Agamben's thought, including issues of **infancy, history** and **messianism**.

The messianic dimension of Agamben's conception of happiness is clear in its reference to Benjamin's work, where the idea of happiness is tightly bound with that of redemption. For instance, in his "Theological-Political Fragment", Benjamin addresses the relation of messianic and historic time and writes that "only the Messiah himself consummates all history, in the sense that he alone redeems, completes, creates its relation to the Messianic" (Benjamin 2002: 305). Constructing an image of two arrows pointing in opposite directions but which are nevertheless reinforcing, Benjamin goes on to say that "the secular order should be erected on the idea of happiness." This is because, while the profane cannot in itself establish a relation with the Messianic, it assists the coming of the Messianic Kingdom precisely by being secular or profane. In other words, while the profane is not a category of the Messianic, it is "the decisive category of its quietest approach", because "the rhythm of Messianic nature is happiness." Happiness allows for the fulfilment of historical time, since the Messianic Kingdom is "not the goal but the end" of history (Benjamin 2002: 305, 306). Agamben takes from the "Fragment" the idea that the profane-historical order must be founded on happiness and, in that, provides passage for the messianic fulfilment of history; or, in Agamben's words, "the idea of happiness appears precisely as what allows the historical order to reach its own fulfillment" (*Po*, 154).

As this formulation of the relationship between redemption and happiness makes clear, for Agamben, the idea of happy life refers to an idea of redeemed life. However, as he sets out in *The Open*, for humanity, such redemption does not occur through a simple reconciliation of animal life and human life, nor a rejection of natural life to become wholly human. Instead, it requires a kind of transvaluation of natural life. Agamben begins *The Open* with a short reflection on a miniature from a Hebrew Bible from the thirteenth century, which represents the "messianic banquet of the righteous on the last day" (*O*, 1). What interests Agamben is that the miniature represents the righteous or "concluded humanity" with animal heads, which could suggest that "on the last day, the relations between animals and men will take on a new form, and that man himself will be reconciled with his animal nature" (*O*, 3). While this might be understood as an indication of the direction that Agamben's own thesis in *The Open* will take, this is, in fact, not the case. Instead, he argues that this representation of the "remnant . . . of Israel, that is, of the righteous who are still alive at the moment of the Messiah's coming" does not indicate or prefigure a new "declension of the man–animal relation". Instead, it indicates the possibility of stopping the "anthropological machine" that operates through the differentiation between man and animal, and the emergence of a new blessed life in its aftermath. In short, for Agamben, the "in-human" life that the inoperativity of the anthropological machine allows for is saved precisely by its being unsavable. That is, keeping in mind that "beatitude" means blessedness as well as extreme happiness, this inhuman life is blessed by virtue of its being absolutely profane (and thus built upon happiness). And for Agamben, this – "what has *never happened* – is the historical and wholly actual homeland of humanity" (*Po*, 159).

HEGEL, G. W. F.

Alysia Garrison

Agamben warns that "a critique of the dialectic is one of the most urgent tasks today" for a Marxist philosophy shored on its wreckage (*IH*, 39). Agamben's overcoming of the dialectic, and his critique of strictly "historiographical" readings of Hegel more generally, develop over several stages, beginning with his first serious engagement in *Language and Death*, the work devoted to the question of negativity in Hegel and **Heidegger**. Here Agamben locates the presupposition of language in **Voice**, the ontological dimension he defines as the "taking place of language between the removal of the voice and the event of meaning" (*LD*, 35). In Voice, language is disclosed as always already captured in negativity. The "supreme shifter", Voice functions like the indicative pronoun "this" in Hegel's *Phenomenology* (*LD*, 36). At the moment sense-certainty tries to take the "this" (*diese*), it is superseded by its negative. Sense-certainty is revealed not as immediate, but engaged in a dialectical process of mediation – at once negating, in the removal of the animal voice, and preserving, in the disclosure of its removal and the event of meaning. The voice of the animal is thus entombed in language as merely a "vanishing trace", "death that recalls and preserves death" (*LD*, 46).

Reading the young Hegel's Jena lessons from 1803–4 and 1805–6, Agamben draws an analogy between the dialectic of voice and language, and the dialectic of master and slave. Like voice, in which the dying **animal** expresses itself as removed in **language**, the master's enjoyment also shows its removal, pure negativity that is "no longer animal but not yet human, no longer desire but not yet work", apparent only in its vanishing (*LD*, 46–7). Confined by meaningful discourse and thus bound by the dialectic, the master cannot fulfill his enjoyment except as a negative articulation. Agamben suggests that the master's enjoyment can only be represented as an animal or divine figure, not a human one: a figure that evokes "only silence, or at best, laughter" (by way of **Bataille** and **Kojève**) (*LD*, 50). This entombed figure of death in language is, for Agamben, the point of fracture at which we can glimpse not only language's taking place, but also the means by which Spirit surpasses the dialectic.

Agamben examines the point of fracture and its overcoming in *Potentialities*, through a reading of Hegel's Absolute, "the fundamental philosophical problem itself" (*Po*, 116). For Agamben, the singular task of philosophy is to absolve the proper of division, to lead *se back to itself. For the Absolute, something only becomes what it is at its end. A process necessarily temporal and historical, the Absolute must fulfill time, ending it, and in so doing gather its moments into space, like a picture gallery (*Po*, 123–4). Having sunk into its night, humanity is consigned to timeless memory, a state of "total memory" in which all memories are present to themselves and therefore have nothing to remember (*Po*, 125). It is at this point of absolutely fulfilled discourse that Hegel's thought, for Agamben, thinks beyond itself; it thinks humankind's entry into "being without nominative", its "separation but also its solidarity" (*Po*, 125). This state may approximate something like species-being in **Marx**: the fulfilled animality of the human that "coincides without residue with human activity and praxis" (*Po*, 127).

In *The Time That Remains*, Agamben considers how the Hegelian dialectic is a secularisation of Christian theology, noting similarities between the Hegelian *Aufhebung* and Pauline messianic (see **Paul**; **messianism**) *katargesis* (99). Luther uses *Aufheben* to translate Paul's verb *katargein*, and in so doing, Agamben suggests, he preserves the term's double meaning as both abolishing and conserving. Hegel, for whom the *Aufhebung* connotes, at once, the lifting, suspension, cancellation and preservation of the thing itself from the prison of immediacy, later seizes upon this polysemy. By developing a science of history upon a messianic foundation, Hegel uses the trappings of Christian theology against theology, a conceptual "weapon" that, in Agamben's account, is "genuinely messianic" (99).

Rending theology **inoperative**, such a gesture resembles Agamben's theory of **profanation**.

HEIDEGGER, MARTIN

Thanos Zartaloudis

The thinker who appears most consistently, implicitly or explicitly, throughout Agamben's work, alongside Walter **Benjamin**, is Martin Heidegger. Heidegger's decisive importance for Agamben is evident throughout his *œuvre*. Furthermore, it was in the formative experience of attending Heidegger's Le Thor seminars (on Heraclitus and Hegel), in 1966 and 1968, that "philosophy became possible" for Agamben, leading him to abandon his legal studies. Agamben and Heidegger also share constant references to Plato and Aristotle, as well as to medieval thought. Furthermore, as for Heidegger, Heraclitus and Hegel are far more centrally important in Agamben's work than may appear at first sight. For instance, Heraclitus's notions of play (*paignion*) and time (*aion*) and Hegel's thinking of negativity and language (through Kojève and Heidegger's readings) are crucial for Agamben's re-orientation on the question of being (see *LD*). The references to Heidegger's work are abundant in Agamben's writings, and he has rethought and furthered the questioning of numerous key Heideggerian concerns, including language, being, power, potentiality, time, death, negativity, nihilism, ontology, authenticity, the open, the proper, *Ereignis/Enteignis*, machination and *poiesis*. Most characteristically, Agamben shares with Heidegger an understanding of philosophy and thought. Philosophy is not a discipline, a list of questions, answers and justifications, methods, forms and even writings. Like Heidegger, Agamben uses the term "thought" to signify the experience of thinking, rather than the cataloguing of arguments, justifications, worldviews and the weighing of pros and cons. Philosophy, hence, is the ever-provisional name for the experience of thought in its power, its potentiality (and impotentiality), which means that philosophical thought is the experience of generativity, incompleteness and encounter: an ever-coming thought.

The turn to the primacy of thinking **potentiality** in Agamben's work crucially follows (with and against) Heidegger's programmatic philosophical path, which could be described, generally, as a rigorous rethinking of the modalities of potentiality and **contingency**. Agamben's strategy of "destruction" (with regard, for example, to aesthetics) also follows Heidegger's understanding of the term not as an annihilation, but as a dismantling (*Abbauen*), a turning towards what addresses us in our wandering (and erring) being. Further, a defining inquiry in Agamben's work into the division between **poetry** and **philosophy** follows and develops Heidegger's earlier interrogation on the "forgetting" of being and the essence of language and poetry; the early work, *Stanzas*, is dedicated, appropriately, to Heidegger. Finally, one of the most significant, continuing and complex interrogations in Agamben's work, as evidenced in particular in *The Open*, entails a rethinking of Heidegger's examination of the concepts of humanity (see **human**) and animality (see **animal**), world and *praxis*, form and **life**.

HISTORY/HISTORICITY

Alysia Garrison

At the negative foundation of philosophy, **Hegel**'s Absolute and **Heidegger**'s *Ereignis*, history for Agamben is not the search for a cause or an **origin**, but the exposition of a fracture – produced through the discontinuity between **language** and speech, the **semiotic** and the **semantic** (in **Benveniste**'s terms), sign system and discourse (in **Foucault**'s terms) (*Po*, 121, 127; *IH*, 59). Only because of this discontinuity – the split between speech and discourse at the site of **infancy**, the transcendental origin of the **human** – is man a historical being (*IH*, 59). Unlike the **animal**, at one with its life activity and undifferentiated from nature (**Marx**), the human becomes a historical **subject** by removing himself from his wordless **experience**, by **abandoning** his infancy. This speechless moment remains in discourse as its condition of possibility, as the passage that shows the "fall" from pure language to the babble of speech. The **enigma** of infancy catalyses thought by designating a *limit*: the transcendental experience of the difference between *langue* and *parole*. This limit, the transition from pure language to discourse, this very instant, "is history" (*IH*, 64).

For Agamben historicity is at once synchronic and diachronic; the human enters history by exposing the discontinuity of language and also the discontinuity of time. Following **Benjamin** and **Nietzsche**, he believes that history is not a linear progression, a sequence of events like the beads of a rosary, but untimely, riddled by gaps, disjuncture and anachronism. In "What Is the Contemporary?" Agamben writes that the contemporary is the one who, throwing time out of joint, "impedes time from composing itself" but also "must suture this break or this wound" (*WA*, 42). The **contemporary** is only able to keep his gaze firmly on time and grasp it by suturing to its fractures: by focalising "that beam of darkness that comes from his own time" (*WA*, 45). It is from the shadow of the contemporary, the exigency to which we cannot fail to respond, that chronological time is urged, pressed and transformed from within by the light that perpetually voyages toward it. By "dividing and interpolating time", the contemporary is capable of relating it to other times, transforming it into a meeting place where the unlived past shows itself for the first time, emerging in the present; this exposition is history (*WA*, 53).

The distinction between individual historical phenomena and **paradigms** helps to explicate Agamben's approach to the problem of history further. At the beginning of his essay, "What is a Paradigm?", Agamben suggests that "misunderstandings" have emerged regarding his use of figures such as *homo sacer* or the concentration **camp** as "merely historiographic theses or reconstructions", as opposed to "paradigms whose role was to make intelligible a broader historical-problematic context" (*ST*, 9). For Agamben, the paradigm exposes history as neither "diachrony nor [. . .] synchrony but [. . .] a crossing of the two" (*ST*, 31). Like Foucault's panopticon, which illustrates both a general functioning of panopticism and also a **threshold** for **modernity**, Agamben's *homo sacer*, the camp, the *Muselmann* and the **state of exception** are analogical, moving from singularity to singularity. Their historicity resides not in any presupposed origin, but in their immanent exposition as *belonging* to a group of historically specific singularities and *suspending* such belonging (*ST*, 17). History for Agamben is a gathering, a relation that holds together individual images at a zone of perfect equilibrium between generality and particularity. This zone is necessarily ontological; paradigmatic ontology is, for Agamben, about being itself, defined in "Philosophical **Archeology**" as "a field of essentially historical tensions" (*ST*, 111). We are returned, then, from *The Signature of All Things* back to *Infancy and History* and the foundational fracture that exposes man as a historical being. By grasping history's discontinuities, historical inquiry sutures the phenomena that unfold through time, transforming the present into an emergent structure with an intelligible relation to its past (*ST*, 32).

HÖLDERLIN, FRIEDRICH

Carlo Salzani

Quotations from the *œuvre* of the German poet Johann Christian Friedrich Hölderlin (1770–1843) adorn Agamben's works in an authoritative and

evocative mode that attests to the influence of Martin **Heidegger**. The
chapter called "The Original Structure of the Work of Art" that appears
in *The Man Without Content* (1970) is construed around a quotation from
Hölderlin defining the work of art as rhythm (*MC*, 94); in fact, Hölderlin's
authority is usually invoked to posit the problem of the separation between
a poetic and a philosophical knowledge, as in the preface to *Stanzas* (*S*,
xvii). Hölderlin's poetic philosophising is proposed through thought-
stimulating citations, like his translation of Heraclitus in "**Se*: Hegel's
Absolute and Heidegger's *Ereignis*" (1982) (*Po*, 118), a quotation from
his poem "Patmos" and a 1795 note on "absolute Being" in "Tradition
of the Immemorial" (1985) (*Po*, 113–14), and his translation from Pindar
and a note on "pain" in *Homo Sacer* (*HS*, 32–3, 185). Hölderlin's citation
from the *Suda* on **Aristotle** appears in "The Thing Itself" (1984) and
"Bartleby, or On Contingency" (1993) (*Po*, 38, 243), and a sentence from
a letter to Böhlendorff, "the free use of the proper is the most difficult
task," importantly epitomises, in "The Passion of Facticity" (1987) and
The Coming Community, the centrality of **love** for the coming **politics**
(*Po*, 204; *CC*, 25). Finally, the paratactic fragmentation of Hölderlin's
later hymns signifies, in *The Time That Remains* (*TR*, 87) and *Il Regno
e la gloria* (Agamben 2007: 260–2, 275), the messianic deactivation (see
messianism; **deactivate**) of **signification**.

HOMO SACER

Anton Schütz

Homo Sacer is, first of all, the title of a study which was first published in
Italian in 1995 and in English in 1998; it explores the relationship of **bare
life** and **sovereignty**. Second, it is the title of a multi-volume series which
has grown out of what it retroactively refers to as its first volume. Only
once it has covered its not entirely premeditated historico–philosophical
itinerary with a substantial sequence of further intermediary part-volumes
will this series see, one day, or so it is announced and expected, its final
instalment dedicated to "form of life".

What has confounded many readers, of the initial study as well as of
the emergent series, is the fact that *homo sacer* had existed as a common
name well before being chosen as a title and a key to the riddle underlying the Western relationship to politics. It was the name given to a
vague but complex figure registered in the grammatico–institutional
inventory of the personnel of archaic Rome, and is recorded as such in
an extant fragment of Sextus Pompeius Festus, one of the pale but well-

instructed scriveners of that inventory. The degree of interest, perplexity and resistance that Agamben's work has elicited, uncommon by any standards, is certainly due, in large part, to its historico-philosophical message and the "all-crushing" aspects of some of its implications (to use an adjective famously coined, in the late eighteenth century, by one Moses Mendelssohn, looking for an appropriate characterisation of the **Kant** of the first Critique). Even so, there is a formal aspect that might have played an important part as well. The decision to introduce the theme of **bare life** by calling upon the *homo sacer* and appointing him as its exemplary carrier or personal representative, the further decision to christen this representative with the name of a perfectly documented, yet tenebrous figure of the Roman institutional *nomenclatura*, thus referring the topic of the study, on its title page, to a long-bygone historical layer, in order then to use the entire study to contradict and correct this first impression and to show just how little "bygone" – indeed, how increasingly momentous – both the motive of bare life and the structure underlying its Roman impersonation have proven throughout the most recent history: all this involves a methodological strategy that stands in plain opposition to a, very generally embraced, philosophical habit – namely, the choice of casting new thought in new conceptual terminology. This had been the preference adopted by Kant, **Marx** and even **Foucault**, among others.

Agamben, instead, entrusts his reasoning – at least at the decisive level of the reader's first encounter with the text – to the representation of a personal character which, however generically named and archivally documented, is taken from the *dramatis personae* of the Western drama. Who is this *homo sacer*, imported from the primeval regions of Roman antiquity and endowed with the role of bare life's silent spokesperson and historical protagonist? Conceptually, he is the site of a conjunction of a passive capacity ("can be killed") with a passive incapacity ("cannot be sacrificed"). Two strict lines determine the status of the *homo sacer*; he is locked out of the politico-legal order's protection, considering that, whoever would kill the *homo sacer*, is not deemed to have committed a murder, yet, at the same time, he is locked in with respect to this "order's" procedures, considering that his exclusion from being sacrifice-worthy is the outcome of a well-defined routine, consecration or sacrification, *sacratio* (*HS*, 81ff.), that he has undergone and survived.

This is the point at which historical issues come into closer sight. Even if our information stems from a grammarian working under the Empire (late second century AD), what a gaze into these sources makes immediately clear is that, at the time at which he writes, the *homo sacer* looks back to a long pre-history. Indeed, far from dealing with a historical singularity that comes complete with a well-defined date of appearance, we are confronted with an immemorial institution, the "being-around" of which in Roman history precedes any assignable historic term. At the same time, the *homo sacer* clearly instantiates the most unsettling aspect of the social arrangement to which he belongs. Agamben's decision to appoint him retroactively to the role of the eponymous hero of **bare life** (itself a notion borrowed from **Benjamin**'s essay, "Critique of Violence") epitomises the argument that the structure of inclusive exclusion or sovereign ban that the *homo sacer* embodies, far from commanding – as it did in Roman times – the existence of a singular and extreme individual fate, supplies the biopolitical order with its compassing paradigm, formulating what can effectively be understood as the default status of any person whatsoever.

Clothing a study intended to be a "response to the bloody mystifications of a new planetary order" (*HS*, 12) in the immemorial garb of the Roman outlaw (while at the same time precisely disputing that he is exclusively out of the law), Agamben also replied to another question, which is how to evaluate the transformations brought about by the centuries that have passed since those early Roman times into which Festus's indications throw just a spark of light. If, despite numberless transformations, evolutions and revolutions during the last centuries and millennia, all destined to improve the structure of the social community and to abolish its most atavistic elements, the blueprint of the *homo sacer* thrives today more than it has ever done, this jars dramatically with the evolutionist mind-set at work in the Western self-description and political philosophy. Does Agamben's thesis about the *homo sacer* belittle, contrary to his own assertions (*HS*, 10), the conquests and accomplishments of democracy? What his argument takes issue with is the claim that the evolutionist theme deserves to be invested with exclusivity rights: that "politics" needs to be understood, as if by sovereign definition, as internal episodes in the life of the political system, its parties, its media, and so on.

HUMAN

Mathew Abbott

The human for Agamben is not a natural kind, but something that must be produced. It would be difficult to overstate the importance of this for his philosophy, for he understands the very **origin** of **politics** as we know it in terms of the conflict between what he variously refers to as "the animality [see **animal**] and the humanity of man" (*O*, 80), "**bare life**/political existence" (*HS*, 8), "animal **voice**" and "human **language**" (*LD*, 44), and "the living being and the speaking being" (*RA*, 147). This conflict, contingent as it is on a kind of convergence between historico-political factors and intractable metaphysical problems, is a highly fraught one, and the category that results from it – the human as the rational and political animal, endowed with the command of language – is therefore fundamentally unstable, always in danger of collapsing into that which it defined itself against. If this is drawn up in different ways in Agamben's books (and arguably with slightly different outcomes as a result), they are all nevertheless united by an image of the human as a being that is delivered over to something it cannot assimilate. The inhuman, the animal, *zoē*, the simply living: these are all names for the inappropriable core of human being. Agamben's political philosophical commitments are based on the claim that the attempt to manage and/or police the border between the human and this inappropriable object is both misguided, because the task can never be completed, and dangerous, because it produces bare life as its remainder.

Foucault is a key influence on Agamben's claims about the nature of **biopolitics**, as are **Arendt**'s investigations into the political **nihilism** that has coincided with the progressive intrusion of natural life into the *polis* since the Industrial Revolution. Important too is **Aristotle**, whose opposition in the *Politics* between animal *phonē* and human *logos* Agamben takes as paradigmatic (see **paradigm**) of the Western political tradition. Yet Agamben's analyses arguably have their foundation in Heideggerian ontology. Specifically, they can be understood as beginning from a transposition of **Heidegger**'s ontological difference on to classical biological categories, where *zoē* (natural life) is equated with the fact of being as such, and *bios* (politically qualified life) with the ontic level of particular beings. This transposition, in which the human appears not just as that being for which being is an issue, but also as the animal for which animality is an issue, allows Agamben to read the distinction between natural life and political life in fundamental ontological terms, and thus serves as the ground for his characteristic blending of ontology and politics. It also allows him to move into territory that Heidegger was usually intent on avoiding, at least with much explicitness: political ontology, or the study of the political stakes of ontology (or indeed, of the political stakes of the ontological question). The Heideggerian problematic of the "forgetting of being" then takes on a biopolitical character, such that what metaphysics tries to forget is not just the fact that beings are, but the fact of biological life itself. Agamben draws up the problems of politics in terms of a Heideggerian understanding of the metaphysical tradition, finding that the Western political space is following a particular metaphysical logic when it works to forge the human through the exclusion of the animal (an exclusion that is always already an inclusion). Does the human forget the animal because it has already forgotten being? Or does the human forget being because it has already forgotten the animal? For Agamben, these two questions are actually equivalent, and the answer to both of them is yes. As he puts it toward the end of *Homo Sacer*:

it may be that only if we are able to decipher the political meaning of pure Being will we be able to master the bare life that expresses our subjection to political power, just as it may be, inversely, that only if we understand the theoretical implications of bare life will we be able to solve the enigma of ontology. (*HS*, 182)

Agamben's political ontological approach to these problems is predicated on the possibility of their transformation: the claim that human beings could **experience** a change in their relation to their lives. This proposition – which is phrased in *The Open* in terms of a demand that we "render inoperative" (*O*, 92) the anthropological machine of humanism – can be understood as a call to abandon definitively any idea of realising a human essence, whether it be through work, philosophy or revolutionary politics. This is not quite to say that Agamben calls on us to abandon the category of the human, or calls for a reconciliation with the animal that subsists within it. As Agamben puts it at the conclusion of the book, his image of redeemed (see **redemption**) humanity entails not "a new declension of the man–animal relation" as much as a "figure of the 'great ignorance'" which lets both of them be outside of being, saved precisely in their being unsavable" (*O*, 92). This is an **ethic** of attentiveness, an ethic that asks us to attend our animal life as something ungraspable. It requires us to "risk ourselves in the 'central emptiness' between human and animal, following through on "an unprecedented inquiry into the practico-political mystery of separation" (*O*, 92).

Important here is the Benjaminian (see **Benjamin**) image of the "saved night" of sexual fulfilment, which Agamben refers to as "the hieroglyph of a new in-humanity" (*O*, 83). In this profane (see **profanation**) fulfilment, the "secret bond that ties man to life" is severed, and the human being takes on a new relation (or rather non-relation) to nature (*O*, 83). This is the gateway to the kind of **happiness** that Benjamin linked to the messianic (see **messianism**), the rhythm of a "worldly restitution that leads to the eternity of a downfall" (quoted in *O*, 82). Agamben's idea of redemption, then, is based not on some quasi-Heideggerian return of the gods, but rather on disenchantment: "the **irreparable** loss of the lost, the definitive profanity of the profane" (*CC*, 102).

HUMAN RIGHTS

Andrew Schaap

Agamben understands human rights not as protections against sovereign power but as conduits of power that are from the outset bound up with the constitution and regulation of subjects. Indeed, he discerns a "secret solidarity" between humanitarian politics and the sovereign power it seeks to contest, for it is through the inscription of human rights within the modern state that life is politicised, brought into relation with the sovereign and therefore subject to biopolitical regulation (*HS*, 133). Human rights discourse represents the *subject* of politics (the **human** in human rights) as **sacred** in the sense of commanding moral respect. It represents the *relation* between political subjects as originating in a virtual social contract between free and equal persons. And it conceives the *space* of politics as constituted through the rational organisation of the state, the legitimate purpose of which is to protect the human rights of its members. For Agamben this is all so much mystification.

First, the true subject of politics is not the human whose life the state is supposed to protect. Rather, he sees a "secret complicity between the sacredness of life and the power of the law" (*HS*, 66). For Agamben (appropriating Hannah **Arendt**), the plight of stateless people reveals the true subject of human rights to be **bare life**. He appeals to the original meaning of sacredness (as life that can be killed without committing homicide) in order to show the ideological nature of its invocation in human rights discourse (as the inviolability of human life). Second, what binds the political community together is not a virtual contract to secure the human rights of all, i.e. the counter-factual but necessary presupposition of the constitutional state. Rather it is the sovereign ban, which renders all political subjects virtually *homines sacri* (*HS*, 111). The "originary political element" of the political community is revealed in the ever-present possibility of the state of exception in which human rights are withdrawn (*HS*, 181).

Third, far from being an aberration of the normal politics of the constitutional state, Agamben claims that the **camp** is paradigmatic of modern politics. As such, the production of bare life within the camp (through the withdrawal of human rights) is consistent with the inscription of bare life within the juridical order (through the declaration of human rights). Just as the writ of *habeas corpus* in 1679 compelled the law to assume the care of the *body* brought before it (*HS*, 125), so the Declaration of the Rights of Man and Citizen inscribed bare life within the law by virtue of the fact of *birth*. The emergence of the exceptional space of the camp therefore reveals the illusory nature of the "citizen" as the bearer of rights that, in fact, originate in the politicisation of the natural life of "Man" (*HS*, 128).

For Agamben, then, "every attempt to found political liberties on the rights of the citizen is in vain" (*HS*, 181). Far from promising emancipation from sovereign power, the more we invoke human rights in social struggles against oppressive forms of social relations, the more we intensify biopolitical subjection (*HS*, 121). In order to conceptualise the "ways and forms of a new politics", political theory should represent the subject of politics not in terms of the rights-bearing human but the figure of the refugee that prefigures the **coming community** (*HS*, 186; *ME*, 16).

$$\boxed{\text{I}}$$

IMAGE

Connal Parsley

For Agamben, the image is something "impossible", since it is the means by which Western metaphysics seeks to reconcile its most central problem: the mediation between the sensible and the intelligible, the unique and the reproducible, the single and the multiple (2004: 138–9). As such a "means", the image is a privileged site for Agamben, constituting a **threshold** and also a **caesura** between the single, unique individual with its intellectual and psychic attributes on the one hand; and **history**, the "in-common" and "social memory" (*Po*, 100) on the other. It is thus always bipolar, tensive and ambivalent; as he writes, "images, which constitute the ultimate texture of the human being and the only means of his possible salvation, are also the place of his incessant lacking to himself" (2007a: 53).

At the most general level, Agamben's critical project critiques and displaces the structures which surround and enable the image as the cipher of the **human**'s divided ethos and "lacking to himself". For example, his accounts of **aesthetics** and **art**, of the **commodity**, representation and **signification**, of Friedrich **Nietzsche**'s eternal return, and his commentary on Guy **Debord**'s society of the **spectacle** all seek to transfigure the manner in which humanity's – and the image's – constitutive caesurae are understood. But without ever systematically negating it outright, Agamben also aims to transform the category of the image itself. For example, he affirms that "the element of cinema is **gesture** and not image." Suggesting Gilles **Deleuze**'s cinematic "movement-image" describes the status of the image in modernity generally, Agamben works to convert it from a "static rigidity", taken wholly out of time, to a dynamic, involuntarily memorial and historically referential display of human gesturality. In this way, Agamben aims to expose the sphere of human *ethos* within the very place of its supposed lack (*ME*, 57). A second, similar displacement of the category "image" can be found in Agamben's casting of the image as the mere byproduct of the activity of the imagination, which he installs (instead of the intellect) as the defining attribute of the human species, and as the place where "history must be decided", thereby attempting to pose an "imagination without images" (2007a: 57).

What is at stake in Agamben's effacement of the image is, above all, the opening of a different relation to historical time. The authors who are most influential for Agamben's thought of the image, Aby **Warburg** and Walter **Benjamin**, as well as medieval scholars like Avicenna and Averroes on whom Agamben often draws in this context, offer ways of understanding the image which potentially reconfigure its metaphysical divisions. Absolutely critical for Agamben is to recognise the image as a dialectically tensive relation between the elements it might be thought to separate: the individual and shared intellect, the sensible and intelligible, and above all, separate historical instants (which in Benjamin's thought, for example, are condensed and abridged within the image). And just as it did for Benjamin, this deeply implicates the image in Agamben's notion of the messianic (see **messianism**); Agamben writes that "each image is charged with history because it is the door through which the Messiah enters" (2004a: 315). It is a matter, he suggests, of being able to see the medium of the image itself – named variously "the being-image of the image", "the image as such" and "the image of images" (2007a: 53–4) – thus bringing its means to visibility. Agamben therefore does not propose a new reading of this or that image, aimed at rendering its contents or its historical context more legible, but emphasises the paradoxical possibility of its visibility itself coming into visibility: not in, but *through*, *each* image.

IMPOTENTIALITY – see 'Potentiality'

IMPROPRIETY/INAUTHENTICITY

Robert Sinnerbrink

The conceptual couple of propriety/impropriety or authenticity/inauthenticity derives from Martin **Heidegger**, though it is also related to the general determination of the proper and the improper. For Heidegger, human being or *Dasein* exists in two modes of being: namely, as authentic (*eigentlich*) or inauthentic (*uneigentlich*) (plus an "indifferent" mode). Inauthenticity defines everyday being-in-the-world: when we are absorbed in ongoing activities, defined by prevailing norms, and inattentive to our own contingent, finite, temporal existence (our *finitude*). Authentic *Dasein*, by contrast, acknowledges and appropriates its existential and temporal finitude (*Being and Time*, §9).

Agamben finds an anticipation of this dialectic between authentic and inauthentic in Heidegger's lectures on the phenomenology of religion. On Agamben's reading, the "authentic does not have any other content than the inauthentic"; it is, rather, a way in which we take up the inauthentic (*TR*, 34). Agamben differs from Heidegger, however, on how we relate to the inauthentic; for Heidegger it is through an appropriation that presupposes an "authentic" or "proper" mode of existence, whereas for Agamben, following St **Paul**, it depends upon the "use" to which we put this impropriety (*TR*, 34). We cannot retrieve or recreate a lost authenticity or essential propriety; we can only make ethical use of the inauthentic, improper identity we acquire in our contingent historical situation.

In modernity, defined via Guy **Debord**'s "society of the **spectacle**", this means the improper, "nullified" identities revealed by the spectacular image-world of **commodities**. Existence within spectacular societies is such that there is no longer any space of authentic or proper being, since everything has been expropriated (see **expropriation**) and commodified under conditions of global capitalism (*CC*, 78–9). The nihilistic global class of the "petty bourgeoisie", heirs of this completely commodified world, "know only the improper and the inauthentic and even refuse the idea of a discourse that could be proper to them" (*CC*, 62). An ethics and politics of the improper would therefore mean finding new uses for the inauthentic that defines our empty modern experience. Lacking any determinate identity, existing essentially as singularity or "whatever being" (see **whatever singularity**), making use of this impropriety for new ends – in language, communication and culture – might transfigure our nihilistic world into a "**coming community**" (*CC*, 78–86).

INDISTINCTION

Paolo Bartoloni

Indistinction is a concept that traverses Agamben's entire opus and is fundamental to the understanding of his philosophical project, centring on the reconceptualisation of life and Western ontology. It is a term that, in Agamben's philosophical semantic field, is not without analogies to others such as suspension and **threshold**, and indicates the moment at which conventional metaphysical oppositions such as potentiality and actuality, authenticity and inauthenticity, humans and animals are given up or become unavailable. It is precisely at these particular junctures that a re-evaluation of ontology can commence. It is in the book *The Open* that Agamben's philosophical treatment of indistinction finds its methodological apex, opening the way for his singularly fascinating and conceptually complex theory according to which a new discussion of **life** must perforce pass from an ontology where the definition of Being, arrived at through differentiating between forms and beings (that is, humans/animals), is suspended. *The Open* begins, emblematically, with the description of a series of illuminations accompanying a Hebrew bible of the thirteenth century, depicting the scene of "the messianic banquet of the righteous" (*O*, 1). Shadowed by heavenly trees and entertained by divine music, the righteous sit at a richly adorned table. Everything conforms to iconic norms apart from the fact that the righteous have the heads of animals (an eagle, an ox, an ass, a panther, a monkey). This might mean, writes Agamben, that on **Judgment** Day the relation between animals and humans will be recomposed in a new form, and that humans will be reconciled with their animal nature (*O*, 3). The remainder of the book is an interrogation of the conflation/indistinction between humans and animals, elaborated through a rich discussion which combines philosophy, theology, politics, medicine and biology. The indetermination that Agamben presents is essentially part of an ongoing dialogue with a number of philosophical figures who are central to his work: namely, **Benjamin, Foucault** and **Heidegger**.

Foucault is the privileged interlocutor with regards to the biopolitical project that Agamben begins with *The Coming Community*, and which finds a culmination in the *Homo Sacer* series. It is in these writings that Agamben enters an insistent discussion of human life based on the distinction between *zoē* and *bios*, or life as such and political life. This distinction, which revolves around an elemental state as opposed to a cultural and political one, the latter directed and determined by language, is the one that is also employed by Western metaphysics to separate humans from other forms of life. This distinction decrees humans' superiority and humans' control on life as such. Thus begins, according to Agamben, the rule of the anthropological machine, whose use of power, violence and the state of exception (**Benjamin, Schmitt**) is still at the basis of modern and contemporary democracies. If distinction is the cause of interminable abuses and exploitation, indistinction or the suspension of the anthropological machine might very well bring about alternative forms of life. To this end Agamben turns to the concept of the **open**, and to the philosopher who has zeroed in on it from the angle of the humans/animals distinction: Martin Heidegger. The central chapter of *The Open*, itself called "The Open", is Agamben's attempt to go deeper into Heidegger's discussion of the open in the famous lectures of the late 1940s, later included in the volume *Parmenides* (1992). The open stands for the authentic experience of unconcealment, and it is therefore an ontological state in which being regains a complete and mutual belonging with the world and Being.

Agamben claims that Heidegger found and took the notion of the open in and from Rilke's eighth *Duino Elegy* – "That it arose out of the eighth *Duino Elegy* was, in a certain sense, obvious" (*O*, 57). And yet this is the only point in common since Rilke's and Heidegger's respective readings are diametrically opposed. Whereas in Rilke the animal is in the open, in Heidegger the animal is unaware of it, and therefore shut out of the open. Humans, on the other hand, are before it and can gain a truthful understanding of the open through an authentic experience of language, which in the later Heidegger equates with poetry. Following in the footsteps of **Plato** and **Aristotle**, Heidegger thus traces the gap separating humans from animals back to language. It is the human's ability to speak, and therefore to enter a dialogue with tradition, that enables human beings to come face to face with the open, and ultimately, with Being.

Agamben conceptualises the open by closely following Heidegger's definition. From Heidegger, he also takes the main distinction between animals (those which are unaware of the open) and humans (those who face the open), as well as the theory of a possible proximity and similarity between humans and animals (*O*, 57–72). It is the latter that enables Agamben to go further. Heidegger compares humans' boredom with the stupefied being of the animal in the open. But whereas stupefaction conceals the world from the animal, boredom, especially if and when understood in the meaning of suspension, has the potential to bring humans into the presence of the world. Through suspending the habitual expectations open to being by life, the original potentiality of simply being as such might emerge. The significant difference between Heidegger and Agamben is that for the latter the moments of suspension are precisely the moments when humans and animals become suspended in indistinction, and when animality and humanity are momentarily reconciled (*O*, 71–92). It is at these moments on the threshold that the anthropological machine comes to a halt.

INFANCY

Paolo Bartoloni

This term is employed by Agamben in the context of the discussion of modern literature, and as a way to expand on **Benveniste**'s distinction between semiotic and semantic. Agamben's interrogation of infancy finds its focus and climax in his book, *Infancy and History*, where he develops the conceptualisation of **potentiality** by relating it to a reflection on **language**, and especially on the concept of **voice**. Human language, according to Agamben, cannot be understood unless it is framed within the *experimentum linguae*: that is, an investigation into the development of language from sound to speech via the acquisition of voice. Within this framework, sound is the elemental state, comparable to **Aristotle**'s *dynamis*, while speech is the transformation of language into discourse, and as such close to the opposite of *dynamis*: *energeia*. The similarities between sound and speech and Benveniste's semiotic and semantic are apparent, yet Agamben takes this distinction further by introducing voice, and locating it in infancy, as a means to enter an analysis of the space and the processes in-between, and of the philosophical implications of potentiality understood here as the capacity "to have a faculty", "to be able" (*IH*, 7). Voice is the relational modus of language, capable of turning into speech but also of reverting into sound. It is in this sense that infancy cannot only be interpreted literally as the stage at which voice transmutes into discourse and grammar through acculturation. It acquires in addition, and more importantly, a paradigmatic philosophical meaning standing for the human ability to will the power towards *energeia* but also to renounce it. In fact, the faculty to do can be matched by the decision not-to-do.

It is this insight that will allow Agamben to write significant pages on **Melville**'s fictive character, **Bartleby**, in books such as *Potentialities*. Infancy is thus an instance of **threshold**: that is, a place or a state in which quotidian activities and habits can be brought suddenly to a halt, suspended in a space of **indistinction** given to re-experiencing the world by introducing a lack of experience. Agamben compares infancy to certain disconcerting events such as those described by Montaigne and Rousseau, and related by Agamben in *Infancy and History* (*IH*, 37–41). These moments, which might be defined as falls into the unconscious, herald existential experiences, which in turn enable Agamben to introduce his bold claim that modern poetry from Baudelaire onwards is founded on a shock. It is a sudden and unexpected stoppage of the natural course of life, as in the cases of Montaigne and Rousseau, that brings about a shock, whose result is to make experience unemployable. It is this philosophical event that leads to an aesthetic production in which what is at stake is not so much "a new experience" as an "unprecedented lack of experience" (*IH*, 41). "It is experience that best affords us protection from surprises, and the production of shock always implies a gap in experience [. . .] To experience something means divesting it of novelty" (*IH*, 41). Shock, infancy and **play** are antidotes to stultifying experience, and the necessary entrance into poetry.

INOPERATIVE/DEACTIVATION

Carlo Salzani

The concept is contained, *in nuce*, in the "Idea of Politics" chapter in *Idea of Prose*, which relates the condition of the dwellers in **limbo**; abandoned to the absence of God, to His forgetfulness, they are irredeemably lost, but it is precisely this loss that means they have no destiny, and they live like letters with no addressee, in the joy of an inestimable hope (*IP*, 77–8). "Idea of Politics" is reproduced almost word for word in the "From Limbo" chapter in *The Coming Community*, to represent the condition of the **whatever singularities**, indifferent to **redemption** because irredeemable, but as such embodying that life, simply **human**, which survives the end of the politico–theological machine (*CC*, 5–7). In the 2001 apostille to the Italian re-edition of *The Coming Community*, Agamben renames this condition "inoperativity".

It is in *Homo Sacer* that Agamben articulates this theme for the first time. "Inoperativity" translates the French term *désœuvrement* (*inoperosità* in Italian, although Agamben often uses the French word), which was first coined by Alexandre **Kojève** in the 1952 essay, "Les Romans de la sagesse", a review of three novels by Raymond Queneau, *Pierrot mon ami* (1942), *Loin de Rueil* (1944) and *Le Dimanche de la vie* (1952). Kojève argues that the three protagonists of the novels, whom he calls "*voyous désœuvrés*" (lazy rascals), embody, in a sense, the wisdom of man living after the end of **history**. The article provoked a *querelle* with Georges **Bataille**, which had a great impact on the following generation in France, and the term entered the philosophical debate, taking a central place in Jean-Luc **Nancy**'s and Maurice **Blanchot**'s reflections. In *Homo Sacer*, Agamben proposes a personal redefinition of *désœuvrement*; it cannot be read merely as absence of work/activity (*assenza di opera*), nor, as in Bataille, as a form of negativity which is sovereign in so far as it has no use (*senza impiego*); rather, it must be read as "a generic mode of **potentiality**, which is not exhausted (like the individual or collective action, intended as the sum of individual actions) in a *transitus de potentia ad actum*" (*HS*, 62). In *Means Without End*, the argument takes the central place that it has retained in Agamben's later works. Human beings as potential beings have no proper *ergon* (work); they are *argos*, without *opera*, inoperative. Therefore,

> **politics** is that which corresponds to the essential inoperativity of humankind, to the radical being-without-work of human communities. There is politics because human beings are *argos* – beings that cannot be defined by any proper operation – that is, beings of pure potentiality that no identity or vocation can possibly exhaust. (*ME*, 140)

The theme of the coming politics is therefore to interrogate this essential inoperativity and this essential potentiality without transforming them into a historical task, by simply assuming this exposition and this creative indifference to any task as a politics assigned to **happiness**.

Inoperativity is central to *The Time That Remains*. The messianic **vocation** (*klesis*) consists precisely in the re-vocation of any vocation; however, this re-vocation does not destroy or annihilate the factitious condition of the world, but rather suspends it in the figure of the "as if not" (*hos me*, *come non*): "it is not another figure, another world; it is the passing of the figure of this world" (*TR*, 25; trans. modified). Use [*uso*] is the form that this deactivation takes: "to live messianically means 'to use' *klesis*; conversely, messianic *klesis* is something to use not to possess" (*TR*, 26). Importantly, this use in the form of the *as if not* does not merely have a negative connotation; it does not constitute a new identity, but rather the "new creature" is nothing but the use and the messianic vocation of the old identity. The old identity is not replaced by a new one but only rendered inoperative, and, in this way, opened to its *true use*. The key term is here *katargesis*, which describes, in St **Paul**'s epistles, the "fulfilment" of the **law** at the arrival of the Messiah (see **messianism**); it comes from the Greek *argeo*, and thus from *argos*, and means "I make inoperative, I deactivate, I suspend the efficacy" (*TR*, 95). *Argeo* translates also, in the Septuagint, the verb that signifies the Sabbath rest. The fulfilment in the use is thus *désœuvrement*, and messianic potentiality is precisely that which is not exhausted in its *ergon*, but that remains potential in a "weak" form. *Katargesis* restores the works – the identities – to their potentiality by rendering them inoperative.

What is rendered inoperative is an activity directed towards a goal, in order to open it to a new use. This does not abolish the old activity, but rather exposes and exhibits it. The essential connection between potentiality and inoperativity means that the sabbatical suspension, which, by rendering inoperative the specific functions of the living being, transforms them into possibilities, is the proper human *praxis*. This operation takes the name, in more recent texts, of **profanation**; it implies the neutralisation of what is profaned, which loses its aura of sacrality and is restored to use, and the creation of a new use is possible only by deactivating an old use, by rendering it inoperative. The new use takes the forms of **study**, **play** and festivity. Study and play free humankind from the sphere of sacrality but without abolishing it; what was **sacred** is restored to a special use, different from the utilitarian form, which opens the gate for a new happiness. Play and inoperativity are brought together in festivity; inoperativity *coincides* with festivity in so far as festivity consists in neutralising and rendering inoperative human **gestures**, actions and works, and only in this way making them festive. What defines festivity is not what is not done in it, but rather the fact that what is done is not so much different from what one does every other day, but is freed and suspended from its "economy", from the reasons and aims that define it during weekdays.

IRREPARABLE

Paolo Bartoloni

The title of the Appendix to *The Coming Community*, "The Irreparable", deals with "the relationship between essence and existence, between *quid est* and *quod est*" (*CC*, 88). Through a fragmentary, aphoristic style Agamben claims to provide a "commentary" on Section 9 of Martin **Heidegger**'s *Being and Time*, and Proposition 6.44 of Ludwig **Wittgenstein**'s *Tractatus*. Agamben's answer to the old metaphysical conundrum, and other philosophers' attempt to shed light on it, is to invoke the notion of the irreparable by which he means the "suchness" (*talità*) of things (*CC*, 97). "The irreparable", Agamben writes, " is that things are just as they are, in this or that mode, consigned without remedy to their way of being" (*CC*, 89). By positing the "as such" of things, essence and existence are mutually appropriated to the extent that the properties of being, be they religious, political or linguistic, are placed under erasure. Revelation is proposed as an example of suchness, in so far as it "does not mean revelation of the sacredness of the world, but only revelation of its irreparable profane state" (*CC*, 89). The advent of Christ introduces an irreparable caesura between the time before and after the second coming, or eschaton; and while Christ's sacrifice is the prelude to humans' salvation, it also implies the impossibility of salvation in the time that remains. Agamben connects this insight to his postulation that hope can only be placed in "what is without remedy" (*CC*, 101) as further evidence of an existence in which life is propelled by the power "to not-not-be" (*CC*, 103). With the concept of the irreparable, and the category of suchness, Agamben intends to conjure up a mode of being whose exposure to the world, and the things of the world, is no longer postulated by the opposition and separation of subject/object, predicate and pronoun, but on the awareness of an irreparable belonging based on mutual relations by which the facing of each other as things as such generates an availability that transcends the objectification of the other.

$$\boxed{\text{J}}$$

JUDGMENT

Jessica Whyte

"As jurists well know," Agamben writes in *Remnants of Auschwitz*, "law is not directed toward the establishment of justice" (*RA*, 18). Neither, he suggests, is it directed towards the verification of truth; "Law is solely directed toward judgment, independent of truth and justice" (*RA*, 18). Elsewhere, he illustrates his contention that "punishment does not follow from judgment . . . judgment is itself punishment" (*RA*, 18), through an examination of **Kafka**'s story, "In the Penal Settlement" (Kafka 1980). Nowhere does the indistinction of judgment and punishment appear more starkly than in Kafka's penal apparatus, which inscribes a sentence repeatedly on the body of the accused, ultimately leading to his death. Kafka's story marks the crisis of law, the point at which judgment becomes its own end and is separated irrevocably from justice. Its significance for Agamben lies in that fact that, in providing an image of a penal sentence that is also, quite literally, a linguistic sentence, inscribed on the body of the accused, it highlights what he sees as the essential proximity between *logos* and law. Logic, he suggests, has its exclusive realm in judgment: "logical judgement is, in truth, immediately penal judgement" (*IP*, 116). It is this insight that links Agamben's earlier works on language to his later works on law, and that orients his account of what he terms "whatever being" (see **whatever singularity**). Such beings, he suggests, exist in a condition of potentiality prior to those linguistic judgments that must divide into classes in order to signify (*CC*, 73). Such beings are not the product of linguistic judgments, and thus they cannot be ascribed juridical identities and subjected to legal judgment.

The problem of judgment reappears in Agamben's account of messianism. In his *Arcades Project*, Walter **Benjamin** records a passage from a letter in which Max Horkheimer disputes his conception of historical incompleteness. "Past injustice has occurred and is completed," Horkheimer writes. "The slain are really slain . . . If one takes the lack of closure entirely seriously, one must believe in the Last Judgment" (Benjamin 1999b: 471). Like Benjamin's, however, Agamben's messianism must be distinguished from eschatology; if there is a Judgment Day, then this "Day of Judgment is not different from any others" (*Po*, 160). The redemption of the past is not something that occurs at the end of time; rather, "[e]very instant is the instant of judgment on certain moments that precede it" (*Po*, 160). In a more recent essay with the title "Judgment Day", Agamben defines photography as that which "captures the Last Judgment" by grasping that which is being lost in order to make it possible again (*Pr*, 25). The "angel of the Last Judgment", he writes, "is also the angel of photography" (*Pr*, 25). Once again, the redemption at stake in this judgment does not occur at the end of time, but at "the end of all days, that is, everyday" (*Pr*, 27).

JUSTICE

Jessica Whyte

If there is a story that exemplifies Agamben's approach to justice, it is, unsurprisingly, written by a figure for whom the law is most often a site of injustice: that is, by Franz **Kafka**. In a short piece entitled *The Idea of Language II* (*IP*, 115–17), Agamben discusses the horrific ending to Kafka's "In the Penal Settlement", in which the officer straps himself into a penal apparatus and attempts to have it inscribe the sentence "Be Just" into his own flesh. The machine, usually so adept at inscribing sentences into the bodies of the accused, cannot write this particular sentence, and destroys itself in the attempt. Agamben offers an interpretation of the machine's destruction in which the officer inserts the injunction "Be Just" into the machine with the precise intent of destroying it. The tale, Agamben suggests, presents the ultimate meaning of language as precisely this injunction, "Be Just", and yet, it is precisely this injunction that language cannot make us understand: "Or, rather," Agamben writes, "it can do it only by ceasing to perform its penal function, only by shattering into pieces and turning from punisher to murderer" (*IP*, 117). Justice, Agamben's earlier works suggest, is intimately bound to the question of the potentiality of language – it is the *sayability* of things, the *thing itself,* which has been captured in language and made inaccessible to us. Justice is the potentiality or sayability that language cannot say without ceasing to be a penal machine, without ceasing to capture the ineffable as its presupposed foundation. This justice, he argues in "The Idea of Justice", should neither be passed over in silence, nor delivered to language (*IP*, 79). Rather, it is that pure possibility of language without which there could neither be language nor transmission.

In his later works, Agamben's account of justice is also an intervention into politico-juridical debates. Justice, he makes clear, is not law, and neither is it judgment. "Law", he notes in *Remnants of Auschwitz*, "is solely directed toward judgment, independent of truth and justice" (*RA*, 18). Agamben frames the possibility of justice in relation to law in terms of what he calls law's "deactivation": "What opens a passage toward justice", he writes, "is not the erasure of law, but its deactivation and inactivity" (*SE*, 64). Agamben's account of the relation of justice to law can be illuminated if we briefly compare it to that of Jacques **Derrida**. In contrast to Agamben's explicit antinomianism, Derrida's work, while sharing the former's refusal to equate law with justice, is animated by another concern: that "[a]bandoned to itself, the incalculable and giving [*donatrice*] idea of justice is always very close to the bad, even to the worst for it can always be reappropriated by the most perverse calculation" (Derrida 2002: 257). For Derrida, law can never entirely satisfy the demands of justice, yet justice none the less demands the calculation of law, which must forever approximate it; indeed, "in their very heterogeneity, these two orders are undissociable" (Derrida 2002: 257). For Agamben, in contrast, law is not a necessary condition of justice, but that which must be fulfilled in the passage to it. "Justice without law", he writes in *The Time That Remains*, "is not the negation of the law, but the realisation and fulfilment, the *pleroma* of the law" (*TR*, 107).

KAFKA, FRANZ

Alex Murray

From Agamben's first published book (*The Man Without Content*) through to some of his most recent publications (the essay "K"), the work of the

Czech–German author, Franz Kafka, has been a pronounced influence on Agamben's work. Whether discussing **aesthetics, politics, ethics** or **law**, Agamben's recourse to Kafka's work is always pivotal, and at times requires the reader to follow Agamben's reading back to Kafka to grasp the importance of his interpretation.

The way in which Agamben makes use of Kafka is linked indelibly to the work of Walter **Benjamin**, who wrote two influential essays on Kafka which outlined a model of reading him that sought to deactivate or render **inoperative** the two dominant modes of reading his work: the psychoanalytic and the theological. Benjamin's example of Dr Bucephalus in Kafka's "The New Advocate" suggests that "study" is the "gate to justice" in Kafka's world. Here the process of study works to "deactivate" the institutions and processes central to all forms of authority. We can then regard Agamben's own process as drawing out the deactivation inherent in Kafka's work with the goal of uncovering in Kafka the glimpse of the messianic (see **messianism**) in which the world will appear only minutely different but utterly transformed.

In *The Man Without Content* (1970) Agamben concludes his study of aesthetics through turning to Kafka as the author who has most come to terms with man's "inability to appropriate his own historical presuppositions" and whose body of work "turns this impossibility into the very soil on which man might recover himself" (*MC*, 112). It is the idea of the world as always transformed and our failure to grasp it by seizing our own historicity that will become an important feature of Agamben's thought, although arguably it is refined and complicated in the later work. He provides a more nuanced account of Benjamin's reading of Kafka in *Potentialities*, in which he outlines more clearly the temporal structure of the messianic (*Po*, 171–4). Kafka's obsession with the strange "parahuman" and "semi-divine" that work to blur the boundaries and divisions between categories is also important for Agamben (*EP*, 91). Agamben, in *Stanzas*, gestures towards Odradek, the strange anthropomorphised bobbin in Kafka, which he suggests is emblematic of the strange world of the commodity in which the subject/object, use value/exchange value split produces the **fetish** and the commodity which, through inference, Kafka exposes. This idea of Kafka exposing the boundaries and divisions between practices has recently been outlined in Agamben's, "K", in which the character K./Josef K from *The Castle* and *The Trial* is read as a figure of **inoperativity**. Undertaking an expansive etymology of "K", Agamben argues that K. should be read as a character who works to open a door and catches a glimpse of what lies beyond the divisions between "high and the low, of the divine and the human, the pure and the impure" (2008a: 26). The other central figure from Kafka who Agamben has explored at length is the man from the country in Kafka's short fragment, "Before the Law". Agamben argues that rather than see the man from the country as maintaining the power of the law by waiting to enter it, his entire purpose was to have the door shut. In *Homo Sacer* he suggests that the open door, *contra* **Derrida**, is law's "being in force without significance" and that, in having the door-keeper close it, the man from the country has opened the way for the messianic reopening of the door beyond the law.

KANT, IMMANUEL

Carlo Salzani

The critique of key concepts from the works of Immanuel Kant (1724–1804) punctuates Agamben's writings. His first book, *The Man Without Content*, opens with a quotation from **Nietzsche** criticising Kant, and the book argues for an overcoming of modern **aesthetics** founded on the Kantian theory. Kant's aesthetic **judgment** is compared to a "negative theology" (*MC*, 43) in so far as it is able to define **art** only as what it is not; it is therefore something like a "mystical intuition" (*MC*, 45). In *Infancy and History*, Agamben identifies the same problem in Kant's notion of **experience**. The transcendental **subject** as simple representation is without content, it is not a concept but a simple conscience which accompanies all concepts; Kant thereby grounds the possibility of experience by positing it in terms of the inexperienceable (*IH*, 32). Only by rearticulating transcendental subjectivity around **language** can this *impasse* be overcome (*IH*, 4–5, 44). In *The Coming Community*, the Kantian schema of possibility is used to define the **whatever singularity**, which is determined only by its relation to all possibilities and is thus only the Kantian empty "**threshold**" (*CC*, 34, 67).

This pure, empty formalism, also central to Kant's notions of law, comes to embody, in *Homo Sacer*, the originary form of **law**; the purely formal character of the moral law founds its claim of universal practical applicability in every circumstance, but law is as such reduced to the zero point of its significance and this exemplifies its character as "being in force without significance" (*HS*, 51–3). The problem of the application of the general norm, or of the relation between general and particular, is briefly touched on in relation to Kant's determinant judgment in *State of Exception* (*SE*, 39), and resurfaces in *The Signature of All Things* (2008) in the definition of **paradigm** and of a philosophical **archaeology** (Agamben 2008: 22–3, 82–4). In *Means Without End*, the Kantian expression "purposiveness without purpose" describes the nature of **gesture**

(*ME*, 59), and in *Remnants of Auschwitz* Kant's notion of time is used in the analysis of the originary structure of subjectivity (*RA*, 109–10).

KOJÈVE, ALEXANDRE

Alysia Garrison

Beginning with *Language and Death* and thinking beyond the horizon of the Hegelian dialectic, Agamben consistently invokes the work of Alexandre Kojève (1902–68), usually in relation to his "disciple-rival", Georges **Bataille**, and the tangled lines between them (*O*, 9). In his lectures, Kojève describes a post-historical figure at which "the animal of the species Homo sapiens ha[s] become human, [has] reached completion" (*O*, 6). Bataille's point of disagreement concerns precisely this animal remnant, a "negativity with no use" that survives the end of history. For Bataille, the joyful excesses of "art, love, play" remain "superhuman, negative, sacred", while for Kojève, the state of "nothing left to do" is given as pure animal praxis, the absence of work found in figures like Raymond Queneau's "lazy rascal" (*O*, 6; *HS*, 61–2). Agamben will critique both philosophers: Bataille for holding fast to the tie between **negativity** and the **sacred**, and Kojève for an inadequately developed notion of **inoperativity**.

For Kojève, the end of history means the end of man, of philosophy, of the tumult of wars and revolutions. What remains "**animal**" and "**human**" in the figures of this condition remains an "open" question. Examining Kojève's thesis, Agamben asks aptly, "what becomes of the animality of man in posthistory?" (*O*, 12). In his review of Queneau, Kojève is the first to present the theme of inoperativity, or *désœuvrement*, later taken up by Blanchot and Nancy. But, as Agamben puts it, "everything depends" on what this inoperativeness means (*HS*, 61). For Agamben, to reach fulfilment, humanity cannot merely take the form of an absence of work, but it must "unwork" or idle what is suspended. Ignoring this suspension, the human being in Japanese "snobbery" recounted by Kojève's footnote continues to negate its animal body, transcending and abandoning the animal, forgetting the internal caesura that separates life from its form (*O*, 11–13).

Contra Kojève, Agamben wants to preserve some of the restlessness in the dialectic, recoded for Agamben as **potentiality** without **actuality**, "a generic mode of potentiality not exhausted", to push the empty form of relation to its extreme: that is to say, to think politics without relation (*HS*, 60–2). If, as Kojève suggests, by 1946 the end of history has already been completed, the camp and his American and Japanese examples reveal that humanity has not reached the happy life, the fulfilled state of harmony

Kojève seeks, but remains divided and captured by modern biopolitics in the continued separation of animal from human life. Agamben's critique of Kojève's Hegelianism enables our thinking of the task of philosophy: the end of the state form along with the end of **sovereignty**. Kojève's end of history thesis posits a state that survives history by merely maintaining an empty form of sovereignty.

KOMMERELL, MAX

Anton Schütz

Agamben dedicated one of his studies dealing specifically with literary critique to Max Kommerell (1902–44), a German writer and literary historian ("Kommerell, or On Gesture", in *Po*, 77–85), calling him the last personality of the time between the wars still to be discovered. He clearly takes from Walter **Benjamin** the impulse to explore this specialist of the limit regions of the written and spoken word – of gesture in Jean Paul's novels, of speechlessness in Heinrich von Kleist's theatre. Benjamin had acknowledged the outstanding quality of Kommerell's work in spite of political antagonism (he was not alone on the left to grant Kommerell this exceptional status). Personal secretary, in the 1920s, to Stefan George, a poet and head of an aesthetising literary circle, Kommerell was, in the 1930s, a representative of the official German culture, later even a member of Hitler's party. (His play, "Prisoners", was, however, prohibited for reasons of being not, at closer looks, an accusation against bolshevism, but against power as such). When he died after an illness, more than a year before the end of the Third Reich, he was Professor of German Philology in Marburg. His short life was that of an unpolitical or politically isolated figure (although he had close relations to all the leading intellectuals of his time, including **Heidegger**, Gadamer and Bultmann), yet one who unquestionably contained major political parameters and zones of indecision. Agamben takes from Kommerell the idea of gesture's grasp upon life and of the (profane) initiation of life through life itself.

KRAUS, KARL

Anton Schütz

The first time Agamben quotes the Viennese satirist, poet and media critic (1874–1936) is in *Stanzas: Word and Phantasm in Western Culture* (1977), relating a Kraus aphorism : "The language of eros, too, contains its meta-phors. The illiterate calls them 'perversions'." In a series of notes about the situationist Guy **Debord** from 1990 – entitled "Marginal Notes on Comments on the Society of the Spectacle" – Agamben remarks that the only writer to whom Debord might accept being compared is Karl Kraus, the revealer of the hidden laws of the spectacle, "in these loud times which boom with the horrible symphony of actions which produce reports and of reports which cause actions" (quoted in *ME*, 77). Agamben goes on to say:

> The punch line with which Kraus, in the posthumous *Third Walpurgis Night* [1936], justified his silence in the face of the rise of Nazism is well known: 'On Hitler, nothing comes to my mind.' This ferocious *Witz*, where Kraus confesses, without indulgence, his own limitation, marks also the impotence of satire when faced by the becoming-reality of the indescribable. (*ME*, 77)

Benjamin's essay on Karl Kraus (1931) is one among those most quoted by Agamben, which is explainable not only in terms of its – obvious – biographical interest (which is decisive for **Scholem**'s interest as well, especially in dealing with the new angel, who would rather liberate by taking, than delight by giving), but also because of the intimate knowledge Benjamin unfolds of the secret relationship between the esoteric and the everyday, the mystical and the profane (see **profanation**), theological categories and materialistic categories, and so on, which provide, prop-erly speaking, the Agambenian zone of operation/inoperativeness (see **inoperative**).

LANGUAGE

Justin Clemens

Drawing on diverse currents of the post-Romantic "linguistic turn" that integrally affected both "analytic" and "continental" philosophical tradi-tions – including the work of Ludwig **Wittgenstein**, Martin **Heidegger**, Walter **Benjamin**, Emile **Benveniste**, Jacques **Derrida** and Jean-Claude **Milner** – Agamben develops, in the course of his work, a strikingly original doctrine regarding the powers of language. This doctrine hinges on the problematic of *deixis*, and draws together all of Agamben's key terms: **infancy, potentiality, poetry**, the messianic (see **messianism**), and so on. As he announces: "In both my written and unwritten books, I have stubbornly pursued only one train of thought: what is the meaning of 'there is language'; what is the meaning of 'I speak'?"(*IH*, 5). If, as Wittgenstein puts it in *Philosophical Investigations*, "The limits of my language are the limits of my world," Agamben wishes to radicalise this insight further. While he believes that thought must take language as its primary material, he thereby aims at something that is *other* to language.

While the essentials of Agamben's doctrine remain unaltered from very early in his career (at least from the late 1970s on), he ceaselessly returns to his own theses in an attempt to refine and specify their import further. Very simply, human beings are held by the Western philosophical tradition as *essentially* bound to two characteristics; they are at once speaking and mortal. Language therefore delivers both the possibility of communication and the necessity of death. In doing so, it functions as the paradigm of **law** (**politics**, theology, religion) in general. Law in general has the structure of an exception, determining its field not simply through violent imposition, but by withdrawing from its referent; the resources for contesting these operations of law can only come from within language itself. This doctrine is very clearly announced in *Homo Sacer*:

As the pure form of relation, language (like the sovereign ban) always already presupposes itself in the figure of something nonrelational, and it is not possible either to enter into relation or to move out of relation with what belongs to the form of relation itself. . . . the nonlinguistic is only ever to be found in language itself. (*HS*, 50)

Agamben's work involves a detailed exploration of this doctrine in often very varied contexts.

From the beginning of his studies on the problem of the negative in language, with Hegel and Heidegger as his privileged interlocutors, Agamben directs his enquiry towards the problem of "sense and reference", to invoke Gottlob Frege's famous article. What guarantees the suture of language to being when truth can no longer be thought of as adequation, when reference has become problematic, when the thinking subject can no longer function as foundation – and what are the consequences of these recognitions for thinking itself? These problems have forced philosophers towards a re-examination of language under such headings as "ostensive definition", "indexicals" and so on. For Agamben, however, reference can no longer be to something that simply exists *outside* language, but is an intra-linguistic phenomenon, bearing upon the problem of the *actualisation* of language (*deixis*). This requires Agamben to rethink Aristotle's actual/potential (see **potentiality**) distinction, which he exemplifies through his attention to great poets, to literary figures like **Melville**'s **Bartleby** and Dostoevsky's Prince Mishkin, and to survivor testimonies.

Agamben's own method is inherently linguistic; the events to which he refers are exemplarily linguistic events (such as **poetry**, philosophy of language, testimony, and so on), and he reads them at once "archaeologically" (see **archaeology**; that is, seeking their "principle"), "genealogically" (that is, seeking their disjunctive unfolding over time, the becoming-patent of their self-dissimulating structure) and "messianically" (see **messianism**; that is, seeking to transform their operations). Agamben, moreover, tends to read various theses that can seem to be about other matters (such as "God") as theses about language itself, and the history of political life as the working-through and final separation of man from language. In a kind of philological modelling drawn from Friedrich **Nietzsche**'s genealogy of **nihilism** – in which the establishment of "truth" as an ideal finishes by undermining itself (the quest for truth ultimately reveals that "truth" itself is a self-denying fiction) – Agamben wants to argue that contemporary nihilism, "the realm of absolutely speakable things", also offers an unprecedented historical opportunity, the possibility that human beings can not only engage in communication, but also now experience "communicability itself". As he puts it in *Means Without End*,

> exactly for this reason, the age in which we live is also that in which for the first time it becomes possible for human beings to experience their own linguistic essence – to experience, that is, not some language content or some true proposition, but language *itself*, as well as the very fact of speaking. (*ME*, 85)

In *Language and Death*, Agamben uses the received term, "nihilism", to designate our own situation, a use which persists, with slight modifications, up to *Remnants of Auschwitz*, where he gives it a new political specificity and a new philosophical sense. As survivors such as Primo **Levi** testify, if the Nazis perpetrated mass industrial genocide in the death camps, another kind of personage emerged as an unintended, unexpected by-product. Often denominated the *"Muselmann"*, this personage is crucial for Agamben in so far as what philosophy had always maintained was the essence of the human (its capacity for speech) had been fully stripped from the *Muselmänner*, who, though *surviving* as a biological organism, could no longer be recognised as human – not only by the Nazis, but by fellow camp inmates themselves. What the death camps thereby also revealed is that "man" (the mortal speaking being) can *really* be separated from his "essence" (speech) and consigned by the most extreme expressions of sovereign power (the camps, contemporary torture) to a kind of undead subsistence. The potential for speech (to speak or not) had therefore been expropriated from the *Muselmänner*; it would be impossible for a *Muselmann* to say "I am a *Muselmann*." As a consequence, survivor testimonies exhibit an extraordinary structure. They testify in language to an experience which the writers did not and could not have had: that is, the experience of being stripped of the possibility of having an experience (that is, language). This at once reveals something essential about the relationship between human language use and political power (humans beings can be separated by power from their own essence) as they contest it (the witness confronts and resists this possibility).

LAW

Connal Parsley

Although Agamben's work contains several analyses of law and legal formations, the horizon of these investigations bears no similarity to that usually attributed to legal thought. Proposing a fundamental opposition between law and **justice** in one of his earliest reflections on the subject (*IP*, 79), Agamben eschews the determination of a discrete entity called "law" – rejecting, also, the classical presumption that law (howsoever derived) could structure an ethical (see **ethics**) "good life", along with the modern liberal project of lawful institutional governance under the rule of law, and more generally all of the central features of juridical discourse: from the value of law as a textual system for creating and transmitting authority, to the very figure of the **human** which it takes for its **subject**. But beginning in earnest with his essay on the problem of law in Walter **Benjamin** (*Po*, 160), Agamben pursues a sustained inquiry into a set of interrelated themes – largely inherited from Benjamin – which underlie the *Homo Sacer* series, as well as Agamben's related work on **messianism** and that on the nature of **language**, *praxis*, oath and **glory** in relation to power (particularly in *The Sacrament of Language* and *Il Regno e la gloria*). This investigation into the intimate relation between the themes of violence, law, the **sacred**, and finally the notion of "**bare life**" which belongs to this constellation, takes the form of an attempt to reckon with and overcome "law in its originary structure" (*Po*, 167): a structure revealed, above all, in the **state of exception**.

What is revealed about the nature of law, in the state of exception? This question gains importance – and obvious relevance to modern constitutional democracy – in light of the constitutive role which Carl **Schmitt** allocated to the fundamentally anti-normative inherent emergency powers of the sovereign (see **sovereignty**), in his account of the paradoxical maintenance of the legal order through its suspension. For Agamben, Benjamin's subsequent extension of this idea in his affirmation that "the 'state of exception' in which we live is the rule" reveals the "hidden foundation" of all law (*Po*, 162): a paradoxical situation where the law is in a perpetual state of suspension and is for that reason, in the final analysis, always indistinguishable from the de-normated **life** it would govern.

In order to think this perpetually suspended law, Agamben draws on a broad intellectual heredity and a variety of different formulations. Amongst these, the most emblematic comes from the 1934 debate between Benjamin and Gershom **Scholem** regarding the conception of law in Franz **Kafka**'s writing, where Scholem characterises the law as "being in force without significance" (see *HS*, 49–62). Agamben generalises this description of law, applying it to Scholem's own account of the Torah in the originary structure of law: in force, but lacking "a determinate content and meaning" (*Po*, 170), a power whose content is reduced to its "zero-degree". This at once entails the separation of legal power from its exercise (or **potentiality** from act), and implies a constitutive indifference between the legal order and life, characterised by lawlessness *anomie* (*SE*, 39). Similarly, in the state of exception (of which the **camp** is Agamben's paradigmatic example), any "content", a positivity called "law", is absolutely secondary to the unremitting force which would apply it – or not – according to an essentially *anomic* or ungoverned principle.

What Agamben emphasises is the conception of sacred political life in relation to law which pertains to this parlous historico-political situation. Extending Jean-Luc **Nancy**'s notion of the **ban** and relating it to the Schmittian proposition that the rule applies to the exception precisely in no longer applying, Agamben characterises this total *nomos* in which there is "nothing outside the law" as one in which the individual being is abandoned (see **abandonment**) both *by* the law and *to* the law's paradoxical topological structure. Agamben suggests it is this abandoned **bare life**, produced in the **caesura** between the **sacred** and profane and held in place by the political mythologeme of the sacred (*HS*, 84) that is the decisive element of the state of exception and Western politics generally. It is also this relation that guarantees a foundational connection between law and violence (see *SE*, 60).

Drawing on Michel **Foucault**'s conception of biopolitical power and tying it to the juridico-institutional power of the sovereign exception as the paradigm of the modern state, Agamben suggests that this originary structure of law constitutes the uniting feature of modern and archaic forms of political power (*HS*, 6). Thus, the legal phenomena which concern Agamben are above all the recurring historical figures which expose this sacred power-structure – for example, *homo sacer*, or the Greek *nomos empsuchon* ("living law") (see *HS*, 173; *SE*, 70–1) – and in which law, legal power and life cannot be meaningfully separated. Importantly, in referring law to the sacralising element of Western political ontology in this way, Agamben directs the thought of law away from a posited origin in either a transcendental authority, or a purely rational act of constitution. Revoked too, in this sense, is the significance of any operative epochal distinction between the theological and the secular (see *IP*, 87; *ST*, 76). Rather, law's hidden foundation, its *an-archic* (see **archē**) relation to life and lawlessness, becomes revealed only through contemplation of the sacred violence engendered within Western thought itself, and its relation to power (or potentiality). This redirection of the thought of law offers us a glimpse, within the dangerous state of exception, of the conditions of a profane, happy life without law's sacred divisions.

An important element of this gesture is the identity which Agamben proposes between the ban structure of law and that of language. As he writes in *Homo Sacer*, in the context of Aristotle's politics, "The question 'In what way does the living being have language?' corresponds exactly to the question 'In what way does bare life dwell in the *polis*?'" (*HS*, 8). This identity, which is first posed in the mid-1980s in *Idea of Prose* (79–80, 99), is also foreshadowed in Agamben's earlier work on linguistic negativity; both remain essential to his account of law as fundamentally negative and divisive (see *TR*, 47). Moreover, in the recent essay, "K", Agamben elaborates the etymological bond between "category" and "accusation", as the cipher of the shared originary **appropriation** of the "thing" into language and law (2008: 15). Against a jurisprudential approach which would see law as a specific linguistic code, culture, institution or genre, Agamben suggests that language as currently understood is bound into the self-same appropriative structure as is law. As such, whereas liberal legalism offers an apparently politically objective law, codified in language, as the prophylactic between the subject and political power, for Agamben subjection within language, and law, means life is always already exposed to **judgment** and violence, and in this way, bare life is always already guilty life; judgment is always already punishment (2009: 38).

The nature of Agamben's critical approach to law means he cannot be understood as calling for the strengthening of juridical instruments, such as **human rights**. But neither, on the other hand, is his attempt to overcome the law's divisions, which gains its impetus from the messianic (see **messianism**) gesture of confronting and overcoming law (see *Po*, 166), a simple "antinomialism". What Agamben attempts, alongside his rethinking of the metaphysics of language, is an overt confrontation with the juridico-normative categories he regards as pervading thought (some of which, like ethics and human dignity (*RA*, 66), are typically offered by other legal scholars as resistances to politico-legal power). This confrontation, part of the broader relationship between the messianic and thought (*Po*, 161), entails that the law itself is not to be destroyed – and still less replaced with another, "better" law. Rather, it is to be rendered **inoperative**: "fulfilled and set aside". Agamben invokes numerous specific figures in direct response to this exigency: **study**, particularly the study (rather than application) of law; the notion of **play**; and the character **Bartleby**. Functioning alongside Agamben's more overt critique of the ban and Schmitt's sovereign decisionism, these figures are of interest to Agamben because of their **use** of the potentialities of the state of exception and its originary, ambivalent **nihilism**, reorienting its newly exposed conditions towards a reckoning with law's originary structure.

LEVI, PRIMO

Jessica Whyte

In *The Drowned and the Saved*, Primo Levi (1919–87) notes that anyone who reads or writes about the history of the Nazi camps today is faced with the desire to "emulate Christ's gesture on Judgment Day", separating the good from the evil, "the righteous from the reprobates" (Levi 1999: 37). From Levi, who survived Auschwitz and went on to write some of the most powerful accounts of life in the camps, Agamben takes a conception of the *Lager* as a grey zone, in which the judgments that apply in the outside world break down. Levi plays a central role in Agamben's attempt to conceptualise a non-juridical **ethics** of testimony in *Remnants of Auschwitz*: "He is the only one", Agamben writes, "who consciously sets out to bear witness in place of the *Muselmänner*, the drowned, those who were demolished and touched rock bottom" (*RA*, 59). From Levi's attempt to speak in the place of those who cannot speak, Agamben develops an account of witnessing in which the witness always speaks in relation to an impossibility of speech.

LÉVI-STRAUSS, CLAUDE

Nicholas Heron

The 1950 essay, "Introduction to the Work of Marcel Mauss", written by the great structural anthropologist, Claude Lévi-Strauss, remains one of the most persistent reference points across Giorgio Agamben's body of work. Of particular interest, for Agamben, is Lévi-Strauss's celebrated elaboration of the concept of the "floating signifier", and the theory of the constitutive excess of the signifying function with respect to all possible signifieds that underpins it.

It is instructive to chart the migration of this concept across Agamben's work, wherein it is progressively extended and, indeed, polemicised so as to articulate a strict counterpoint to his own methodology. In *Homo Sacer*, it is first employed by simple extension in support of his critique of the scientific mythologeme of the purported "ambivalence of the sacred", as it was construed in the human sciences of the early part of the twenti-eth century; this ambivalence, he suggests, exists solely in the minds of researchers ("*mana* really is *mana* there," as Lévi-Strauss efficiently states; Lévi-Strauss 1987: 57). In an important section of *The Time That Remains* (*TR*, 101–4), it is then inserted into a more general theoretical frame-work which has its discrete linguistic heritage in Troubetzkoy, Bally and Jakobson, and its ultimate philosophical outcome in **Derrida** – the global development of which is now presented under a new cipher: **degree zero**. In this account, the deconstruction of the primacy of the signified in the metaphysical tradition results in a paradoxical preservation of the form of signification itself beyond any determinate contents – a "linguistic 'state of exception'", as he explicitly formulates it elsewhere (*HS*, 25). In *Signatura rerum*, this same lineage undergoes a decisive new inflection. Here, it is reconfigured as an extreme point in his own theory of signatures and is, accordingly, submitted to a new charge: that of an "absolutisation" of the **signature** (Agamben 2008: 78). In a more recent essay again (Agamben 2009: 158), finally, Agamben has returned to his initial point of departure, but from a perspective that completely overhauls the usual chronology; perhaps the ambivalent status which accrues to those floating signifiers through which we represent "religious" phenomena to ourselves, he sug-gests, is but a relic of originally sabbatical human actions with respect to which the forces of religion (and of **law**, which is consubstantial with it) have sought to intervene in order to capture at its centre.

LIFE

Catherine Mills

Agamben's work is littered with references to conceptions of life, though he argues that "life" is not a biological concept but a political one. In keeping with this, his own approach to the philosophy of life is to attempt to grasp the ways that life has been central to the history of Western **poli-tics**. Several of his texts have made contributions to this project, including *Homo Sacer*, *The Open* and an important essay in *Potentialities* in which he discusses Gilles **Deleuze**'s formulation of an impersonal life, understood as akin to a non-biologistic vital principle or force. However, Agamben's approach to the concept of life is distinct from that of theorists working in the tradition of Spinoza, Bergson and vitalistic approaches to the concept of life. For one, he rejects notions of a vital force or resistance in biological life itself. Instead, his point of reference is typically **Aristotle**, in either *The Politics* or *De Anima*. Indeed, that the Ancient Greeks did not have a unified concept of life and instead isolated and identified several variants is especially productive for Agamben's own thinking about life.

Aristotle's *Politics* is most significant for Agamben's conception of the role of life in **biopolitics** in *Homo Sacer*. Aristotle defines and differenti-ates life in relation to political community, suggesting that, whereas the household is mostly closely associated with the life of reproduction, in contrast the *polis* is most concerned with the good life – not living but living well. Agamben notes that the distinction made by Aristotle between bio-logical life (*zoē*) and political life (*bios*) effectively excluded natural life from the *polis* in the strict sense and relegated it entirely to the private sphere. Regrettably, Agamben remains blind to the gendered dimension of the relegation of natural life and reproduction to the household and exclusion from the realm of politics, although feminists have long argued that the association of femininity with natural, biological life is a consistent element of the Western political imaginary. Instead, for Agamben, this distinction between natural life and political forms of life is first and foremost the start-ing point for the emergence of biopolitical sovereignty that includes life in politics only through its exclusion. The category of "**bare life**" emerges from within this distinction, in that it is neither *bios* nor *zoē*, but rather the politicised form of natural life. Immediately politicised but nevertheless excluded from the *polis*, bare life is the limit-concept between the *polis* and the *oikos*. Bare life is understood as life that is abandoned to an "uncondi-tional power of death": that is, to the sovereign right over death or the sov-ereign ban (*HS*, 90). As he states, "not simple natural life, but life exposed to death (bare life or sacred life) is the originary political element" (*HS*, 88).

The danger of biopolitics is not that it collapses forms of life into natural life as it is often supposed, but rather that it relentlessly separates one from the other and provides the condition for the production of bare life. Thus, as it is formulated in *Homo Sacer*, Aristotle's division provides the concep-tual *arthron* that drives the originary biopolitical structure of Western pol-itics. The problem that contemporary political thought must face, then, is not only to discover the originary relation that underpins and gives rise to this aporia, but also to find a way to think beyond it. The task for Agamben is to transform this biopolitical *aporia* into a *euporia* – to transform the lack of a way into a felicitous way or path (*Po*, 217). The task of moving beyond this aporia gives rise to notions such as that of "**happy life**" and "form-of-life"; it may also be seen as the motivation for Agamben's reflections on the relationship between human and animal life in *The Open*.

The Open takes up Aristotle's differentiation of life in *De Anima*, to suggest that this indicates that "life" has no positive content as such, but that the division of life "passes first of all as a mobile border within living man" and provides the necessary condition for the decision on what is human. It is by virtue of the division of life that a hierarchy of vegetal, animal and **human** life and the economy of relations between them can be established. Because of this, the question of life itself turns into a question of humanism. Or in other words, any attempt to think the concept of life outside the frame given to Western philosophy by Aristotle and the divisions it institutes will necessarily entail questioning the presuppositions of humanism – of what it is to be human and what relation the being so identified bears to those excluded from that designation. From this, then, Agamben's reflections in *The Open* turn towards Heidegger's extended concern with humanism, especially in his discussions of the mode of the being of the human, as opposed to other animals, in *The Fundamental Concepts of Metaphysics* and elsewhere. Heidegger's discussion revolves around issues of captivation, boredom and the open-ness of being that he takes to be characteristic of the human but lacking in the animal.

The conclusion that Agamben reaches is that the human and animal are not radically distinct, for "the jewel set at the centre of the human world . . . is nothing other than animal captivation" (*O*, 68). But what distinguishes the human from the animal is its capacity to suspend this captivation, thus allowing for the "appearing of undisconcealment as such" (*O*, 68). But Agamben is not satisfied with simply having shown that man and animal are not "separated by an abyss", as Heidegger argues they are. This is not to say that he urges a return to a biologistic understanding of the human as simply another animal, albeit one with unique capacities such as reason or language; on this point, Agamben accepts Heidegger's critique. Instead, he urges that man (*sic*) appropriate his animality as pure abandonment. At this point, Agamben turns to Benjamin for a way of thinking pure abandonment, not as a reconciliation of man and animal, but in order to bring about a "new and more blessed life, one that is neither animal nor human", which is "beyond both nature and knowledge, beyond concealment and disconcealment" (*O*, 87). This life is not simply redeemed or reconciled in the sense of simply re-integrating natural and non-natural life through, for instance, reducing one to the other. Instead, it is "outside of being" – that is, external to the

Heideggerian opposition of animal and man on the basis of the openness to being, and instead characterised by beatitude or **happiness**.

LIMBO

Jessica Whyte

Limbo re-appears throughout Agamben's *œuvre* whenever he wants to exemplify a condition beyond both salvation and **judgment** (*CC*, 6; *IP*, 77–8; *Pr*, 54). In a section of *The Coming Community* entitled "From Limbo", Agamben recounts Saint Thomas's view that those children who die prior to baptism, and thus with no fault but original sin, are condemned to inhabit limbo for eternity. What is conceived as a non-afflictive punishment, which consists exclusively in the lack of a vision of God, is, Agamben suggests, instead their greatest joy; as they have always already forgotten God, his judgment cannot touch them, and He is impotent in the face of their "neutrality with respect to salvation" (*CC*, 6). These figures are beyond judgment and thus beyond the reach of the law. Throughout a number of texts (*IP*, *CC*) Agamben reads various figures as exemplifying this limbo-like condition of neutrality with respect to divine judgment, amongst them the characters of Robert **Walser**, Herman **Melville**'s "**Bartleby** the Scrivener" and the freed convict in **Kafka**'s "In the Penal Settlement", who has outlived the machine that was to sentence and execute him. If we wish to find the realm of those **whatever singularities**, without substantive identity or condition of belonging, it is to limbo, Agamben suggests, that we should turn our attention.

LOGOS

Robert Sinnerbrink

The Greek term *logos* has been variously translated as "word", "saying", "reason", "**language**" and "account", and is arguably central to Agamben's understanding of language. In Ancient Greek thought, to have knowledge is to provide a *logos*: a reasoned account of a thing's nature, expressed in language. Aristotle defined the human being as a "rational animal"; we possess the power of reasoned speech as distinct from the natural cries of animals, and human moral capacity and **politics** depend upon having *logos* (*Politics* 1253a). The ethico-political problem is thus located in the passage from *phone* (speech) to *logos* (reason/language) (*LD*, 87).

Logos also defines the metaphysical-theological conception of language; revelation – "In the beginning was the Word" (*en arkhē en ho logos*) – concerns not God but "the fact that the word, that language exists" (*Po*, 41). Revelation through language is linked with the **Voice** as its metaphysical foundation: "a voice that, without signifying anything, signifies signification itself . . . voice as pure indication of an event of language" (*Po*, 42). This metaphysical Voice, moreover, articulates the relation between *phone* and *logos* through a double negativity: the absent or removed voice, and that which remains unsayable by discourse (*LD*, 84–5).

How to experience language in a way that undoes the privileging of the Voice? This would require rethinking the Aristotelian definition of human beings as *zōon logon echōn* – living beings using language (*S*, 156). What is essential in the Greek way of thinking *logos*, for Agamben, is not the conjunction between living being (*zoē*) and language (*logos*) but the *articulation* that both divides and links them together. *Logos* can thus be rethought as the "fold that gathers and divides all things in the 'putting together' of presence" (*S*, 156).

LOVE

Paolo Bartoloni

In the essay entitled "The Passion of Facticity" in *Potentialities*, Agamben engages with the notion of love in the work of Martin **Heidegger**, refuting the view that Heidegger's writing is devoid of love. He claims that: "Heidegger was [. . .] perfectly conscious of the fundamental importance of love, in the sense that it conditions precisely the possibility of knowledge and the access to truth" (*Po*, 186). Agamben not only provides an interpretation of some central passages of *Being and Time*; but he also rehearses his own understanding of love which will be developed in later writing, such as in *The Time That Remains*. In "The Passion of Facticity" love as passion is seen as one of the inherent attributes of being, so much so that it must "find its place and proper articulation in the Being-already-in-the world that characterizes Dasein's transcendence" (187). It is through love that *Dasein* experiences its thrownness (the *Da*) in the world, and it does so in a manner that is quintessentially related to the discussion of openness and unconcealment in so far as love is one of the fundamental guises of *Dasein*'s potentiality. Agamben emphasises this passage when he writes that "Passion, *potentia passiva*, is therefore the most radical experience of possibility at issue in Dasein: a capacity that is capable not only of potentiality [. . .] but also, and above all, of *impotentiality*" (201). According

to Agamben, love brings *Dasein* face to face with the possibility to be
but also not-to-be, leading towards experiencing truth and knowledge
as well as concealment and opacity. Love is, therefore, the access to the
knowledge of the incessant experience of belonging and "nonbelonging"
of *Dasein*, which is also the struggle between the "I" and the "other", the
subject and object of love, which are continuously implicated in a process
of union and separation. As if to echo his reading of love in Heidegger's
work, Agamben writes his idea of love as follows: "to live in intimacy with
a stranger, not in order to draw him closer, or to make him known, but
rather to keep him strange, remote" (*IP*, 61). The idea of love as the union
that keeps apart had already been explored by Agamben in his investigation of medieval poetry in *Stanzas*. In the chapter called "The World and
the Phantasm: The Theory of the Phantasm in the Love Poetry of the
Duecento", Agamben proposes a reading of the *dolce stil novo*, including
Dante's and Cavalcanti's poetry, in which the poetic experience of love
is described as the physical entrance of the "spirit" of love by the eye and
through the eye. Love penetrates the subject as an image of the beloved
that, by turning into its spirit, bids farewell to the actual person. It is in
this sense that love in medieval poetry is the narration of an image which
is rooted in memory and melancholia. Love, as *agape* and *caritas*, assumes
a central importance in Agamben's later works, and especially in *The Time
That Remains*, where the revolutionary figure of St Paul is presented as
imbued with a message in which love ascends to theological and political
meanings not only as the indispensable encounter with truth and God but
also, and more importantly, as the coming together of a new community.

MARX, KARL

Jessica Whyte

There is something initially curious about Agamben's location of his
project within that of "an integrated Marxian analysis" (*ME*, 82). Karl
Marx (1818–83) is best known for *The Communist Manifesto*, written with
Friedrich Engels, and for his great three-volume work, *Capital: A Critique
of Political Economy*. "The history of all hitherto existing society", we read
in the former, "is the history of class struggles" (Marx and Engels 1848:
1). In Agamben's work, however, both class struggle and the critique of

political economy are largely absent, and we find only unsparing criticism of the so-called "communist states" founded in Marx's name. There
are, none the less, several key areas in which Marx's thought is decisive
for Agamben's own, and which make it meaningful to position the latter
within a Marxian, if not a Marxist, heritage. Foremost amongst these are
Marx's formulation of the **commodity** form, his critique of rights, and
his account of the proletariat as a non-substantive subject that must negate
itself in order to secure general emancipation.

In *Means Without End*, Agamben suggests that Marx's theorisation of
commodity fetishism was "foolishly abandoned" in the Marxist milieu of
the 1960s (*ME*, 76). From Marx, Agamben takes a vision of commodification as a structure of separation, which represents human powers as the
objective properties of the world of things. Agamben's account of the
contemporary society of the spectacle as "a capitalism that has reached
its extreme figure" (*ME*, 76) is indebted to Marx, but to a Marx filtered
through both Walter **Benjamin** and Guy **Debord**. Second, while Marx
appears nowhere in Agamben's critical account of the ambiguous man/
citizen link that underlies modern rights declarations, this critique can
none the less be seen as a continuation of the inquiry that started with
Marx's essay, "On the Jewish Question" (1843). There, the latter had
already posed the question: "Who is the *homme* as distinct from the
citoyen?" (Marx 1843). For both thinkers, it was with the modern declarations of rights that "politics proclaims itself to be a mere *means*, whose
end is life in civil society" (Marx 1843), and both aspire to a condition in
which *bios* and *zoē*, or life in the state and life in civil society, are no longer
separable. None the less, Agamben argues that, ultimately, Marxism, like
anarchism, has failed to formulate the problem of the state correctly, and
thus ended up "identifying with an enemy whose structure one does not
understand" (*HS*, 12).

Despite this implicit critique of the supposed "workers' states",
Agamben's later works attempt to uncover another Marx – one resistant
to substantive identities that could be represented by a state. In *The Time
That Remains*, Agamben suggests that his conception of the subject as the
subject of its own desubjectivation "permits more than one analogy with
the Marxian proletariat" (*TR*, 31). In contrast to the working class as a
sociological category, Agamben sees the proletariat as a non-substantive
subject that must negate itself (as proletariat) in order to liberate itself and
all of society. In a discussion of the messianic, and the revolutionary, vocation, he argues that the revolutionary vocation of the proletariat is not a new
factical vocation but the nullification, or hollowing out, of every vocation.
The proletariat thus lays bare the contingency of every factical vocation
– the split between the private individual and her social position – while

enabling the deactivation of every separation. Thus, in his view, "the fact that the proletariat ends up over time being identified with a determinate social class – the working class that claims prerogatives and rights for itself – is the worst misunderstanding of Marxian thought" (*TR*, 31).

MELVILLE, HERMAN

Arne De Boever

Herman Melville (1819–91) is a North American (US) novelist who also wrote short stories, essays and poetry. Agamben often refers to the titular character from Melville's story, "**Bartleby**, the Scrivener", a **law** copyist who renounces copying and ultimately gives up writing altogether. Agamben does not read this as a gesture of disempowerment, but as a step towards the thought of a **potentiality** that would not pass into **actuality**: "a complete or perfect potentiality that belongs to the scribe who is in full possession of the art of writing in the moment in which he does not write" (*Po*, 246–7). Other works by Melville, such as the story "Billy Budd, Sailor" or the novella *Benito Cereno*, both of which investigate **life**'s political (see **politics**) relation to law, can be read through the lens of Agamben's work as well. What makes Melville a particularly interesting author for Agamben is an aspect of his writing that Gilles **Deleuze** has also emphasised: the ways in which Melville's ethical (see **ethics**) and political project is linked to an exploration of speaking and writing otherwise. Although Bartleby's formula, "I would prefer not to," is the best example with respect to Agamben's work, Deleuze's analysis of Billy Budd's stutter in *Essays Critical and Clinical* can provide additional insights into how, through a reflection on **language**, an ethics and politics beyond sovereign violence can become possible. For Agamben, it is through Bartleby's formulaic use of language that another experience of language, not as meaning-making but as such, can emerge. Such an experience is linked throughout Agamben's work to an ethics and politics of **inoperativity** and **whatever singularity**.

MESSIANISM

Catherine Mills

Attention to the messianic, and the correlative necessity of rethinking time and **history**, is a consistent feature of Agamben's work, from early texts such as *Infancy and History*, through to more recent texts such as *The Time That Remains*. In *Infancy and History*, he addresses the perceived necessity of a new conception of time adequate to the revolutionary conception of history outlined by Marxism (see **Marx**). Taking up this, task, Agamben turns to alternative sources such as Gnosticism and Stoicism, as well as both Walter **Benjamin** and Martin **Heidegger**, to emphasise the disruption of time and man's fulfilment as resurrection or decision in that moment. The model for this conception of time, he suggests, is the notion of *cairos* (*kairos*), "the abrupt and sudden conjunction where decision grasps opportunity and life is fulfilled in the moment" (*IH*, 101). Represented as a young man running on his toes, with a long forelock but bald at the back of his head, Kairos personifies fleeting opportunity, which can be grasped as it approaches but not once it has passed. Opposed to time as *chronos*, *kairos* signifies the propitious and fleeting moment that one must take hold of or forever let pass; it is a "between time" which is nevertheless full of possibility. With this rejection of chronological time in favour of the cairological as the moment of authentic history in mind, we can turn to Agamben's more recent discussions of messianism and time.

In *The Time That Remains*, Agamben proposes an interpretation of Pauline theology that emphasises its messianic dimension, and argues that **Paul**'s "Letter to the Romans" actually aligns conceptually with the messianic threads that run through the thought of Benjamin. Focusing most specifically on Benjamin's text, "On the Concept of History", Agamben argues that Benjamin reappropriates Pauline messianism, which itself should be understood as concerning not the founding of a new religion, but the abolition or fulfilment of Jewish law. Benjamin's main target in these aphorisms is a "historicism" or "universal history" that emphasises progression, unity and continuity, in the place of which he proposes a theologically inspired conception of historical materialism. The importance of this conception of historical materialism for Benjamin is its capacity to release the irruptive power of the historical moment through properly grasping its relation to the present. As he writes in the seventh thesis, this does not mean recognising the past moment "as it really was". Instead, it means "appropriating a memory as it flashes up in a moment of danger" (Benjamin 2003: 391). The past appears as fleeting image, which historical materialism attempts to grasp and wrest free of the weight of conformism epitomised by progressivism. The historical image is not to be aligned with a temporal continuum or narrative of past–present–future but is appropriated to "blast open the continuum of history". The historical moment allows for an irruption in the "empty homogenous time" to which historicism condemns humanity, since it is the site of a "time filled full by now-time *[Jetztzeit]*" (Benjamin 2003: 395).

In *The Time That Remains*, Agamben specifies messianic time as distinct both from the time of prophecy, which is always future referential and announces the coming of the Messiah, and from the *eschaton*, or the eschatological concern with the last day and end of time. Taking up Paul's term for the messianic event – *ho nyn kairos*, or "the time of the now" – Agamben develops a conception of messianic time as neither irremediably "to come" nor the end of time, but instead a "time that contracts itself and begins to end . . . time that remains between time and its end" (*TR*, 62). This conception of a time contracting itself is best articulated for Agamben through the notion of "operational time" developed by the linguist Gustave Guillaume. Guillaume proposes "operational time" as a way of isolating the time that it takes for the human mind to construct an image of time, to which the actual image constructed is always referred back. Thus, Guillaume generates a new "chronogenetic" representation of time that is no longer linear but three-dimensional. It allows time to grasped as "a pure state of potentiality", alongside "its very process of formation" and "in the state of having been constructed" (*TR*, 66). This means that in so far as humans construct and represent chronological time, in doing so, they produce another time which is not a supplement to chronology, but which is internal to the very process of understanding time as chronological.

Relating this to the problem of messianic time, Agamben suggests that a definition of messianic time can be yielded from this, in that it is not end-time nor futural time, but rather "the time we take to bring [time] to an end, to achieve our representation of time"; "messianic time *is the time that time takes to come to an end*" (*TR*, 67). But as such, messianic time is not external to or opposed to chronological time – it is internal to it, and in fact that which *contracts* chronological time and begins to bring it to an end. This contraction of time, Agamben suggests, is rather like the muscular contraction of an animal before it leaps – an image that beautifully highlights the fullness and power of messianic time. While not the leap itself, messianic time is akin to that contraction that makes the leap possible; it is the time "left to us" before the end and which brings about the end. As *kairos*, the time of the now, this operational time is neither identifiable with nor opposed to chronological time, but is instead internal to it as a seized and contracted *chronos* – as "the pearl embedded in the ring of chance" *kairos* is "a small portion of *chronos*, a time remaining" (*TR*, 69). Thus, according to Agamben, Pauline messianism identifies two heterogenous times – "one *kairos* and one *chronos*, one an operational time and the other a representational time", the relation of which is identified in the term "*para-ousia*", which literally means next to, and more specifically, being beside being, being beside itself. In this way, messianic time "lies beside itself, since, without ever coinciding with a chronological instant, and without ever adding itself onto it, it seizes hold of the instant and brings it forth to fulfilment" (*TR*, 71). Agamben avers that the result of this, as Benjamin writes in "On the Concept of History", is that every moment is "the small gateway in time through which the Messiah might enter" (Benjamin 2003: 397; *TR*, 71).

MILNER, JEAN-CLAUDE

Justin Clemens

Jean-Claude Milner (1941–) is a French linguist who works in the heritage of Chomskyan linguistics, Lacanian psychoanalysis, and political activism. This singular confluence means that Milner takes seriously the possibility of linguistics as an empirical science, as he recognises the necessary limits of any such science. Milner's very clear formulations of the status of modern, post-Galilean science also draw on the theories of such historians as Alexandre Koyré and Karl Popper. In *Introduction to the Science of Language* (1989), Milner identifies three key characteristics of modern science:

1. the mathematisation of empirical phenomena
2. an essential relationship with technology as the practical application of science
3. the essential role of falsifiable propositions in science.

Milner deploys these headings to make a set of further distinctions regarding the study of languages:

i. the *factum loquendi*, the brute fact *that* there are beings that speak
ii. the *factum linguae*, that *what* a being speaks merits the name of language
iii. the *factum linguarum*, that one can discriminate language from non-language and that languages can be discriminated from each other (they are at once diverse yet homogeneous)
iv. the *factum grammaticae*, that languages are describable in terms of properties.

In an extremely important but under-discussed review of Milner's work (1990; republished in *Po*, 62–76), Agamben relies heavily on these distinctions in order to delimit both the role of philosophy proper and its object; philosophy essentially deals with the *factum loquendi*, which Milner explicitly excludes from the purview of science. Philosophy is therefore an experiment with examples of **language** that exceed the grip of properties (that is, those phenomena which can be brought under a law identified by science).

MUSELMANN

Jason Maxwell

Making only a brief appearance near the end of *Homo Sacer* (*HS*, 185), the *Muselmann* receives much closer attention in *Remnants of Auschwitz*, Agamben's investigation of the Nazi concentration camps. Meaning literally "the Muslim", *Muselmann* was a name given to those inhabitants of the camps who, due to their brutal treatment by the SS, had ceased to respond and interact with their environment. Ignored by other prisoners, this figure was beyond the point of concealing his dire condition, thereby effectively condemning himself to death during the next round of executions. For Agamben, this figure proves so important because it is the sole figure truly to experience the full horror of the camps – only by being reduced to a mute existence prior to extermination was the *Muselmann* able to feel the full force of the Nazis' dehumanisation. Borrowing from Auschwitz survivor Primo **Levi**, Agamben regards the *Muselmann* as the "complete witness" who nevertheless cannot bear witness (see **witnessing**), precisely because he has been stripped of every relational and linguistic capacity, even before his death prevents him from testifying in the traditional sense of the term.

For Agamben, this paradox reveals that the *Muselmann* not only is situated at the divide between life and death but also occupies the point between the human and the inhuman. He declares that "[t]here is thus a point at which human beings, while apparently remaining human beings, cease to be human. This point is the *Muselmann*" (*RA*, 55). Oddly enough, it is precisely this capacity to be stripped of the traditional markers of humanity that calls into question the essence of the human itself, leaving Agamben to conclude paradoxically that "*the human being is the inhuman; the one whose humanity is completely destroyed is the one who is truly human*" (133). Agamben believes that the final lesson of Auschwitz should be to undermine the legitimacy of all existing legal and juridical concepts that infiltrate **ethics**. Because traditional categories like dignity and respect were rendered fundamentally useless within the concentration camp, Agamben demands a new set of ethical principles that would be better attuned to the human's open **potentiality**.

NAME

Jason Maxwell

In one of the brief and elliptical chapters that make up *The Idea of Prose*, Agamben's interrogation of the unsayable leads him to declare that "what one cannot speak of, language can nevertheless perfectly name" (*IP*, 105). While the unsayable does not completely exceed the grasp of language – after all, it possesses a name – it nevertheless escapes it in every other way. Agamben suggests that philosophy has always been invested in exploring this strange fact, noting that the discipline "pursues, in the name, the idea" (*IP*, 106). But what would it mean to pursue the idea in the name? Although the chapter in *The Idea of Prose* offers little explanation, Agamben's essay, "Tradition of the Immemorial" (published in the same year), provides a more explicit account of the importance of the name. Here, he writes that "discourse cannot say what is named by the name" (*Po*, 107). Discourse presupposes the existence of the name and relies upon it to function smoothly, and it is precisely because of the mysterious existence of language itself that discourse cannot adequately account for names themselves.

Perhaps the significance of Agamben's exploration of the name can best be understood through his critique of Jacques **Derrida** and deconstruction. In his essay "Pardes: The Writing of Potentiality", Agamben includes three passages where Derrida explains that his conceptual vocabulary – most notably, "*différance*" and "trace" – should not be considered names in the traditional sense of the word since these terms do not refer to concrete things so much as the infinite play of signifiers. Agamben goes on to explain that "[w]hat is unnameable is *that there are names* . . . what is nameless yet in some way signified is the name itself" (*Po*, 211). For Derrida, language is nothing more than a self-referential system. As Agamben sees it, the limitations of this approach, which inevitably result in the trap of complete textualism, are evident from its inability to see that self-referentiality is always displaced on to the level of pure potentiality, not within language itself. In this respect, "the name can be named and language can be brought to speech" (*Po*, 217).

NANCY, JEAN-LUC

Carlo Salzani

Jean-Luc Nancy (1940–) is a French philosopher and a personal friend of Agamben (cf. *WA*, 26). His essay, "*La Communauté désœuvrée*" ("The Inoperative Community", 1983; book with the same title 1986), gave origin to the debate about the idea of community, of which *The Coming Community* must be considered a response, though Nancy's work is not explicitly quoted. This debate is already mentioned in an early essay, "Tradition of the Immemorial" (1985) (*Po*, 113), and in *Means Without End* (*ME*, 117). *La Communauté désœuvrée* popularised the term *désœuvrement* and is also extremely important for Agamben's development of the theme of **inoperativity**, but whereas Nancy connotes the term as "absence of production" in the constitution of the community, Agamben broadens its scope and relates it to the theme of **potentiality**, thereby defining it as the proper human *praxis* (cf. *HS*, 61). The other major reference to Nancy is to *L'Impératif catégorique* ("The Categorical Imperative", 1983), from which Agamben derives the notion of **ban**, fundamental for the whole *Homo Sacer* project (cf. *HS*, 28; *ME*, 112; *Po*, 162). Nancy identified the ontological structure of the **law** as that of abandonment and conceived the entire history of the West as the "time of abandonment"; however, Agamben argues that his description remains inside the form of law and does not conceive any way out of the ban (*HS*, 58–9). Other minor references to Nancy relate to **language** (*Po*, 113; *ME*, 116), **love** (*Po*, 204), and **Bataille** and **sacrifice** (*HS*, 113).

NEGRI, ANTONIO

Carlo Salzani

A brief excursus in *Homo Sacer* (*HS*, 42–4) discusses the thesis of the Italian philosopher and politician Antonio Negri (1933–), proposed in his 1992 book, *Il potere costituente* (English trans. *Insurgencies: Constituent Power and the Modern State*). Whereas for Negri constituent power is irreducible to any constituted order, for Agamben it still partakes in the **ban**-structure of **sovereignty**. The strength of Negri's book, however, lies for Agamben in its emphasis on constituting power as "constitution of potentiality", which opens the way for a new articulation between **potentiality** and **actuality**, thereby returning **politics** to its ontological position.

NIETZSCHE, FRIEDRICH

Robert Sinnerbrink

The thought of German philosopher Friedrich Nietzsche (1844–1900) is important for Agamben, in particular the concepts of **nihilism**, **art** as will to power, and eternal recurrence. Nihilism, for Nietzsche, is the cultural-historical condition in which "the highest values devalue themselves": when transcendent sources of normative authority (God) lose their legitimating authority (*The Will to Power*, #2). For Agamben, the metaphysical determinations of the human (split between *bios* and *zoē*), of language (founded in the negativity of the **Voice**) and of **biopolitics** render modern democracies nihilistic (*CC*, 63). None the less, the possibility exists of transfiguring this nihilistic condition through the composition of a **coming community** of singularities defined by "whatever being" (see **whatever singularity**) (*CC*, 62–7).

Agamben also devotes attention to Nietzsche's thinking on art. Nietzsche rejects the Kantian (see **Kant**) emphasis on *aesthesis* (sensuous feeling of the spectator), considering art from the viewpoint of its creator (*MC*, 1–3). None the less, Nietzsche's "artist's metaphysics" articulates the most extreme point in modern **aesthetics** (*MC*, 85). For Nietzsche regards art, encompassing all forms of *poiesis*, as an expression of the metaphysics of *will to power* (the vital willing of being). The most extreme nihilism – the recognition that the world is meaningless chaos – provokes the (unbearable) thought of the eternal recurrence: that existence, without meaning or aim, recurs eternally. The response to this abysmal thought is *amor fati* – to "will the circle of the eternal recurrence as *circulus vitiosus deus*" (*MC*, 90). The overman or "man of art", however, will be capable of this love of fate, transforming the chaos of existence into the affirmation of its eternal recurrence. This is the deeper meaning of Nietzsche's dictum that art "is the highest task of man, the truly metaphysical activity" (*MC*, 91).

None the less, Agamben also criticises Nietzsche's eternal recurrence. **Melville**'s figure of **Bartleby**, whose refrain "I would prefer not to" remains suspended between occurrence and non-occurrence (*Po*, 267), is an attempt to disrupt the cycle of "innumerable repetitions" that would convert **potentiality** into **actuality** (*Po*, 268). Similarly, the eternal recurrence signals the most extreme expression of the loss of **gesture** in modernity, a hyperbolic attempt to transfigure this loss into fate: "*Thus Spoke Zarathustra* is the ballet of a humanity bereft of its gestures" (*IH*, 152; *ME*, 52). Nietzsche both diagnoses and fulfils modern nihilism.

NIHILISM

Yoni Molad

Nihilism, or in Nietzsche's definition, the devaluation of all values, is for many thinkers the most important consequence and defining feature of modernity. Over and above understanding nihilism as a historical process or cultural phenomenon, Agamben's thought contributes to the understanding of modern nihilism in two significant ways: by showing the nihilism and self-cancellation inherent in the formal structures of human sciences, institutions and actions, and by alluding to the redemptive **potentiality** of nihilism itself. Developing Nietzsche's definition, Agamben understands nihilism not only as devaluation but as the continual existence and power of that which has been devalued. In a similar way to Nietzsche, Agamben believes that rather than maintaining a reactionary or merely critical attitude towards nihilism, our task is to put it to a new use by realising its redemptive potentiality.

Agamben's ethics is one of a fulfilled nihilism: the realisation that the world as such is as it is, that therein lies its wonder, and that there is no **vocation** or pre-given destiny for the species (*CC*), and hence no historical or political tasks for human beings to fulfill (*O*). Agamben shows, through many examples in his work, that only those who lose their way and experience nothingness can catch a glimpse of a truly human happiness. For Agamben, the human is a workless animal whose redemption lies not in finding the true path, but in losing its way *in the right way*.

Agamben describes our epoch – as a consequence of the development of nihilism, expressed most clearly in the nullity of life in the society of the spectacle – as the epoch that does not wish to be an epoch (*IP*): the epoch in which nihilism finally finds a positive cultural expression and reveals its true significance, bringing to light the human condition, and the potentiality for its redemption, in an unprecedented way. The structural nihilism in **art, politics** and **language** is revealed through Agamben's description of a process by which all three are reliant upon a negative foundation that is obscured through a series of exclusions, splits and aporias. For Agamben, the nihilistic status of modern art results from the split between the experience of the work of art by the modern artist on the one hand and the spectator or critic on the other, who face each other as two sides of the same nihilistic coin: the artist who creates without content but with only a self-negating empty will to create, and the spectator who critiques and judges not on the basis of the work itself but through a negative structure of an artwork, the creation of which they must suppress. The negativity which appears in the forms of the ready-made, which shows the reversibility of artwork and industrial product, and of pop-art, which blurs the distinction between industrial and artistic production, effaces the distinction between artworks and other objects, thus dragging art into ruin, but at the same time reveals the inherent negative structure of human action, and hence the critical force of nihilistic art.

In *Language and Death*, Agamben exposes the negative foundation of language, its possibility of signification guaranteed by mortality alone, and the use of this negativity to distinguish human beings from all other living creatures, separating nature from culture, human language from animal voice. Agamben argues that the idea that language is grounded in death or silence (or what he terms **Voice** as distinguished from language or mere non-signifying sound) presupposes a sacrificial myth in which the social bond between human beings is symbolised and ritualised by **sacrifice**, and **life** is made **sacred**. This myth attempts to "cure" the ungroundedness of human action by ritualising violence as the foundation of a community. The exclusion of the human voice from signifying language grounds what Agamben argues, *contra* Carl **Schmitt**, is the most fundamental distinction of Western politics: the sovereign **ban** that functions through a distinction between *bios* and *zoē*. Just like language, law and the politics that depend on it can only function by separating from within themselves a sphere where they cannot apply. In order for politics to be possible, Agamben argues, human life must be abandoned by law and placed in a permanent state of exception, thus becoming **bare life**. This bare life is the negative foundation of sovereign power, the **state of exception** in which the law can only apply by being in force without significance (*HS*). In this way the law maintains its force and value despite its self-cancellation and devaluation, revealing its nihilistic structure.

Far from bemoaning the permanent state of exception in which we live, Agamben wants to show that the emptying out and nullification of all historical tasks and forms of community demand that we bring about a real state of exception in which we can think the end of history and the end of the state simultaneously (*ME*), thus no longer concealing the negative foundations of the species and demanding sacrifices from each other, be they political, ethical or economic, as a consequence. Agamben suggests that rather than searching for new ways to cover over the essential nothingness of the human condition, it is our task to profane our nihilism and put it to free use. In direct confrontation with **Derrida**, who Agamben charges with maintaining the force of signification despite emptying it of any referent, and **Scholem**, who wishes to maintain the law in force as indecipherable, Agamben wishes to overcome this nihilism of language on the one hand, and law on the other, by exposing the void that exists between voice and *logos*, life and law, and finding in that void the possibility of an ethos and a community.

NUDITY

Connal Parsley

For Agamben, nudity is marked by a heavy theological heredity. Following and extending the analysis of Erik **Peterson**, in a recent collection of essays entitled *Nudity* (*Nudità*), Agamben argues that the relation between nudity and clothing coincides with the problem of human nature in relation to **grace**. According to Christian theology, Adam and Eve were not simply "naked" in the Garden of Eden but were clothed in grace, and after the Fall – having been deprived of their glorious garment – they were forced to wear the human clothing of sin and hypocrisy. They were, therefore, only ever "naked" for a few brief, negative moments of dis-covery, and this situates nudity – as well as the "human nature" of which it is, for Agamben, the analogue – as possible only in relation to, first, divine grace (without which it is thought sinful, imperfect and in need of completion) and, later, its apparently secular counterpart: clothing. This theological analysis of nudity corresponds to Agamben's account of "**bare life**". Just as, for Agamben, the political mythologeme of *homo sacer* presupposes and produces bare life as its ultimate content, so too are nudity and human nature produced and presupposed by their theological "veiling" (2009: 95). Nudity is therefore a theological "**signature**" – a *dispositif* which binds nudity to clothing, and nature to grace.

Agamben affirms that this means we ought not to search for a more originary, prior state of nudity – one does not exist. Rather, the theological *dispositif* itself must be understood in order to neutralise it, thus rendering simple, profane nudity possible (2009: 98). Everything therefore depends on our grasping the fact that nudity consists only in the privative moment of its unveiling (2009: 112). This presents for Agamben a potentially transformative occasion of pure "knowability", by the very virtue of its revelation that there is no object of knowledge – no underlying nature or nudity – to reveal.

OIKONOMIA – see 'Government'

OPEN

Mathew Abbott

Agamben has devoted an entire book – *The Open* – to exploring this Heideggerian concept. Heidegger, in his later works, borrows the term from Rilke but employs it differently, using it as one of his names for being *as such*. As Agamben shows, the difference consists in Heidegger's criticism of what he took to be Rilke's overly metaphysical rendering of the being of **animals**, and a subsequent attempt at undoing his reversal of "the hierarchical relationship between man and animal" (*O*, 57). In the eighth elegy, Rilke seems to indicate that the animal possesses a relation to being that exceeds that of the **human** in its intensity and immediacy. The animal, as Rilke puts it, can see the open "with all its eyes", while the human, caught in the frame of **language**, can never enter its "pure space" (quoted in *O*, 57). Heidegger takes issue with this idea, claiming that it stems from Rilke's misunderstanding of what reveals itself in the experience of *aletheia*: that it is the human's dwelling in language that forms the condition for experiencing the co-belonging of concealment and unconcealment that marks the truth of being.

In his engagement with this conflict, Agamben turns to the threefold thesis of Heidegger's *Fundamental Concepts*: "the stone is worldless [*weltlos*]; the animal is poor in world [*weltarm*]; man is world-forming [*weltbildend*]" (quoted in *O*, 51). While the stone simply has no world, the animal is *deprived* of world; unlike the stone it has access to a set of beings depending on its specific "disinhibiting ring" (quoted in *O*, 55), but unlike the human it can never experience the being of those beings. As the example of the bee continuing to drink honey after the removal of its abdomen indicates, the animal is captivated by its environment, "wholly absorbed in its own disinhibitor" (*O*, 52). As such, the difference between the human and the animal is not only that the human is in language, but also that the human is the animal that "has awakened *from* its own captivation *to* its own captivation", the animal that "has learned to become bored" (*O*, 70). For Agamben, Heidegger's ontology of animality affirms but also problematises the human/animal distinction, because "the jewel set at the center of the human world and its *Lichting* [clearing] is nothing but animal captivation." This to say that the "wonder that beings *are*", which Heidegger prized as the true calling of authentic *Dasein*, is just an exposure to the "essential disruption" in the human that allows it to experience the fact of its being alive as uncanny (*O*, 68).

Agamben turns to **Benjamin** to bring out the messianic (see **messianism**) dimensions of these problems, as hinted at by Heidegger in his link between world poverty and the "yearning expectation" that marks creatural life in **Paul** (quoted in *O*, 61). Following through on and eventually rejecting the implication that animal life is life in need of **salvation**, Agamben posits a theory of **redemption** as synonymous with a "pure abandonment" (*O*, 80), in which life is "saved precisely in its being unsavable" (*O*, 92).

ORIGIN/*ARCHĒ*

Thanos Zartaloudis

A philosophical **archaeology**, a term employed by Immanuel **Kant** to refer to his science, is a paradoxical experience. Such a philosophical inquiry, or archaeology, into the origin of things poses itself as historical, yet cannot but interrogate its own origin as such. Yet, since for Kant philosophy is the gradual unfolding of human reason, which is neither simply empirical nor a matter of mere intellectual concepts, philosophising takes place in a paradoxical time that can never be identified with a chronological date in the conventional historical sense. Thus, Agamben writes:

> We could provisionally call "archaeology" the practice which, within any historical investigation, has to do, not with the origin, but with the question of the point from which the phenomenon takes its source, and must therefore confront itself anew with the sources and with the tradition. (*ST*, 89)

Any philosophico-historical inquiry must confront this constitutive dishomogeneity and the way in which it has been reconstructed as a particular type of a negative relation to a pseudo-transmission of the supposedly original state of tradition.

   Such a form of division between an original state and a historical state is problematic for it is based on an ideology of **potentiality**, where potentiality is exhausted in the transition from an original state to a conventional or established state. There is, then, for Agamben, an important precaution that should be observed every time one presupposes that a pre-historic original stage prevailed in the times preceding the moment of a historical split. Consider, for instance, the relationship between religion and law, and in particular the division between the presumed earlier religious sphere (a so-called pre-law state, where law and religion were indistinguishable) and the later profane juridical sphere. Agamben writes, in a key passage:

> It is essential, in situations of the sort, to have the shrewdness not to simply project onto the presupposed "primordial indistinction" the characters, which,

later on, are going to define the religious and profane spheres. [. . .] The pre-law (if one were to admit that a hypothesis of the sort makes sense) cannot be only a more archaic law; in the same way, that which lies before religion as we know it historically is not only a more primitive religion; it would be a good idea here to avoid the terms "religion" and "law", trying instead to imagine an x, for the definition of which we need to take all possible precautions, indeed practicing some sort of archaeological *epoché* which suspends – at least provisionally – the attribution to it of the predicates which we use habitually whenever we refer to religion and to law. In this sense, as well, prehistory is not homogeneous with history, and the point at which it emerges is not identical to what comes into being through it. (*ST*, 90)

Before such a presumption of a fringe of ultra-history, archaeology does not try to grasp some chronological site, or a meta-historical structure, or transcendental or unconscious categories. What is at stake is "an *archē*: but it is an *archē* which, as with Nietzsche and Foucault, is not diachronically displaced into the past, but rather ensures the coherence and the synchronic comprehensibility of the system" (*ST*, 92).

This paradoxical conditioning means that a philosophico-archaeological investigation must in fact discover its object rather than presuppose it. In this sense, one can speak of needing to discover the paradoxical memory of the past *in* the present: neither "preceding chronologically the present" nor "simply exterior to it" (*ST*, 95). A philosophico-archaeological investigation seeks the condition of possibility in the historical *a priori* that is, however, contemporaneous and immanent *in* the present. The archaeologist retreats back towards the present. This practice is contrary to the conventional theoretical approaches that understand such a retreat as a vision of repression or of progress on the grounds of victorious or mawkish, subaltern paradigms of history. Regression is not towards prehistory or the unconscious. What opens up is a point of emergence, the present as a futural-past, as that which "we had neither been able to live nor think" (*ST*, 99) – that is, an aspect of the present that can be called the non-lived (or unlived). Agamben writes:

The point of emergence, the *archē* of archaeology, is that which will happen, that which will become accessible and present only when the archaeological inquest will have fulfilled its operation. It has therefore the form of a futural past, that is, of a future perfect. (*ST*, 106)

Archaeology is philosophically understood in this sense as meaning that the *archē* towards which archaeology regresses is not a chronological *topos*, but a force that immanently operates in history and that continuously pulls us towards its explosive radiation. The *archē* in question remains always a field of bipolar tension between point of emergence and becoming, between arch-past and present. As something that is supposed to have already happened and which yet, in a genuine paradox, cannot yet be hypostatised in any chronologically identifiable event, "it is solely capable to guarantee the intelligibility of historical phenomena, of 'saving' them archaeologically within a future perfect, yet grasping not its (in any case unverifiable) origin, but rather its history, at once finite and untotalizable" (*ST*, 110).

P

PARADIGM/EXAMPLE

Steven DeCaroli

The paradigm first makes its thematic appearance in Agamben's sixth book, *The Coming Community*, thus coinciding with his first explicit political reflections. *The Coming Community* was published in 1990, immediately following both the break-up of the Soviet Union and the Tiananmen Square crackdown in Beijing, and was conceived not only as a response to these events, but also as a contribution to a debate concerning the possibility of envisioning a community which has no criteria for belonging. In the wake of the collapse of state socialism, writers such as **Blanchot**, **Bataille** and **Nancy** began to ask whether a community could form in the absence of specific membership criteria (be they religious, ideological, racial and so on) so as to avoid turning these criteria, which govern inclusion, into powerful means of exclusion, particularly when communities begin to speak in the language of purity. Agamben's foray into this debate began by reconceiving the relationship between the individual and the community as that between the whole and the part, or the general and the particular, and it is in this context that the paradigm (or the example, which is used synonymously) is introduced.

The third chapter of *The Coming Community*, entitled simply "Example", opens with a discussion of the antinomy of the general and the particular which, Agamben tells us, "has its origins in language" (*CC*, 9). The familiar antinomy to which Agamben refers arises when, in the act of calling something a tree, or a plough or bitter, the concrete singularity of that thing is transformed into a member of a general class defined by a property held in common. "The word 'tree'", Agamben explains, "designates all trees indifferently, insofar as it posits the proper universal significance in place of singular, ineffable trees" (*CC*, 9), and in so doing transforms singularities into members of a class – a procedure that closely resembles the formation of political communities in so far as membership is granted according to characteristics held in common. Thus, language, like politics, is perpetually caught between the universality of its generalised expressions and the singularity of those denominated entities which, while they are the ground of this generalisation, remain inadequately represented by it. In considering the problem, Agamben argues that there exists a concept that escapes this antinomy: namely, the example: "Neither particular nor universal, the example is a singular object that presents itself as such" (*CC*, 10). In other words, the example is simultaneously a simple member of a set as well as the defining criteria of that set. By providing its own criteria of inclusion, the example remains ambiguously positioned alongside the class of which it is most representative, neither fully included in a class nor fully excluded from it. The importance of this formulation is made evident in Agamben's future writings, for not only do the ambiguities of inclusion and exclusion appear prominently in his next book, *Homo Sacer*, where he takes up the paradoxical nature of sovereignty, but the concept of the paradigm assumes an increasingly important role in Agamben's more recent efforts to clarify his theoretical methodology.

In *Homo Sacer*, Agamben draws on the work begun in *The Coming Community* to extend his analysis of politics by arguing that the logical structure of sovereignty parallels that of the example. Following Carl **Schmitt** in understanding **sovereignty** as a **state of exception** – whereby the sovereign, who, though included within the political order, nevertheless occupies a foundational position outside of that system from which s/he can declare the **law**'s suspension – Agamben shows that, just as the example is at once excluded from that of which it is nevertheless a part, so too the sovereign remains included within the very juridical order in relation to which s/he stands as an exception. "From this perspective," Agamben concludes, "the exception is situated in a symmetrical position with respect to the example, with which it forms a system" (*HS*, 21). Throughout *Homo Sacer*, Agamben introduces a broad array of exemplary figures whose ambiguous conditions illuminate not sovereignty as such, but the biopolitical logic that the sovereign exception both reveals and disguises. The most controversial of these examples has been the concentration **camp**, which he speaks of as "the fundamental biopolitical paradigm of the West" (*HS*, 181). Regarding the camp not as an historical anomaly, but as the current condition of political life, Agamben argues that the extra-legal circumstances that the camp makes possible have been gradually extended to entire civil populations.

Not unexpectedly, this claim has brought with it a number of criticisms. What exactly does it mean for a camp to be the paradigm of modern political life? In what capacity is the concept of a paradigm being used here? In response to such questions, as well as to some general misunderstandings regarding his historical method, many of Agamben's more recent interviews and writings have sought to clarify how paradigms fit within his methodological approach. The most significant result of these reflections has been the publication of *The Signature of All Things*, a book devoted to methodology that opens with a lengthy first section entitled, "What is a Paradigm?" What is immediately made clear is that the paradigm must be understood in terms of Agamben's relation to Michel **Foucault**. Agamben's work has, from the very earliest writings, employed concrete historical figures, but the use of these historical examples must not be confused as being part of a properly historical project. Similar to Foucault's reflections on the panopticon, each of the figures that populates Agamben's research – *homo sacer*, the *Muselmann*, the concentration camp – has a double nature. They are not merely discrete historical phenomena, but are primarily understood in their capacity as examples: which is to say, in their capacity to "establish a broader problematic context that they both constitute and make intelligible" (*ST*, 17). In an effort to make clear how examples function, Agamben uses the first section of *The Signature of All Things* to trace, in effect, a brief genealogy of the concept. In it we are told that **Aristotle**, in the *Prior Analytics*, was the first to describe the special logical movement of the example, a logical structure which distinguishes it entirely from both induction and deduction. The example, Aristotle writes, is neither the ascending movement of parts to the whole, nor the descending movement of the whole to its parts, but rather a relation of part to part. Thus, for Agamben, the example presents us with a "peculiar form of knowledge" which ultimately calls into question the particular–general relation as a model of logical inference. In so far as the example proceeds from particular to particular, its epistemic character remains unconnected to general categories of any kind and so, Agamben suggests, must be understood as analogical – inasmuch as analogy is a cognitive process in which particulars are associated without reference to generalities. The example, Agamben explains, is simply the deactivation of a particular from its normal usage, such that it both constitutes and makes intelligible "the rule of that use, which cannot be shown in any other way (*ST*, 18)", thereby never separating its exemplarity from its concrete particularity.

In presupposing the impossibility of general rules in certain cases, the paradigm shares an important affinity with Immanuel **Kant**'s writing on aesthetic judgment. Recognising this connection, Agamben writes, "nowhere, perhaps is the paradoxical relation between the paradigm and generality as forcefully formulated as in *The Critique of Judgment*" (*ST*, 20). For Kant, the necessity entailed by aesthetic judgments is achieved without the assistance of general rules; thus, when one claims that something is beautiful, it is merely "the exhibition alone of the paradigmatic case that constitutes a rule, which as such cannot be applied or stated" (*ST*, 21). Consequently, when Agamben uses examples in his writings, they are more than merely historical facts referenced to clarify a historical lineage, or, as Agamben writes, they "are not hypotheses through which I intend to explain modernity by tracing it back to something like cause or historical origin" (*ST*, 31). Rather, their use is designed to "make intelligible a series of phenomena whose kinship had eluded or could elude the historian's gaze" (*ST*, 31). And what is made intelligible is precisely that analogical, perhaps discursive, form of knowing through which the present is conceived, that can neither be explained with reference to an origin, nor conveyed by way of rules. Paradigms, then, are less about understanding the circumstances of the past than they are about bringing into the open the intelligibility of the present.

PARODY

Alex Murray

Agamben devotes an essay in *Profanations* to a discussion of parody, providing a brief yet wide-ranging exploration of the term that challenges the traditional definition of it as a comic or grotesque representation of something serious. Instead, he places it more in the realm of a **profane** literary space that reveals that **language** cannot have access to the thing itself.

The essay begins with a discussion of the Italian poet and novelist, Elsa Morante (1912–85), who was a friend of Agamben's, focusing on a novel in which a character is accused of being a Parody. Agamben then proceeds to outline parody through ancient, medieval and modern definitions. In all of these he finds a literary form that is a separation from a dominant form. Following an Ancient definition, Agamben will suggest that the "parodic loosening of the traditional link between music and *logos*" creates the space in which prose can emerge (*Pr*, 40). In this sense literary prose is "marked" by this "separation from song". The mark of that which it is not is crucial for Agamben. It is a form of literary language that, in carrying a residue of that which it parodies, "renders indiscernible" divisions and distinctions (*Pr*, 43). This notion of rendering division **inoperative** is crucial in all of

Agamben's work, and in his work on literature we may want to recall the way in which **poetry** struggles to differentiate itself from **prose**, with the end of the poem the point at which the poem "reveals the goal of its proud strategy: to let language finally communicate itself without remaining unsaid in what is said" (*EP*, 115). So parody, as a literary form, is about the presentation of the unsaid, a revelation that language always contains division and disorder: "if ontology is the more or less felicitous relationship between language and world, then parody, as paraontology, expresses language's inability to reach the thing and the impossibility of the thing finding its own name (*Pr*, 50). Parody is therefore "marked by mourning", presenting the negative foundation of all language.

PASSIVITY

Alex Murray

The term passivity is not a major concept in Agamben's work and appears exclusively in relation to the discussion of Aristotle and **potentiality/ impotentiality** that appears in the essay "On Potentiality". It is important that passivity is not given its usual pejorative meaning here, the focus instead being on the way in which "every human power is *adynamia*, impotentiality". Impotentiality is the power not to do, the welcoming of the "non-Being" by potentiality. This welcoming is characterised by Agamben as a "fundamental passivity" (*Po*, 182). It is fundamental in the sense that it is ontological for Agamben, rather than a condition of weakness that is forced on to the **subject**. So **Bartleby**, as the great figure of Agambenian potentiality, is not passive; nor is he active. Instead he exploits the fundamental passivity of being by suspending, rendering **inoperative** the movement from potentiality to actuality. So if Agamben's politics are "passive", it is only in the sense that they use an understanding of fundamental passivity that exists to challenge and disrupt, rather than advocating some sort of weak a–politicism.

PAUL

Connal Parsley

Agamben is one of a number of contemporary scholars to undertake primarily non-theological analyses of St Paul, the so-called Apostle to the Gentiles (c.5 BC–c.67 AD). Agamben's commentary on Paul's "Letter to the Romans", published under the title *The Time That Remains*, is influenced by and dedicated to one of the most significant of these – Jacob **Taubes** – but it is nevertheless unique in certain key respects, which display the importance of Paul to Agamben's account of **politics**, and his related conceptions of the messianic (see **messianism**) and historical (see **history**) time.

Agamben's reading attempts to "restore Paul's letters to the status of the fundamental messianic text for the Western tradition" (*TR*, 1). It frequently does so by referencing and developing the German politico-philosophical approach to Paul, via Martin Luther's translation. This constitutes a major thematic in Agamben's reading: building on Walter **Benjamin**'s thesis that Karl **Marx**'s "classless society" is "a secularization of the idea of messianic time" (*TR*, 30), Agamben highlights the importance of a number of Pauline concepts to key German thinkers such as Max Weber, Marx, Martin **Heidegger**, G. W. F. **Hegel**, and Benjamin himself. Agamben is thus able to find in Paul conceptual resources, central to the Western philosophical tradition, for his transformative critical project.

Amongst these – which include specific conceptions of terms like vocation, class, Hegel's *Aufhebung*, Heidegger's dialectic of the proper and improper, and the distinction between time as lived and as represented – none is more important than the *leimma* ("remnant"), which Agamben names as the "only real political subject" (*TR*, 57). From Agamben's interpretation of Paul's status as *aphōrismenos* ("separated"), there emerges a complex critique of **law**, faith, political identity, representation and universalism; this distinguishes Agamben from those who (like Taubes) suggest that Paul can be understood as founding a new people or religion, as well as from those who (like Alain Badiou) argue that Paul can be used to found a universalism, howsoever conceived. For Agamben, Paul, himself situated ambiguously between Judaic and Hellenic identity and culture, founds only a fracture which complicates and renders **inoperative** Jewish law and the Pharisaic ideal of clearly separating law from non-law, Jew from non-Jew (*TR*, 46). Thus, Paul offers Agamben an important confirmation and elaboration of his own theoretical commitments, such as his critique of identitarian politics, and his response to the inherently divisive and exclusive operation of *nomos*.

Paul's special status in Agamben's work is reaffirmed by Agamben's insistence on a "secret appointment" between Paul and Walter Benjamin. Not only does Agamben treat the messianic as "a paradigm of historical time" (*TR*, 3), against what Benjamin called the "empty homogenous time" of history; he also attempts to move beyond a merely conceptual connection – already intuited by Taubes – to establish a *textual* link between

Paul's letters and Benjamin's *Theses on the Philosophy of History*, using the same philological attentiveness that marks his reading of Paul. Proposing that both writers articulate a messianic "time of the now" (Paul's *ho nyn kairos* and Benjamin's *Jetztzeit*), and that both emphasise the messianic abridgment of historical time, gathering it within figures (Paul) and images (Benjamin) by a citational rather than chronological logic, Agamben himself "recapitulates" history and demonstrates the secret "appointment" between chronologically separate historical moments. By placing the texts of these two writers in a chronologically indeterminate "constellation whose time of legibility has finally come" (*TR*, 145), Agamben suggests that Paul and Benjamin are **contemporaries** (*WA*, 52–3).

PETERSON, ERIK

Nicholas Heron

Today, the name Erik Peterson is principally known – if, indeed, it is known at all – for a single footnote appended to the "legendary conclusion" (Schmitt 2008) of his 1935 treatise, *Der Monotheismus als politisches Problem*. In it the central contention, which, as critics have observed, indubitably guided his entire presentation, receives its clearest and firmest expression: "The term 'political theology' was, as far as I know," he writes, "coined by Carl **Schmitt** . . . Here we have tried to demonstrate, by a concrete example, the theological impossibility of any 'political theology'" (quoted in Schmitt 2008: 132).

Peterson's "concrete example" is, of course, the orthodox dogma of the Trinity. According to Peterson, the concept of political theology itself, the earliest strata of whose history he patiently reconstructs in the treatise (in particular, through reference to Philo of Alexandria's notion of "divine monarchy"), is theologically incompatible with the Christian belief in a triune God. In Christianity, as the adversaries of the Arian heresy well understood, the theological idea can no longer be realised politically, and for the apparently simple reason that the triune God has no analogue in the world of created nature. According to Peterson, the Trinitarian creed in effect liberated the Christian faith from the claims of the *Imperium Romanum* and, in this way, marked the definitive eclipse, as the title of his treatise suggests, of monotheism as a *political* problem. For him, accordingly, as one critic has aptly summarised it, "no one could legitimately claim that the modern cult of the state found its roots in Christian theology" (Stroumsa 2005: 137).

It is Peterson's argument, together with Schmitt's belated response from 1970, that (much like the "esoteric dossier" between **Benjamin** and Schmitt on the **state of exception** for its prequel) forms the propulsive nucleus for what is Agamben's most extended work to date: *Il Regno e la gloria* (2007). His singular intervention, with respect to this debate, however, hinges not so much on what the two authors say, as on what they do not say. Indeed, if Peterson grounds the authority of his argument in the testimony of the Cappadocian Father Gregory of Nazianzus, in the opposition he traces between the monarchy of a single person alone and that of the triune God, he none the less strikingly neglects to mention – in what, for Agamben, amounts to "something like a conscious repression" (Agamben 2007: 26) – that the very oration from which the citation is drawn is itself grounded in the distinction, absolutely central to the Trinitarian doctrine, between God's nature and his economy. It is the sense of precisely this distinction, and its protracted afterlife in the history of the West, that Agamben seeks to develop in his book. His own contention, positioned somewhere between that of Peterson and that of Schmitt, is that political theology indeed continues, even after the consolidation of the Trinity; but that it assumes a decidedly different, indeed mysterious form. It is, paradoxically, in the unfolding of the divine *oikonomia* that the locus of the theologico-political is to be sought: which is to say, in that discourse – not strictly political but "economic" – that undertook to elaborate the theological paradigm for the divine government of the world.

PLATO

Thanos Zartaloudis

In Agamben's writings and thought, Plato is a key reference. Agamben's readings of the Platonic writings are as unconventional as they are decisive, and they genuinely renew the interest in Plato in a meaningful manner. Plato's writings figure in a variety of Agamben's works, the most crucial of which are *The Man Without Content*, which is an implicit rethinking of Plato's writings on the *polis* and art, and *The Coming Community*, where the key Platonic notion of "erotic anamnesis" is reread with regard to the taking place of linguistic being and language as such. For instance, Agamben writes: "The movement Plato describes as erotic anamnesis is the movement that transports the object not toward another thing or another place, but toward its own taking-place" (*CC*, 2; see also *S*, part 1). Plato's dialectics are considered in the essay "What is a Paradigm?" in *The Signature of All Things* (2009), while in *The Idea of Prose* (1995) Plato figures explicitly and implicitly throughout in the consideration of the idea of prose as well as in several other crucial meditations in this work. In *The End of the Poem: Studies in Poetics* Agamben considers the Platonic reception of poetry and art. The most detailed and explicit reference to Plato appears in the collected essays on Plato and language in the first part of *Potentialities* (1999). It is in these collected essays that Agamben explores the conception of the Platonic Idea in relation to the understanding of language's taking place and the thinking of thought itself (see also **Aristotle**). Plato's thinking on language is approached from the contour of the wider problem of the status of linguistic expression and existence in contemporary capitalism and nihilism. Agamben writes in the "The Idea of Language" that "contemporary thought has approached a limit beyond which a new epochal-religious unveiling of the word no longer seems possible" (*Po*, 45). Plato's approach to language with regard to its taking place and the conception of transcendence as *epekeina* is, then, contrary to conventional readings, a rethinking of language in its irreparable profanity: that is, a rethinking of the transcendence of linguistic being within language and through the particular human experience of linguistic existence as such. The thing itself is the thing *of* language and it emerges no longer as an obscure object for knowledge, but as that through which beings are known in language, the very sayability or knowability (communicability) of linguistic being, the pure dwelling of beings in language (see also **Heidegger**). It is in this manner that Plato can say that philosophy is "the supreme music" (*Po*, 46).

PLAY

Alex Murray

Agamben's explorations of play are most clearly found in the essay "In Playland" from *Infancy and History* and in *Profanations*. Play is best understood as a form of **profanation** and temporal disruption that deactivates both the logic of capital and the temporality that governs it.

In the earlier essay, Agamben contrasts ritual with play, arguing that ritual can be aligned with synchronic time while play works on a model of diachronic time. Yet both contain residues of the other and there has never been a society governed by pure play or pure ritual. The language here is clearly that of Claude **Lévi-Strauss** and Agamben would never substantially return to the language of structural anthropology after *Infancy and History*. But here it allows him to take the very simple act of children playing with toys and to extrapolate from it an entire approach to constructing time. Play and ritual can be understood by their relation to the calendar. Ritual works to support calendar time, providing those festivals and events that structure it. Play "on the other hand, though we do not know how and why, changes and *destroys* it" (*IH*, 77). The disruptive nature of play is linked to the commodity. Here Agamben suggests that the toy, while produced as part of the practical–economic, can, through play, work to disrupt that sphere, putting it to a new **use**.

The disruptive nature of play is given further articulation in *Profanations* in which Agamben suggests that play is the inappropriate use of the **sacred**. It is here that he also articulates in more detail the relationship between capitalism and the sacred. Both the sacred and commodification are attempts to separate objects from one sphere and place them in another, whether it is the sacrifice of an animal which renders its flesh as the property of the sacred sphere, or the attribution to an object (a handbag) of an exchange value that separates it from any use, separating things from themselves. This division, however, has to cover over "the residue of profanity in every consecrated thing and a remnant of sacredness in every profaned object" (*Pr*, 78). The necessity to hide the remnants that exist in the process of division is essential to all forms of authority and control.

Returning to **Benveniste**'s essay on play that he explored in *Infancy and History*, Agamben again outlines play's ability to challenge the logic of both the ritual and the sacred. If the power of the sacred is linked to the way it combines myth and rite, then "play breaks up this unity: as ludus, or physical play, it drops the myth and preserves the rite; as iocus, or wordplay it effaces the rite and allows the myth to survive" (*Pr*, 75–6). In this way play **deactivates** the power inherent in the sacred residues that characterise **law**, economics or politics. In *State of Exception* Agamben highlights play again as central to the deactivation of power: "one day humanity will play with law just as children play with disused objects, not in order to restore them to their canonical use but to free them from it for good" (*SE*, 64). Play therefore becomes both the pathway to, and practice of, a messianic (see **messianism**) or redeemed (see **redemption**) time.

POESIS – see 'Poiesis'

POETRY/POETIC

William Watkin

One-third of Agamben's published output is concerned with literature and the arts, with poetry taking the foremost place in his considerations.

Agamben is a post-Heideggerian (see **Heidegger**) thinker in terms of considering poetry (*Dichtung*) as the only possible access to truth in an age of metaphysical destitution. Thus he accepts the central qualities of poetry as being singular, presentative and having a special relationship with **language** as such. For Agamben, like Heidegger, poetry most powerfully presents language as an immediate medium for the support of thought. The emphasis in poetry on language as such, or on the **semiotic** over and above the **semantic**, allows us to see or attain open access to language as pure mediality. That said, early work in *Stanzas* and *Language and Death* warns us from looking to the poetic as a simple solution to the dependence on negation and ineffability in relation to language that is typical of Hegelian (see **Hegel**) and Heideggerian thinking on the foreclosure of metaphysics.

Where Agamben differs from Heidegger and certain other post-Heideggerian thinkers on poetry is that he moves from a generalised conception of semiotic singularity to specific technical readings of the effects of prosody. In *Stanzas*, for example, the stanza becomes a means of opening up the line of scission in metaphysics between signified and signifier, converting imposed division into a two-dimensional mediality which he later considers in relation to **potentiality**. In *Idea of Prose*, **caesura** defines the means by which philosophical and poetic thinking can only exist in a relation of tensile suspension, the semiotic overrunning sense in **enjambment** but then being arrested by a sudden *ekstasis* of thought in caesura. In *The End of the Poem* the prevalence of enjambment in poetics becomes a means of defining the tensile relation between two modes of thinking, philosophical and material. The development of semiotic effects such as onomatopoeia becomes an essential consideration of the **voice**, further developed in terms of politics and ontology in texts such as *Remnants of Auschwitz* and *The Open*.

Finally, poetic structure as such comes to present the essential category of time within Agamben's metaphysics. The reading of projective recursion in the poem "L'Infinito" in *Language and Death* is an early prototype of messianic (see **messianism**) kairatic involuted time in the later *The Time that Remains* with its concentration on the rhetorical devices of *typos* and *antitypos*. Exemplary of what he terms "cruciform retrogradation" (*TR* 82), the means by which a poem prefigures semiotically what is to come, and manner in which one must reconsider and reread what has already occurred to get a full sense of poetic finitude, come to be the presentative act of the temporal category *per se*, clearly influenced by Husserlian conceptions of protention and retention.

For Agamben, poetry presents access to the possibility of a thought of indifference to come due to its emphasis on the semiotic over the semantic, special relationship with language as such as pure medium, and ability to present access to messianic projective, recurrent, involuted temporality.

POIESIS/POESIS

Robert Sinnerbrink

The Greek term *poiesis* means "making" or "bringing forth"; it is the root of our term "**poetry**" via the *poesie* and *poesy* of romanticism. **Heidegger** interprets *poiesis* as a bringing-forth into truth (*aletheia*) that is also a making; *poiesis* is linked, rather than opposed, to *techne*, a making or know-how in art, craft and what we today call technology. Agamben draws upon but also transforms Heidegger's reflections. Human *poiesis* or poetry is understood as *pro-ductive activity*: "*Poesis*, poetry is the very name of man's doing, of that productive action of which artistic doing is only a privileged example" (*MC*, 59). In the *Symposium*, **Plato** defines poiesis as the "pro-duction" of something, bringing it out of concealment and non-being into the light of truth (*MC*, 59). For Plato, every art is a kind of poetry, pro-duction into presence; nature too has the character of *poiesis* in so far as it brings itself into presence. For **Aristotle**, *techne*, the skill of the craftsman and work of the artist, is also a species of *poiesis* as the pro-duction into presence. This *poiesis*, unlike that of nature, always involves the imposing of a shape or form (*MC*, 60). In modernity, this Greek sense of *poiesis* is transformed into *work* as willed practical activity (***praxis***) (*MC*, 59). The Greek unitary status of things not coming from nature is broken thanks to technology, the industrial revolution and an alienating division of labour (*MC*, 60). Human poetic activity is now understood as having a dual status, divided into aesthetic works of art and (mass-)produced things.

Poiesis, as the origin of poetry, is also essentially linked to **language**; poetry expresses the "taking place of language", the *experimentum linguae* of language communicating itself. The metrical character of poetry, its contrasting dimensions of sound and sense (expressed through **enjamb-ment**), articulates both semiotic and semantic spheres (*EP*, 109). Poetry, however, comes to an end; it is defined by its collapse into silence, an "endless falling away": "The poem thus reveals the end of its proud strategy: to let language finally communicate itself, without remaining unsaid in what is said" (*EP*, 115). Poetry offers an experience of language in which the negativistic conception of its ineffability is potentially overcome.

POLITICS

Jessica Whyte

Politics, Agamben argues in *Homo Sacer*, is experiencing a "lasting eclipse" (*HS*, 4) in which both theory and praxis are "imprisoned and immobile" (*HS*, 11). And yet, in this same work, he gestures towards a "completely new politics", which, he suggests, has never been more possible than it is today (*HS*, 11). To grasp the point of intersection between Agamben's critique of what he sees as the nihilistic and empty spectacle of contemporary politics, and the new politics to which his works gestures, it is necessary to grasp that his understanding of political life today stems directly from his analysis of what he sees as an "aporia that lies at the foundation of Western politics" (*HS*, 11). From **Aristotle** onwards, he argues, the political realm has been predicated on a *caesura* that divides the human into a political and natural **life**, and isolates what he terms "**bare life**" (*HS*, 4). In this division of man's private life in the home *(oikos)* and his public life in the state, he locates the fundamental problem not only of ancient politics, but also of contemporary politics. A process that begins with the attempt to banish natural life from the *polis* culminates in the "lasting eclipse" of politics today, and in "the assumption of the burden – and the 'total management' – of biological life, that is, of the very animality of man" (*O*, 77). Agamben thus draws a connection between the Aristotelian conception of politics and contemporary instances of the politicisation of life. Turning to Michel **Foucault**'s account of **biopolitics** – that is, the modern process whereby the state began to concern itself directly with the biological life of its population – he argues that Western politics has *always* been biopolitics, as the political realm was originally predicated on a *caesura* that divides the human into a political and a natural life, and isolates what he refers to as bare life.

This isolation of bare life, Agamben argues, finds its structural analogue in the metaphysical definition of the **human** as a *zoon logon echon* – a living being with *logos*. Reflecting on Aristotle's argument that the **animal voice** expresses only pleasure or pain, while human speech expresses the **just** and the unjust, he identifies a caesura in the human in the passage from the animal *phone* to human *language*. "The living being has *logos*", he writes in *Homo Sacer*, "by taking away and conserving its own voice in it, even as it dwells in the *polis* by letting its own bare life be excluded, as an exception, in it" (*HS*, 8). Agamben's account of metaphysics therefore consists in problematising precisely this notion of human life, or *logos*, as an "additional capacity". In isolating bare life, Agamben suggests, Aristotle is aiming to discover what is proper to man *qua* man, and whether man *qua* man has a *work*. From the isolation of a specific "work of man", which Aristotle sees as a particular form of life (life according to *logos*), he derives the end of politics. Politics thus enables man to *actualise* the rational capacity Aristotle had isolated as definitive of human life, and to live according to what is proper to him; the *polis* is the place in which the metaphysical determination of man as a living being with *logos* is actualised. "The political, as the work of man as man," Agamben argues, "is drawn out of the living being through the exclusion – as unpolitical – of a part of its vital activity" (Agamben 2007: 6). Both politics and metaphysics, he suggests, are founded on the exclusion of that life that men share with other living beings, and on a separation between life and politics that is the essential presupposition of sovereignty. "Political power as we know it", he writes, "always founds itself – in the last instance – on the separation of a sphere of naked life from the context of the forms of life" (*ME*, 4).

In *Homo Sacer*, Agamben turns his attention to modern politics, and depicts his project as an attempt to bring together Foucault's insights with Hannah **Arendt**'s account of the totalitarian states, in order to examine what he terms "the hidden point of intersection between the juridico-institutional and the biopolitical models of power" (*HS*, 6). This leads him to an examination of the **state of exception** and of that bare life that he sees dwelling in this zone of indistinction between law and fact. Only if we are able to decipher the state of exception, he argues, will it be possible to develop a clear understanding of the differences between the political and the juridical, and between life and law. Only then, he suggests, "will it be possible to answer the question that never ceases to reverberate in the history of Western politics: what does it mean to act politically?" (*SE*, 2). Agamben's contention is that, today, politics has been eclipsed because it has been aligned with the problem of sovereignty, and thus "contaminated with law" (*SE*, 2). Only an engagement with the state of exception, he suggests, will enable us to think a non-juridical politics capable of reversing this eclipse.

To this point, this appears to be a despairing account of political possibility, and, indeed, Agamben has often been critiqued for a supposed pessimism. None the less, it precisely from the darkest depths of modern biopolitics, from amongst the lives that border on death, that he believes a new politics of creative potentiality may emerge. This new politics, he suggests, will not restore the division between natural and political life that was central to classical politics, but finds its condition of possibility precisely in the contemporary cohesion of life and politics. While this politics remains gestural, its problem, Agamben writes, is whether it is "possible to have a *political* community that is ordered exclusively for the full enjoyment of worldly life" (*ME*, 114). Agamben's political life would not be a vulnerable, fearful life, like that which provides the support for Hobbesian social contract theory, but what he terms a **happy life** – an "absolutely profane 'sufficient life' that has reached the perfection of its own power and of its own communicability – a life over which sovereignty and right no longer have any hold" (*ME*, 114–15).

In Agamben's work, "genuinely political paradigms are sought in experiences and phenomena that are not usually considered political or that are considered only marginally so" (*ME*, ix). His attempt to articulate the bases of a new politics thus begins from phenomena such as **profanation**, which he frames as a praxis capable of returning things to free **use**, his related account of the desacralising potential of **play**, and his attempt to found a community without identity on a particular experience of **love**. What links these, and what enables us to shed light on the often obscure territory of Agamben's new politics, is his suggestion that "politics is the sphere of pure means" (*ME*, 60). Such a politics would offer an escape both from utilitarian subject–object relations and political instrumentalism, and from substantivist conceptions of politics which find their model in a work (state-building, for instance), and which presuppose stable identities and exclusions. If humans had something we had to be, whether an identity or a vocation, he suggests, "there could not be any community but only coincidences and factual partitions" (*ME*, 10). A politics of means without ends would thus be a politics of singularities without identity, of beings with no "nature", no task and no biological destiny: a politics, in short, of potential beings. Only such a politics, Agamben contends, can overcome the bloody forms of inclusion and exclusion presupposed by any community founded on identity.

PORNOGRAPHY

Jessica Whyte

Those who turn to Agamben's short piece, "The Idea of Communism" (*IP*, 73–5), aiming to discern his views on an idea that is once more at the centre of philosophical discussion may be surprised to find that the piece is entirely devoted to the question of pornography. And yet, it is precisely in pornography, in his view, that "the utopia of a classless society displays itself", albeit "through gross caricatures of those traits that distinguish classes and their transfiguration in the sexual act" (*IP*, 73). The "truth content" of pornography, he writes there, is its display of a claim to happiness that can be grasped in every moment. This happiness, he suggests, in an insight that will inform his later treatment of pornography in

Profanations, is never a natural condition, and pornography is not simply a lack of clothes. "To demonstrate that the potential for happiness is present in every least moment of daily life wherever there is human society: This", he writes, "is the eternal political justification of pornography" (*IP*, 74). Pornography, on this reading, shows us our unfulfilled dreams, alerting us to the possibility of **happiness** and messianic (see **messianism**) fulfilment that lies in every moment.

When Agamben returns to the problem of pornography, in *The Coming Community* and again in *Profanations*, his treatment is more ambivalent as he situates it in the context of the commodification of the body in the society of the spectacle. Pornography, which now appears as the apotheosis of the spectacle, simultaneously frees sexuality from its naturalisation or sacralisation, he suggests, *and* separates it into a realm in which it can only be consumed but not used. If pornography appears as a "midwife" of the future society, this is because, in denaturalising and desacralising sexuality, it opens the space for "a new collective use of sexuality" (*Pr*, 91). Not merely a celebration of pornography, however, Agamben's work positions it as an **apparatus** that attempts to capture pure means, the human capacity for erotic behaviour without end, such that the "solitary and desperate consumption of the pornographic image replaces the promise of a new use" (*Pr*, 91). Faced with this capture, Agamben suggests that our task is to find a new **use** for this denaturalised and desacralised eroticism. This strategy owes something to the Situationists, as evidenced, for instance, in Renée Viénet's proposal for "Experimentation in the *détournement* of romantic photo-comics" and pornographic photographs (Viénet 1967: 213), which aimed to "bring to the surface the subversive bubbles that are spontaneously, but more or less consciously, formed and then dissolved in the imaginations of those who look at these photos" (Viénet 1967: 213). Put to a new use, it is advertising and pornography that "escort the commodity to the grave like hired mourners" (*CC*, 50).

POTENTIALITY/IMPOTENTIALITY

Kevin Attell

Agamben's theory of potentiality is most concisely presented in three texts: "On Potentiality", "Bartleby, or On Contingency" and the "Potentiality and Law" chapter of *Homo Sacer*. This dictionary has a single entry for potentiality and impotentiality because the two are so intimately connected in Agamben's thought that they can be said to be the same thing. Indeed,

the first point that must be made about potentiality is its constitutive
co-belonging – and ultimate identity – with impotentiality.

The essential intimacy of potentiality and impotentiality is the key
point in Aristotle's polemic with the Megarians in Book Theta of the
Metaphysics, on which Agamben draws heavily for his own theory. Against
the Megarian position that all potentialities are always actualised and
that the only potentialities that exist are those that pass into act, Aristotle
asserts that in order for there to be potentiality at all, and therefore for any
sort of change to happen, the potentiality to be or do something must also
equally entail the potentiality not to be or do that thing. "Every potentiality (*dunamis*)", he writes, "is impotentiality (*adunamia*) of the same
and with respect to the same" (*Met* 1046a 32). If this were not the case,
then all potentialities would immediately realise themselves as particular
actualities and all potentialities-not-to would always have been absolute
impossibilities, or more simply, there would *be* only a static and unchang-
ing actuality. Thus, potentiality as such must pose some resistance to or
independence from actualisation, and this resistance or independence is
the potentiality *not* to pass over into the act. This potentiality-not-to is
what Aristotle calls *adunamia* or impotentiality. To avoid an easy misunderstanding, it must always be kept in mind that in Agamben's usage
"impotentiality" (*impotenza*) does not mean inability, impossibility or
mere passivity, but rather the potentiality not to (be or do), which is the
constitutive counterpart to every potentiality to be or do. For Agamben,
the necessity of an impotentiality in every potentiality is the "cardinal
point on which [Aristotle's] entire theory of *dunamis* turns" (*HS*, 45), and
it is on this basis that he will develop his own doctrine of potentiality. He
writes: "Of the two modes in which, according to Aristotle, every potentiality is articulated, the decisive one is that which the philosopher calls
'the potentiality not to be' (*dunamis mê einai*) or also impotentiality (*adunamia*)" (*CC*, 35; trans. modified). The reason *adunamia* is the decisive mode
of *dunamis* is not that it is more powerful or pervasive, but that it is what
distinguishes potentiality from actuality and enables potentiality to "have
its own consistency and not always disappear immediately into actuality"
(*HS*, 45). Thus, "all potentiality is impotentiality" (*Po*, 181).

This leads us then to ask how precisely such a potentiality–
impotentiality realises itself in act, and what the relation between actuality
and potentiality is. Indeed one of the most important, though difficult,
aspects of Agamben's theory of potentiality is his account of the passage
from potentiality to act. The difficulty arises once impotentiality and
potentiality are identified with one another, for if it is easy enough to
imagine potentiality realising itself in the act, how do we understand the
passage to act when this is equally the product or result of a modification

of impotentiality, the "decisive" mode of potentiality? Or, as Agamben puts it, "*How is it possible to consider the actuality of the potentiality to not-be?*" (*Po*, 183). For Agamben, Aristotle's account of the passage from potentiality–impotentiality to act is found in "two lines that, in their brevity, constitute an extraordinary testament to [his] genius" (*Po*, 183): namely, *Metaphysics* 1047a 24–6, which he translates as "A thing is said to be potential if, when the act of which it is said to be potential is realized, there will be nothing impotential". (Agamben cites this sentence and rehearses this argument in each of the three texts noted above.) Agamben's reading of this cryptic and highly debated sentence differs from most interpretations in that he takes it not as a description of potentiality or possibility, but as an account of the precise way potentiality realises itself in the act. Everything hinges here on the meaning of the final clause of the sentence, "there will be nothing impotential" (*outhen estai adunaton*). In contrast to the more orthodox – and tautological – interpretation of this sentence as saying that "what is possible (or potential) is that with respect to which nothing is impossible (or impotential)" (*Po*, 183), Agamben claims that rather than giving a criterion for possibility (namely, that the realised act not be an impossibility), the three words *outhen estai adunaton* specify "the condition into which potentiality – which can both be and not be – can realize itself. What is potential can pass over into actuality only at the point at which it sets aside its own potential not to be (its *adunamia*). To set im-potentiality aside is not to destroy it but, on the contrary, to fulfill it, to turn potentiality back upon itself in order to give itself to itself" (*HS*, 46). The reason this actualising negation or "setting aside" of impotentiality is not its destruction or elimination is that potentiality and impotentiality are not in fact opposite or contradictory to one another; rather, they co-exist, indeed are one and the same, on the plane of potentiality or future contingency (where the principle of non-contradiction does not apply), and thus the fulfilment or act of potentiality is also equally the fulfilment or "act of impotentiality" (*Po*, 183). That is to say, because they together constitute the originary structure of the potentiality that realises itself, *both* modes of (im)potentiality pass into the act, though in different ways. Thus Agamben reads the double negation in Aristotle's phrase "there will be nothing impotential" as indicating a particular kind of negation – namely, "privation" (*sterêsis*) – which is closer to a sort of self-suspension than cancellation. The inherently two-sided structure of potentiality–impotentiality means that in the passage to act, impotentiality must set itself aside, suspend and turn back upon itself, and yet not be totally destroyed or left behind, making actuality not just the realisation and fulfilment of the potentiality-to-be (i.e. being), but also the privative negation (and fulfilment) of the potentiality-to-not-be: the potentiality not to not be (i.e. not not-being). For further discussion of the passage from potentiality to act or *energeia*, see **actuality**.

The centrality of this doctrine of potentiality for Agamben's thought can hardly be overstated, as it constitutes the ontological underpinning of virtually all of his work from the mid-1980s on, especially that concerning sovereignty. "Potentiality (in its double appearance as potentiality to and potentiality not to) is that through which Being founds itself *sovereignly*, which is to say, without anything preceding or determining it (*superiorem non recognoscens*) other than its own ability not to be" (*HS*, 46). Because being arises out of and is grounded on the anterior internal modification or self-suspension of (im)potentiality, a process that in *Homo Sacer* he will liken to the self-suspension of the sovereign ban, Agamben calls for "a new and coherent ontology of potentiality . . . [one that will replace] the ontology founded on the primacy of actuality and its relation to potentiality" (*HS*, 44) and will enable us truly to follow Aristotle's affirmation of the "autonomous existence of potentiality" (*HS*, 45), which is the ultimate object of what might be called Agamben's "dunamology" or "potentiology".

PRAXIS

Robert Sinnerbrink

The Greek term *praxis* is traditionally contrasted with *poiesis*. While *poiesis* refers to pro-ductive activity, *praxis* refers to willed practical activity. In modernity, however, *praxis* has become the dominant way of understanding human productive activity: "all of man's doing – that of the artist and the craftsman as well as that of the workman and the politician – is praxis, that is, manifestation of a will that produces a concrete effect" (*MC*, 68). Moreover, *poiesis* has been transformed into work understood as a form of *praxis*: "this pro-ductive doing, in the form of work, determines everywhere the status of man on earth, understood from the point of view of praxis, that is, of production and material life" (*MC*, 59). The Greeks, however, made a distinction between *poiesis* and *praxis*. *Poiesis* is the pro-duction into presence, the passing of something from nonbeing to being, from concealment to truth understood as unveiling (*aletheia*); *praxis* (from *prattein*, meaning "to do") refers to the will that finds expression in practical action. **Aristotle** ranked *poesis* higher than *praxis* because *poesis* brings something into being, into the light of truth, whereas *praxis* has its roots in the natural condition of humans as living beings, whose principle of motion (will, desire, volition) characterises **life** more generally (*MC*,

69). Work (performed by slaves) was considered even lower than *praxis*, because it meant submitting to biological necessity, which was thought incompatible with the condition of being free (*MC*, 69).

Western culture has progressively obliterated the distinctions between these three kinds of human doing – *poiesis*, *praxis*, work – and this can be tracked both in the convergence of *poiesis* and *praxis*, and in the elevation of work to the "rank of central value and common denominator of every human activity" (*MC*, 70). From Locke's theory of property and Adam Smith's account of the source of wealth, to **Marx**'s thesis that work is the expression of our very humanity, all human doing becomes interpreted as *praxis* or concrete productive activity (as opposed to theory or reflective thought). *Praxis*, in turn, is conceived as starting from work, from "the production of material life that corresponds to life's biological cycle" (*MC*, 70). Even though Marx's thought is refused today, we none the less regard the human as "the living being who produces and works" (*MC*, 71). This interpretation assumes the biological basis of work as defining human activity; *praxis* is interpreted as will and vital impulse, as linked to an interpretation of life and of "man as a living being" (*MC*, 71).

Agamben goes on to link this "biological" account of *praxis* to the way **aesthetics** has blurred the distinction between *poiesis* and *praxis*, shifting towards "the interpretation of art as a mode of praxis and of praxis as the expression of a will and a creative force" (*MC*, 71). Whether in Novalis's definition of poetry as "wilful, active, and productive use of our organs", **Nietzsche**'s identification of art as expression of the will to power, or the Situationist project of a practical realisation of the alienated creative impulses expressed in art, modern art and culture are interpreted metaphysically as forms of *praxis* expressing the artist's creative will.

PROFANATION

Anton Schütz

Composed of *pro* ("out of", "away from") and *fanum* ("temple, sanctuary, holy site or district"), the Latin verb *profanare* means "to defile, desacralize, give back a sacred object to profane use". What is at stake in Agamben's argument in connection to the rather *recherché* word "profanation" is not exhausted thereby. Underlying it is an attack directed against another word, which is also of Latin provenance and connected to a seemingly identical meaning. This is the word "secularisation", of very common use especially among people interested in European-type social science and history. Agamben's study of profanation refers to it sometimes in an explicit, constantly in an implicit way. Remarkably, there is, in the word *secularisation*, or for that matter in *secular* or *secularism*, no trace of any component that would explicitly refer to religion, to the holy, to God or the gods, or indeed to a sanctuary. Latin *saeculum* means simply "lifespan" and "century". It is not immediately clear, therefore, how it can serve to refer to the transformation of something religious into something non-religious, or to its removal from the religious sphere to the non-religious sphere of the public space, as in the claim that "all significant concepts of the modern theory of the state are secularized theological concepts" (Schmitt 1985: 36). The solution to the riddle lies in the fact that, in the language of the Ancient Church and subsidiarily of an extended millennium of European history, the words "*this* century" (*hoc saeculum*) stood for "this world", as opposed to the other, eternal or heavenly world. The modern term secularisation, which refers to this divide, provides, as Agamben explains, only a flashy but misleading piece of new-speak destined to distract from its effective role, which is the role of a powerful enabling device for what it allegedly helps to leave behind. The fact of undergoing secularisation not only fails to prevent a society from perpetuating its power-addicted institutions and *dispositifs*, but also, by substituting secular – for instance, legal – for "religious" ways of imposing and justifying power, it provides society's power routines with a new lease of life. In that sense, secularisation offers an instance of that addictive dependence on the void which Agamben diagnoses in diverse ramifications of modernity analysed in the context of his comments on **degree zero**, both in the context of Paul and of method. He also qualifies secularisation as a "form of repression" which, by "leav[ing] intact the forces it deals with by simply moving them from one place to another, . . . does nothing but displace the heavenly monarchy onto an earthly monarchy, leaving its power intact" (Agamben 2007: 77). Profanation, on the contrary, "neutralizes what it profanes" (ibid.). To profane is to lift the barriers of separation encountered in solemn forms religious as well as secular, in order to give them back to **use**. Use, conversely, is intrinsically profane to the precise extent to which it lifts separation.

PROSE

Jason Maxwell

Within his corpus, Agamben speaks very little of prose in explicit terms. Even in the book which bears the word in its title – *The Idea of Prose* –

this form of writing only receives attention in one brief chapter. Here, Agamben argues that the single feature that distinguishes prose from **poetry** is **enjambment**, explaining that the typical markers of poetry, including "[q]uantity, rhythm, and the number of syllables", are all elements that can be found within prose (*IP*, 39). As Agamben sees it, even poetry that does not include enjambment is merely a poem with "zero enjambement", while prose is fundamentally incapable of possessing this characteristic. In short, prose could be defined as writing where metrical and syntactical elements do not clash. Because prose writing implicitly asserts that form does not participate in the creation of content, it suggests that this content exists independently of its articulation in *language*.

Agamben concludes his chapter by pointing out that Plato directed his attention toward an idea of language that was "neither poetry nor prose, but their middle term" (*IP*, 41). What is this middle term that exists between poetry and prose? Simply speaking, it is the basic existence of language itself. Beyond the capacity to signify this or that proposition – which proves to be the perpetual preoccupation of prose – language consists of the capacity to signify as such. In this respect, the "idea of prose" could easily be understood as "the idea of the idea", as it seeks to communicate language's fundamental **communicability**.

For Agamben, philosophy is the discipline that adheres most rigidly to the beliefs embodied in prose writing, as it aims to achieve a perfect correspondence between word and thing. In its pursuit of pure representation, philosophy demands that language have a transparent signifying function. Agamben challenges these assumptions, calling for a form of creative criticism that would complicate the strict barriers that have been erected between philosophy and poetry, thereby creating the possibility of an authentic experience of language in itself. In *Stanzas*, for instance, he reminds us that "every authentic poetic project is directed toward knowledge, just as every authentic act of philosophy is always directed by joy" (*S*, xvii). Only by assuming the values and methods of the other discourse can poetry or philosophy ever hope to succeed in becoming aware of language as language. Indeed, within *The Idea of Prose* itself, the highly literary quality of the writing calls attention to itself in a way that undermines typical philosophical protocols. Paradoxically, this indirect approach offers the clearest path toward grasping language in its pure **potentiality**.

R

REDEMPTION

Sergei Prozorov

One of the most original aspects of Agamben's philosophy is its recovery of the problematic of redemption. In contrast to other contemporary continental philosophers, who demote or dismiss this problematic, Agamben makes the question of redemption his central concern and insists on its political significance, thus recommencing the discourse of messianic (see **messianism**) politics, inaugurated by **Benjamin**. Agamben's esoteric polemic with **Derrida** since the 1970s focuses precisely on the possibility of redemption, which Derridean deconstruction leaves indeterminate, "thwarted" or "paralyzed" (see *LD*, 39; *SE*, 64; *TR*, 102). In contrast to Derrida's refusal of the very problematic of the "ends" (of man, history or politics) and the insistence of the inaccessibility of the eschaton, Agamben rejects the pathos of infinite deferral and asserts the possibility of redemption in the here and now, any moment in time being a potential *kairos* of a radical break.

At the same time, Agamben's understanding of redemption is distinct from a theological solution of the kind proposed, for example, by the "radical orthodoxy" of John Milbank, who affirms an exit from contemporary **nihilism** *back* into the ontological plenitude of eternal life. For Agamben, redemption introduces no new positive content, nor does it restore positivity to the tradition that nihilism has rendered vacuous. We can never go back on nihilism but it does not follow from this that the horizon of redemption is itself to be annulled. Agamben affirms a minimalist if not outright empty understanding of redemption that should none the less be held rigorously distinct from its absence. The only thing that can be redeemed is what Agamben calls the **irreparable**, "[being] consigned without remedy to [one's] way of being" (*CC*, 90). Thus, redemption does not consist in reclaiming what was lost or making the profane sacred but rather in the "irreparable loss of the lost, the definitive profanity of the profane" (*CC*, 102). Whatever is saved in Agamben's redemption (and what is saved is always whatever – see **whatever singularity**) is saved only as **unsavable**.

The idea of the redemption of the irreparable can be grasped with the help of **Hölderlin**'s phrase from *Patmos*, made famous by **Heidegger**:

"where danger grows, grows saving power also" (see, for example, *MC*, 102; *RA*, 75). Agamben has repeatedly asserted the possibility of redemption on the basis of precisely the same conditions of modern **nihilism** that he described as catastrophic. Agamben's thought is therefore the very opposite of utopianism. Moreover, nihilism is the *only* possible basis for radical change, which would otherwise be doomed to perpetuating the work of the negative, vainly applying it to nihilism itself. Yet, as Agamben demonstrates (*LD*, 84–98), nothing is more nihilistic than a negation of nihilism. Any project that remains oblivious of the extent to which the ideals it valorises have already been devalued and deactivated would only succeed in plunging us deeper into nihilism.

And yet, Agamben paints a convincingly gloomy picture of the present state of things only to undertake a dialectical reversal at the end, finding in our very destitution the condition for the possibility of redemption, whose description is entirely devoid of fantastic mirages. In the redeemed world "everything will be as is now, just a little different" (*CC*, 57). The "saving power" does not make danger disappear, but rather consists in the emergence of new possibilities of the free **use** of whatever exists as irreparable. Rather than lead us out of nihilism, this understanding of redemption consists in its reclaiming as an ethos in its original sense of "dwelling place".

Thus, Agamben's Benjaminian approach to redemption should be distinguished from Theodor **Adorno**'s philosophical strategy of contemplating things from the perspective of redemption in the mode of the "as if". Against this strategy, which Jacob **Taubes** dismissed as the "aesthetization" of the messianic, Agamben rather opts for the logic of the "as not" (*hos me*) that he reconstitutes in his analysis of St **Paul**'s epistles (*TR*, 23–34); this consists in the revocation and undermining of every **vocation** or identity, rendering it inoperative without constituting a new one. In this logic, redemption is no longer a fictitious perspective from which a subject contemplates the world, but rather a real condition of the dislocation of the subject. This is the "tiny displacement" (*CC*, 53) that redeems us *from* the irreparability of the world perceived as oppressive necessity *to* its irreparability grasped as immanent transcendence: "how the world is – this is outside the world" (*CC*, 106).

This logic of the redemption of the irreparable is at work in Agamben's philosophy from his first book onwards. In *The Man Without Content* (108–15), he seeks the redemption of art from the nihilism of modern **aesthetics**, but what is to be redeemed is not the content of any particular cultural tradition, but precisely its loss and forgetting that only retains the aspect of transmissibility (see **transmission**), i.e. pure **potentiality** to signify that exceeds any signified content. The same logic is applied in subsequent books: for example, the redemption of the object of desire from both knowledge and possession in its phantasmatic recasting (*S*, 124–30), of the human experience of **historicity** from the dialectic (*IH*, 112–15), of **language** from its negative foundation of the unsayable (*LD*, 66–81), of **community** from the principle of identity through its recasting as whatever being (see **whatever singularity**) (*CC*, 63–5), of both humanity and animality from their confinement in the anthropological machine (*O*, 33–8, 81–92), of faith from law through the grasp of the messianic *kairos* (*TR*, 129–37), of any human practice whatsoever through a **profanation** that returns it to the sphere of free use (*Pr*, 73–91).

The most controversial deployment of this logic is practised in Agamben's writings on **politics** (*HS*, 187–8; *SE*, 59–64), in which he affirms the redemption from the sovereign (see **sovereignty**) **ban** through a transformation of the fictive **state of exception**, in which the power of suspending the operation of the norm is restricted to the sovereign, into a Benjaminian "real state of exception", in which this anomic power is reappropriated by the entire society. In this manner, the **bare life** produced and confined by the biopolitical (see **biopolitics**) logic of sovereignty is redeemed as **happy life**, a life that is stripped of every identity, vocation or task and consists solely in the **inoperative** being-in-common.

S

SACRAMENT

Anton Schütz

While in classical Latin the legal term *sacramentum* designates both an oath and a sum of money deposited as a pledge by each party to a lawsuit, *sacrament* in its current use refers to a religious operation. Agamben synthesises both and offers an instance of the tendency that characterises his twenty-first-century writing at large – the tendency of looking ever more closely into the concepts, fault-lines and zones of indecidability that are on offer in the legal and theological archive. Increasingly detailed accounts of topics such as the economic genealogy of social organisation in *Il Regno and la gloria* (2007), the legal history of self-obligation in *Il Sacramento del linguaggio* (2008), or the sacrament as a procedure that generates objective effects by dint of its mere taking-place, in *The Signature of All Things* (2008/trans. 2010), put new emphasis on the complex articulation of ancient, medieval and current elements. The common theme here is that of the operation of sacralisation, and that of the possibility for phi-losophy to name and deactivate its grasp. Cast into a term elaborated by Alexandre **Kojève** and Raymond Queneau, Georges **Bataille**, Maurice **Blanchot** and Jean-Luc **Nancy** (*HS*, 28, 61f.), the Agambenian stress on the **inoperative** (*inoperosità* in Italian and *désœuvrement* in French) presents a refined alternative to the programme of deconstructionism, whose "building/unbuilding" theme it replaces with a consecration/ **profanation** theme and its focus on **bare life**. In order to achieve the *homo sacer*'s peculiar state of precarious abeyance or life-as-debt, the sacralising operation plays two moves at once; it transfers a person's life to the gods while refusing to take it. "When a commander consecrates his life to the gods of the underworld in order to ensure victory, [the sacred life constituted] through this solemn act of *sacratio* or *devotio* has been given over to the gods and belongs exclusively to them" (2007: 78). Early Christian theology offers a consistent body of sacramental doctrine, focusing specifically on the "indelible mark" conferred by some sacra-ments. Augustin's (354–430) relevant treatises ascribe an objective or *ex opere operato* efficacy especially to these "one-off" sacraments (baptism, ordination). According to Augustine, if correctly celebrated, these unfold their effects regardless of whether they are administered by a priest or an impostor. While the paradigm of a validity *ex opere operato* is crucial, for instance, for all positive law, Agamben portrays this validity that results as the automatic result of a self-sufficient mere procedure, under the heading of "zero-signatures" (2007: 78). Finally, the sacrament extends its effects into yet another key context – the law-creating force of oath, curse and language at large, analysed in *Il Sacramento del linguaggio: Archaeologia del giuramento* (*The Sacrament of Language: Archaeology of the Oath*) (2008; not yet published in English), his most systematic discussion of performa-tive speech to date. In order to make words "reliable", language itself must transform into a sacrament. However, the issue here is not of secularisa-tion, or of a road leading from "religion" to "law". In order to carry the yoke of lasting effects, the oath has never been more "religious" than it is today, while conversely it has never become more "legal" than it had been in its earliest instantiations.

SACRED

Steven DeCaroli

It is necessary to bear in mind that, for Agamben, the sacred is not prima-rily a religious concept, but a juridical one. The figure of the *homo sacer*, which anchors Agamben's most complete treatment of sacredness and without which no proper understanding of the concept can be achieved, is a juridical term drawn directly from ancient Roman jurisprudence. Thus, in order to see how the sacred intersects with the **law**, it is necessary first to acquaint ourselves with his reflections on the ontological condition of the juridical order.

In the opening pages of *Homo Sacer*, Agamben draws a critical distinction between two terms used in classical Greek to refer to what we mean by the single term "life": *bios* (political life; the way of life proper to an individual or group) and *zoē* (natural or biological life; the sheer fact of being alive). Whereas in the Ancient World the maintenance and administration of natural life (*zoē*) were largely confined to the home (*oikos*) and were therefore excluded from the concerns of the *polis*, in modern times political institutions have increasingly drawn natural life into the sphere of their regular operations. Reoriented in this manner, modern state power has increasingly made the lives of its citizens a central concern, thereby producing a distinctive social order characterised by the intrusion of the state into all facets of daily life. Michel **Foucault** has called this modern form of social administration "**biopolitics**" and Agamben borrows the term directly. In contrast to Foucault, however, for whom biopolitics represents a historical shift, Agamben maintains that the inclusion of *zoē* within the political order is absolutely ancient. For Agamben, sovereign (see **sovereignty**) power has always placed biological life at its centre, only now the modern state has made this explicit, rendering the distinction between the human and the citizen, between fact and right, all but indistinguishable. What is revealed in this conclusion is that the primary activity of sovereign power, both in modern times and ancient, has been the production of a biopolitical body, a body that Agamben refers to as "**bare life**" or, on occasion, as "sacred life".

But what does Agamben mean here by "bare life" and how is it associated with the sacred? From the outset we must recognise that bare life is not synonymous with natural life (*zoē*). Natural life is life entirely without relation to law, whereas bare life is life *excluded* from law: not an original state, but the condition of having been stripped of every legal quality. In an identical manner, and in keeping with a long history of scholarship on the subject, the sacred is properly understood precisely in these terms. Thus, to make something sacred is to remove it from the human world, from the sphere of profane law, and deliver it over to divine law. While Agamben provides numerous examples of bare life, the one that best exemplifies this exclusionary status is *homo sacer* – the sacred man. According to Roman law, *homo sacer* is the term used to designate the status of an individual who, having committed a serious crime, is stripped of all protections granted by the juridical order, including his right not to be killed. But according to Roman statutes, while one is permitted to kill the *homo sacer* with impunity, one is "not permitted to **sacrifice** this man" (cited in *HS*, 71), thus creating a double exception. This dual prohibition – that the sacred man can be killed and yet not sacrificed – signals his exclusion from both profane law and divine law. Regarding this ambiguity, Agamben concludes, "this ancient meaning of the term *sacer* presents us with the enigma of a figure of the sacred that, before or beyond the religious, constitutes the first paradigm of the political realm of the West" (*HS*, 9).

Following a well-established line of anthropological and linguistic research, Agamben emphasises the ambivalence ascribed to the meaning of the word sacred, which ranges from the auspicious to the accursed. The sacred designates not only venerated objects excluded from the sphere of the profane, but applies equally to persons or things deemed untouchable, accursed or contaminated. In these cases, it is not from the profane order that objects are excluded, but from the divine – in so far as they are unsuitable for use in sacrifice. As we have seen, the figure of *homo sacer* mirrors this sacred ambivalence. His status is defined precisely by "the particular character of the double exclusion into which he is taken and the violence to which he finds himself exposed" (*HS*, 82). This violence, which is classifiable neither as sacrifice nor as homicide, in so far as the life exposed to this violence has been subtracted from both human and divine law, opens a sphere of human existence, marked by sovereignty, in which bare life – a truly sacred life – appears. To quote Agamben directly, "The sovereign sphere is the sphere in which it is permitted to kill without committing homicide and without celebrating a sacrifice, and sacred life . . . is the life that has been captured in this sphere" (*HS*, 83).

But if we are to accept this understanding of sacredness as a type of exposure to violence, what are we to make of common claims regarding the sacredness or sanctity of life? For instance, what are we to make of efforts to extend and enforce **human rights**? For Agamben, these efforts, though well intended, invariably reproduce conditions of violence, for though modern democracies are "constantly trying to . . . find, so to speak, the *bios* of *zoē*" (*HS*, 9) – that is, to find a way of life proper to life as such, either through legal policies or the extension of rights – the continual failure to unite *zoē* with *bios* has created precisely what these efforts wish to avoid: namely, conditions under which bare life remains the rule. The fundamental misconception that gives way to this failure is that sacredness is somehow essential to life itself. For Agamben, this only appears to be the case. In fact, the very idea of the sacredness of life appears only as a consequence of sovereignty and, more specifically, as a consequence of having been excluded from the juridical order that the sovereign makes possible. Consequently, and despite every political movement that champions human rights as a foil against state power, it is precisely in conceiving life as sacred that the separation of bare life from political life, upon which sovereignty rests, takes effect. "The sacredness of life, which is invoked today as an absolute fundamental right in opposition to sovereign power", Agamben writes, "in fact originally expresses precisely both life's subjection to a power over death and life's irreparable exposure in the relation of abandonment" (*HS*, 83). Extending rights to cover more and more humans merely follows the same logic that produces bare life: that is, it covers people with the protection of the law by *including* them. The problem with this is that every time one includes someone under rights, even human rights, exceptions can and will be made.

Thus, for Agamben, political movements that align themselves against state power cannot rely on claims regarding the sacredness of life. Instead, political action must begin precisely by rethinking the relation between life and politics as such, and must do so by conceiving of this relation outside of the constraints of biopolitical sovereignty because the danger inherent within biopolitics is not that political life and natural life are collapsed, but rather that they are kept separated. Any future politics not grounded in the logic of sovereignty must employ a concept of life that is not premised on the juridical separation of natural life from political life, *zoē* from *bios*, from which bare life emerges, but must instead make such a separation impossible. This form-of-life, in which the sacralisation of life (and the separation and exclusion sacredness entails) is prevented, is what Agamben calls a profane life. Rather than found community on juridical inclusivity, the outcome of which has invariably been exclusion and violence (think here of the way the "universal" political rights of eighteenth-century Europe were perfectly capable of excluding non-whites and women), what is called for instead is the rendering **inoperative** of the distinction between the sacred and the profane so that the sacred can no longer be used as a mechanism for exclusion.

SACRIFICE

Steven DeCaroli

According to Agamben, all objects designated by the term **sacred** have this in common: they, in some way, belong to the gods and so are "removed from the free use and commerce of men" (*Pr*, 73). Consequently, any attempt to make use of such objects – that is, to violate their special unavailability – is to commit a sacrilege. If to make sacred – that is, to consecrate – is the act of removing an object from the human world and delivering it over to the sphere of divine law, the reverse act of returning something that was once sacred to "the free use of men" (*Pr*, 73) is to profane. Following the work of Henri Hubert and Marcel Mauss, Agamben maintains that sacrifice is always the social practice that regulates and sanctions the passage of an object from the profane order to the sacred, and religion is the cultural practice that governs and determines the sacrificial act. "Religion", Agamben writes, "can be defined as that which removes things, places, animals, or people from common use and transfers them to a separate sphere" (*Pr*, 74). And, according to Agamben, it follows from this that not only is there therefore no religion without the idea of separation, but every other form of separation "contains and preserves within itself a genuinely religious core" (*Pr*, 74).

Agamben's first important discussion of sacrifice occurs at the end of *Language and Death* where, in speaking of the ungroundedness of man – having "no foundation except in his own action" (*LD*, 105) – he associates religious sacrifice, and in particular its exclusionary function, with the founding of communities. "At the center of the sacrifice", he writes, "is simply a determinate action that, as such, is separated and marked by exclusion; in this way it becomes *sacer* and is invested with a series of prohibitions" (*LD*, 105). But that which is forbidden is not simply excluded from society; "rather it is now only accessible for certain people and according to determinate rules" (*LD*, 105). In this way, he concludes, "it furnishes society and its ungrounded legislation with the fiction of a beginning: that which is excluded from the community is, in reality, that on which the entire life of the community is founded" (*LD*, 105). Thus, for Agamben, sacrifice functions to separate the sacred from the profane, to exclude one from the other, and in so doing gives rise not only to the myth of political authority, but to the violence that accompanies it. "All human action," he writes, "inasmuch as it is not naturally grounded but must construct its own foundation, is, according to the sacrificial mythogeme, violent" (*LD*, 105). In the *Homo Sacer* series, as well as in *Profanations*, Agamben describes in great detail this intersection of authority and violence, demonstrating just how close a connection there is between the "sacrificial function" and the operations of political power, even in our secular age.

SAUSSURE, FERDINAND DE

Paolo Bartoloni

A Swiss linguist (1857–1913), Saussure is the author of the core text, *Course in General Linguistics*, published posthumously in 1916. His work on language and its structure have had a vast influence, and have been adopted in various disciplines from literature and psychoanalysis to philosophy. Saussure postulated a theory of the sign based on the distinction between the signifier (a word, for instance) and the signified (a thing, be it organic or inorganic), and claimed that, although there exists a relation between these two events of the sign, this relation is arbitrary and depends on the context of signification and speech. He also argued that language must be understood as the relation between an apparatus of words, grammar and syntax (*langue*), and the particular use that individuals make of this apparatus (*parole*). Saussure's theory of language is thus context-driven, and predicated upon the performability of language according to particular abilities. In his philosophical work Agamben focuses not so much on the poles of Saussure's linguistic equation – that is, *langue* and *parole* – as on experience in between *langue* and *parole*. As he writes in *Infancy and History*, "the site of a transcendental experience [. . .] lies in that difference between language and speech (Saussure's *langue* and *parole* – or rather, in **Benveniste**'s terms between semiotic and semantic) which cannot be encompassed and which every reflection on language must confront" (*IH*, 6). Agamben approaches this site by employing several categories characteristic of his philosophical discourse, including **potentiality**, **infancy**, **indistinction** and **voice** to conduct his investigation and critique of Western metaphysics and **politics**.

SCHMITT, CARL

Daniel McLoughlin

Carl Schmitt (1888–1985) was a German jurist and political philosopher, whose most famous and important work was published during the Weimar Republic (1919–33). His ideas appear throughout Agamben's diagnostic political works, *Homo Sacer*, *State of Exception* and *Means Without End*: in particular, his theory of **sovereignty** and his diagnosis of the dissolution of the Eurocentric *nomos* of the modern nation-state. While deeply opposed to Schmitt's politics, Agamben's interest in Schmitt derives from his insights into the nature of law and the state, their relation to political domination, and his criticisms of the liberal status quo. While taking up a number of Schmitt's central concepts, Agamben also uses them to critique Schmitt himself.

Schmitt's work is controversial due to both its theoretical content and his political involvements. He was deeply critical of the attempt of liberal theory to ground the existence and legitimacy of the law in foundational universal principles such as human rights, or the neutrality and objectivity of the rule of law. For Schmitt any legal system is born of political conflict, deriving its existence and legitimacy from a constitutive act of violence, a groundless decision for a particular form of political order. The continued survival of the state depends upon its ability to identify the enemy (revolutionaries or hostile states) and, if necessary, to do battle with them. Schmitt's fundamental philosophical concern was the preservation of political order, and he saw liberal neutrality as a threat to the survival of the state in the context of Weimar's profound political instability. Schmitt's Weimar work legally justified dictatorial state powers, most famously in *Political Theology* and its definition of the sovereign as "he who decides on the exception", and he worked as an adviser to the conservative Papen government, which operated under almost constant emergency rule during the final crisis of Weimar. Most controversially, Schmitt joined the Nazi party after they came to power in 1933, writing a number of works in their service. Debates still rage over the continuity between this work and Schmitt's Weimar justification of an authoritarian state.

Schmitt's definition of the contingent ground of the legal order in sovereignty is central to Agamben's *Homo Sacer* project, which he sees as having parallels with **potentiality** as the contingent ground of the human. Agamben is, however, critical of Schmitt's rendering of the problem of sovereignty in terms of dictatorship. Instead of the decision on the enemy, however, Agamben argues that the foundation of the legal order is a decision that produces **bare life**. Further, in *Homo Sacer*, he is critical of Schmitt's reduction of sovereignty to the problem of "who in the political order was invested with certain powers" (*HS*, 12). Instead, what is at stake in the sovereign decision is nothing less than the limit and originary structure of the political order as such. Finally, in *State of Exception*, Agamben argues that the Roman institution of dictatorship, through which Schmitt had traced the history of emergency powers in *Dictatorship* (1921), is not the appropriate genealogical origin for the state of exception. Rather, the genealogy of the state of exception should, Agamben argues, be traced back to the *iustitium*, a "standstill" or "suspension of the law". The *iustitium* is not the creation of a determinate magistracy, as is dictatorship, but rather the production of a juridical void, in which every magistrate and indeed every citizen "seems to be invested with a floating and anomalous *imperium* that resists definition within the terms of the legal order" (*SE*, 43).

Agamben's account of the camp as the "*nomos* of the modern" develops from and critiques Schmitt's *Nomos of the Earth* (1950). In this text, Schmitt argues that *nomos*, the appropriation and division of land, is the founding violence of the law. For Agamben, however, the originary violence of the law is the appropriation and division of life through the sovereign exception. While Agamben agrees with Schmitt's diagnosis that the order of the modern nation-state entered into a lasting crisis after World War One, he disagrees on its cause, citing a breakdown in the mechanisms through which life is captured by law. The reordering of the nation-state system after World War One, and the attendant phenomenon of mass statelessness, disproved the modern presumption that an individual automatically belonged to a state by virtue of their birth, and the camp is then the mechanism through which the state directly assumes the management of life amidst this crisis.

The problem of sovereignty first appeared in Agamben's work in the 1992 lecture, "The Messiah and the Sovereign: The Problem of Law in Walter Benjamin". Agamben's own interest in Schmitt appears to derive from Benjamin's engagement with the German jurist, a debate that Agamben reconstructs in *State of Exception*. At stake in this "Gigantomachy Concerning a Void" is the relationship between anomie and law involved in the limit of the juridical order. Much of Schmitt's work was an attempt to shore up the modern state order in the epoch of its dissolution, and according to Agamben, he does this by opening a space for the state to act outside the legal system in the interests of preserving the state. By contrast, in texts such as his *Critique of Violence*, Benjamin attempts to think a revolutionary violence that is outside the law. For Agamben, the decisive move in this debate is Benjamin's *Theses on the Philosophy of History*, which reads: "the tradition of the oppressed teaches us that the state of emergency in which we live is not the exception but the rule" (Benjamin 1999: 248–9). This thesis puts Schmitt's attempt to harness anomie to law in check, as, when the exception becomes the rule, "the machine can no longer function . . . Sovereign decision is no longer capable of performing the task that *Political Theology* assigned it: the rule, which now coincides with what it lives by, devours itself" (*SE*, 58). Instead of the state provision of law and order, backed by the occasional reference to emergency powers, the Nazi state is characterised by the total suspension of the law and the administration of disorder.

SCHOLEM, GERSHOM

Anton Schütz

Gershom or Gerhard (as he was called before he emigrated) Scholem (1897–1982) was Walter **Benjamin**'s friend and was briefly a teacher of Hebrew. He was born into a German (more precisely, Silesian) Jewish family of assimilated background and decided early on in life to return to his Jewish roots. From 1915 until his emigration to Palestine in 1923, Scholem maintained a close friendship with Benjamin during the formative years of their early intellectual careers, both in Berlin and later, during the First World War, in Switzerland (Scholem 1981). They corresponded between 1932 and 1940 (Scholem 1992). It was Scholem, along with Theodor W. Adorno, who oversaw the German edition of Benjamin's *Collected Writings* originally undertaken by R. Tiedemann and H. Schweppenhäuser. After emigrating, Scholem exerted a considerable influence internationally on scholars of Jewish history; he was professor of Jewish Mysticism at Jerusalem University and a member, later President, of the Israel Academy. Agamben, who met him in the 1960s in Rome, was initially interested by Scholem's writing in connection with messianism and by the correspondence between Scholem and Benjamin. The gradual appearance, in his work from *Homo Sacer* onward, of the concept of **degree zero**, a philosophical theme that increasingly takes centre-stage, is related to a topic that was a regular feature of this exchange: namely, Scholem's and Benjamin's discussion of Kafka (*HS*, 50ff.). The question of degree zero pertains to the authority retained over a subject population which no longer locates any meaning in it. A law – the word being taken in its most general sense ("we mean by this term the entire textual tradition in its regulative form, whether the Jewish Torah or the Islamic Torah, Christian *dogma*, or the profane *nomos*"; *HS*, 51) – whose validity is still admitted and recognised exercises its social effects, while its meaning has gone, disappeared beyond recovery: "there", Scholem remarks, "the Nothing appears" (*HS*, 51).

SEMIOTIC/SEMANTIC

William Watkin

Of the two terms it is the semiotic which primarily concerns the early work of Agamben as a means of problematising the predominance of sense over sound in our tradition. That said, while he turns in his early work to the semiotic as a means of overcoming this tradition, typified by **Hegel** and **Heidegger** in *Language and Death*, at no point does he advocate a thinking of pure semiotics or even the destruction of metaphysics via semiotics. The semiotic, for him, is as much a part of metaphysics as supersensuous modes of philosophical thinking. The semiotic in Agamben's work is not to be taken to mean the science of signifying systems. Rather the semiotic is the raw fact of material **signification** as such. It is non-signifying signification, or the potential (see **potentiality**) to signify without signifying anything in particular. This is encapsulated in his theory of the singularity of the whatever (*quodlibet*) (*CC*, 1).

In his work, the semiotic takes three key forms. The first, found in *Infancy and History*, is **language** as such in its **infancy**, or the fact that there is language prior to or separated from the metaphysical insistence on language signifying some thing. The second, again in *Infancy and History* and later developed in *Remnants of Auschwitz*, is inherited from French linguist **Benveniste**, whose theory of the semiotic in relation to indicative forms such as *deixis* presents a language which both draws attention to itself as pure medium, and which presents, through shifting, one of the few instances where one can move across the imposed division between the semiotic and the semantic. Finally, in relation to poetry, it is the basis of Agamben's conception in *The End of the Poem* of the definition of poetry as prolonged hesitation between sound and sense, as well as being the key term in poetry's ability, through the predominance of the semiotic, actually to suspend the false division/relation between semiotic and semantic.

SIGN/SIGNIFICATION

William Watkin

Although Agamben writes extensively on the sign and the **semiotic** in his early work, it would be wrong to see him as anything other than a virulent critic of post-Saussurian (see **Saussure**) conceptions of **signification**. While accepting the predominance of language as signification within Western thought, the view he takes in *Stanzas* is that this is both typical of Western differential and hierarchical metaphysical thought, and source of our inability to access the truth of thought as such: namely, **language**. The placement of language within a bifurcated technical unit called the sign is, according to Agamben, a historical disaster for language. The results are that language is assumed to be bifurcated, that the signified is placed above the signifier as the prime directive of language, and that the true **Voice** of language as pure medium for thought is presented permanently under negation. All three elements are presented in the traditional demarcation of the sign as Sd/Sr. The bar here indicates imposed scission, hierarchy and negation in one simple gesture.

Typical of Agamben's early thinking, however, is the means by which the bar as negation, source of all our problems with language, negation and truth, is turned into a potential solution to the problem. In crossing out language the sign at least gives us negative access to language. Using the Italian conception of the poetic stanza as a room, Agamben argues for an expansion of the bar into a two-dimensional room-like space for language. Language here becomes pure medium for support of meaning, not the negated part of signification.

The sign is reconfigured in *Infancy and History* and *Remnants of Auschwitz* through interaction with **Benveniste**'s conception of signification in relation to *deixis* and desubjectivisation. For Benveniste the sign's semiotic preconditions are that it is at all, and that it is not all other signs. This comes to represent language as such for Agamben as the potential to signify nothing specific, and subjective Being in its withdrawal. Like the sign, Being is there as not being other beings; thus subjectivity is defined as coming to presence as negated.

SIGNATURE

Kevin Attell

The term "signature" appears late in Agamben's *œuvre* but the concept is in keeping with motifs dating back to his earliest texts. "The Theory of Signatures" is one of three essays collected in the 2008 volume, *The Signature of All Things: On Method*.

Agamben presents the signature as a third term to be added to the double logic of linguistic signification, one that in fact precedes and enables the functioning of **signs**: "Signs do not speak unless signatures make them speak" (*ST*, 61). A signature is the operator of the passage from the semiological to the hermeneutic (**Foucault**), the semiotic to the semantic (**Benveniste**), or *langue* to *parole* (**Saussure**). "[S]ignatures", Agamben writes, "find their own locus in the gap and disconnection between semiology and hermeneutics," and the signature is "what enables the transition from one to the other" (*ST*, 59). The gap that separates these two distinct realms, which depend on one another in an irreducible game of oscillating logical priority, is the ambiguous and problematic space that, for Agamben, has largely determined the aporias of thought after the linguistic turn. While Agamben traces a history of the "theory of signatures" back through baroque, Renaissance, medieval and early Christian thinkers, this historical survey prepares for his addition of the problematic of the signature to contemporary (generally speaking, post-structural) philosophical debates.

In response to the structural irreducibility of the play between *langue* and *parole*, Agamben grants primacy and privilege to this third term, which is neither a signifier nor a signified, but a practical and historical mark of the efficacious sign's existence itself: "Before (or better, together with) being the place of signification, language is the place of signatures, without which no sign would be able to function" (*ST*, 76). The signature is a sort of residual mark of the sign's primordial and constitutive split into semiotic and semantic, and the reading of signatures, then, is akin to the *experimentum linguae* in which what is experienced or thought is not "this or that signifying proposition", but "the pure fact that one speaks, that language exists" (*IH*, 5).

SIGNIFICATION – see 'Sign'

SOVEREIGNTY

Arne De Boever

Although **politics** is a significant component of all of Agamben's work, the closing section of *The Coming Community*, "Tiananmen", arguably marks a new entrance of the state into his writings. Agamben's interest there in what he calls "the disjunction between **whatever singularity** and the State organization" (*CC*, 86) – captured by the image of the tank man on Tiananmen square – is translated in *Homo Sacer* into an investigation of the couple **bare life**/sovereign power. While *Remnants of Auschwitz* develops the ethical (see **ethics**) dimension of this investigation through an exploration of bare life's relation to **witnessing**, *State of Exception* contains Agamben's historical, philosophical and political analysis of the state that sovereignty produces. Finally, *Il Regno e la gloria* explores the other side – next to sovereignty – of what Agamben calls the power-machine: namely, **government**.

Traditionally defined as supreme power within a territory, sovereignty emerged in modern political thought through the writings of Jean Bodin (1530–96) and Thomas Hobbes (1588–1679), both of whom are discussed in *Homo Sacer*. Agamben understands sovereignty to be political–theological. He insists on "the paradox of sovereignty": taking up an inside/outside position with respect to the **law** that is similar to how a god relates to his creation, the sovereign, "who [is] outside the law", can "declare that there is nothing outside the law" (*HS*, 15). Whereas Hobbes is thus usually understood as a contract theorist who imagines people giving up some of their rights to an all-powerful and indivisible sovereign so as to be united in a commonwealth or state, Agamben draws out the dark side of this imagination by arguing that "in Hobbes, the foundation of sovereign power is to be sought not in the **subjects**' free renunciation of their natural right but in the sovereign's preservation of his natural right to do anything to anyone" (*HS*, 106). Thus, sovereignty produces a **state of exception**.

In such a state, **life** is internally excluded in the space that is supposed to guarantee its protection; it is reduced to bare life. This is the biopolitical (see **biopolitics**) logic of sovereignty, which Agamben equates to the logic of **abandonment** or **ban**, and which, he argues, permeates the history of Western democracy, from Ancient times until the present. Today, the exception has become power's rule of operation. Agamben calls the space that is opened up in such a situation a "**camp**" (*ME*, 39). The third part of *Homo Sacer* argues that the camp is the "biopolitical paradigm of the modern" (*HS*, 118). For his theory of the sovereign as he who decides on the state of exception, Agamben relies on Carl **Schmitt**'s *Political Theology*. The notion of bare life, however, he adapts from Walter **Benjamin**'s essay, "Critique of Violence", which he argues to have triggered Schmitt's book (*SE*, 52–64). Agamben borrows the notion of biopolitics from the first volume of Michel **Foucault**'s *The History of Sexuality*. For his discussion of abandonment or ban, he turns to Jean-Luc **Nancy**'s essay, "Abandoned Being".

Agamben's theory of sovereignty contradicts the common perception of the period after the Second World War as the era of sovereignty's decline through transnational developments such as **human rights** declarations and European integration. In a chapter in *Homo Sacer* called "Biopolitics and the Rights of Man", Agamben demonstrates, however, that the logic of human rights is nothing but the logic of sovereignty, since human rights are powerless outside of the context of the nation-state and produce a space of the human in which the non-human (concretely, *homo sacer*, and "virtually", all of us; *HS*, 115) is excluded (*HS*, 126–35). This chapter appears, with some revisions, as "Beyond Human Rights" in *Means Without End* (*ME*, 15–35). There, he also discusses a model for European integration that would go beyond the logic of the nation-state, which in his view continues to shape European politics (*ME*, 24). His insistence on the continued importance of sovereignty was proven justified after the September 11 terror attacks, when the US, instead of reconsidering its role in international politics, chose to fortify its sovereignty. It is partly because of this return of sovereignty in twenty-first-century politics that Agamben's work has found such resonance.

In *Homo Sacer*, Agamben's analysis of sovereignty gives way to an examination of potentiality that poses an "objection against the principle of sovereignty" (*HS*, 48). One example of such an objection is Herman **Melville's Bartleby**. The first part of *Homo Sacer* closes with a discussion of the messianic (see **messianism**) dimensions of such an objection against political–theological sovereignty. The connection between messianism and sovereignty is also the topic of the essay, "The Messiah and the Sovereign: The Problem of Law in Walter Benjamin", published in *Potentialities*. But how is one to imagine this in concrete legal and political terms? In the final chapter of *State of Exception*, Agamben calls for a "deactivation of the device that, in the state of exception" (*SE*, 88), ties law to life. Earlier on in the book, it appears that such a dismantling would produce not the destruction of the law but rather its "deactivation and inactivity" (*SE*, 64). This point is repeated in a book that is not a part of the *Homo Sacer* series but which reads like Agamben's solution to the problems of sovereignty: *The Time That Remains*. Here, Agamben turns to Saint **Paul's** "Letter to the Romans" as a resource for the liberation of humanity from the violent nexus between life and law. In this book, as well, humanity's task is to render the law **inoperative** (*TR*, 88–112). Agamben associates this with a notion that, like bare life, he adapts from Walter **Benjamin**, and which he opposes to sovereignty: divine violence. Here, Georges **Bataille's** notion of sovereignty becomes central to Agamben's project, as well.

The final instalment of the *Homo Sacer* series, *Il Regno e la gloria*, no longer focuses on sovereignty but on governmentality. If sovereignty is political–theological, the logic of governmentality is that of theological economy or *oikonomia* – specifically, of the economy of the Trinity through which God governs on earth. From Agamben's perspective, and in response to the arguments of some of his critics, the separation of powers thus did not free humanity from sovereignty. Rather, sovereignty operates in tandem with governmentality, and it is this double-sided power machine that the *Homo Sacer* series ultimately analyses.

SPECTACLE

Deborah Levitt

While the term spectacle appears in a number of works, including *Stanzas*, *The Coming Community*, *Homo Sacer* and *Profanations*, Agamben engages it most definitively in *Means Without End*. In order to grasp Agamben's deployment of this concept, it is helpful to understand its genesis in the work of Guy **Debord**, and the way that, for Agamben, it both names the current state of capitalism and points toward its "positive possibility": that is, the precise terms of its own imminent overcoming.

According to Debord, "[t]he spectacle corresponds to the historical moment at which the commodity completes its colonization of social life" (1995: 29). If the development of an earlier phase of capitalism was marked by the use-value of things being superseded by their exchange-value, and of relations between men that were thus mediated by things whose ideational auras and metaphysical shimmer occluded their status as crystallisations of human labor, "'the society of the spectacle' names a social relationship between people that is mediated by images" (1995: 12). As the commodity approaches pure idea, media as such expands in hitherto unfathomable ways and alienated consumption takes its place alongside alienated production as a social and economic demand. As Debord has it, in this society of the spectacle, "[a]ll that was once directly lived has become mere representation" (1995: 12).

In an essay which seeks to "collect Debord's inheritance today", Agamben defines the spectacle as "[t]he becoming-image of capital". "[T] his is", Agamben explains, translating Debord's maxims into his own terms, "nothing more than the commodity's last metamorphosis, in which exchange value has completely eclipsed use value and can now achieve the status of absolute and irresponsible sovereignty over life in its entirety" (*ME*, 76). In another essay in the same volume, "In This Exile", Agamben makes very clear that the terms he has used here – which relate the society of the spectacle to a relation between sovereignty and life – are not accidental, and that he sees spectacle as intimately bound with the exigencies of biopolitics. As capital becomes image, so too does intimate bodily experience, and the indetermination of public and private that is characteristic of the space of camp also characterises the body of the porn star. While it is the former that is Agamben's best-known figure, it is in fact the manner in which both insist in the same logic and structure that marks the originality of Agamben's thought most generally, and of his conception of spectacle in particular. But linking the development of the society of the spectacle to the ascendance of the modern biopolitical regime does not exhaust Agamben's extension of Debord's concept.

Agamben sees the possibility for a politics and community to come emerging not from a space outside the spectacle, but rather from an extension of its own expropriation of the language of human being. "Capitalism", he explains, "not only aimed at the expropriation of productive activity, but also, and above all, of the linguistic and communicative nature of human beings." The spectacle, according to Agamben, is the extreme form of the expropriation of communicativity, of the **common**.

> But this also means [he continues] that what we encounter in the spectacle is our very linguistic nature inverted. For the same reason, the spectacle still contains something like a positive possibility – and it is our task to use this positive possibility against it. (*ME*, 82–3)

Contemporary spectacular politics is this experience of a human language that is so alienated that what once appeared only in and as the content or truth of its propositions, now shows itself as language itself, as the fact of speaking. What remains is not to heal this alienation of communicativity, but to see it through to its own end without ends, without origin or destiny, without foundation or vocation. "Only those who will be able to carry [the spectacle and its expropriation of linguistic being] to completion . . . will become the first citizens of a community with neither presuppositions nor a state" (*ME*, 85).

SPINOZA, BARUCH

Justin Clemens

Baruch Spinoza (1632–77) is one of the great post-Cartesian philosophers of the seventeenth century. Of Portuguese–Jewish background, Spinoza was expelled from the Jewish community of Amsterdam for his heretical opinions regarding scripture, and made a living as a lens-grinder while working on his radical philosophical texts; his thinking made him notorious as "the atheist Jew of Voorburg". Agamben alludes to Spinoza throughout his work, usually regarding the problem of the articulation of ontology and **ethics**. Following Spinoza's *Ethics*, Agamben announces in *The Coming Community* that "*Taking-place, the communication of singularities in the attribute of extension, does not unite them in essence, but scatters them in existence*" (*CC*, 19); he later glosses Spinoza's remarks about the devil being the "weakest of creatures" in order to suggest that "Evil is only our inadequate reaction when faced with this demonic element" (*CC*, 31; see also *ME*, 129 on Spinoza's critique of "repentance"; *RA* on ethics as other than "guilt" and "responsibility"). If Spinoza's ontology and ethico-political thought continue to have a deep impact upon contemporary European philosophy – notably in the work of Gilles Deleuze and the Italian Autonomists – Agamben's own most interesting direct commentary hinges on a little-read work of Spinoza's, the *Compendium grammatices linguae hebraeae*, unfinished at the latter's death and published posthumously. The treatise is a study in Latin of the Hebrew language, in which "Spinoza illustrates the concept of immanent cause – that is, an action in which agent and patient are one and the same person – with the Hebrew categories of the active reflexive and the infinitive noun" (*RA*, 111). This short commentary exemplifies Agamben's practice, his attentiveness to "marginal" writings, to theses regarding the articulation of language and being, to the places at which such an articulation in-discriminates activity and passivity, where heterogeneous terms find their paradoxical nexus in an **enigma**.

STATE OF EXCEPTION

Alex Murray

The term "state of exception", which first appears in *Homo Sacer* and is greatly expanded in the book of that name, identifies the ways in which politics and law are completely intertwined. The relationship between law and politics has always understood the judiciary as maintaining autonomy yet, as Agamben suggests, the very idea of politics is about the possibility of the rule of law becoming suspended in the state of exception.

It is clear from the introduction to *Homo Sacer* that understanding the state of exception is of importance in moving beyond the "weakness" that had characterised Marxist (see **Marx**) and anarchist theories of the state. The central flaw in these approaches was the belief that a suspension of the power of the state was essential to its overcoming. The rule of law that protected the state was to be suspended in the "exceptional" time of revolution in order for a stateless society to emerge (*HS*, 12). The reality of the modern state is, as Benjamin suggested, that the exception has become the rule and that the extraordinary conditions of the state's overcoming are part of its regular function. The exceptional suspension of the rule of law happens so often that one cannot treat the state as a solid, impervious concept. What emerges, under Agamben's analysis, is that the state has routinely suspended its own rule of law to preserve the rule of law, and the traditional model of the state needs to be understood in these terms.

The centre of *State of Exception* is Agamben's intricate reconstruction of an esoteric debate between Walter **Benjamin** and Carl **Schmitt** on the place of extra-legal violence. Schmitt's *Political Theology* is important in both *Homo Sacer* and the *State of Exception*, being the text that defined the state of exception as intrinsically linked to the construction and exercise of **sovereignty**, with the sovereign "he who decides on the state of exception". For Agamben the exceptional nature of the sovereign act of suspending or altering the law has resulted in it remaining unconnected to the ordinary production of law while, paradoxically, becoming its centre. The fact that the sovereign exception is both within and outside the law means that it is both illegal as well as the epitome of the legal system: "The fact is that in both the right of resistance and the state of exception, what is ultimately at issue is the question of the juridical significance of a sphere of action that is itself extrajuridical" (*SE*, 11).

Agamben argues that Schmitt's theory of the state of exception in *Political Theology* was an esoteric response to Benjamin's 1921 essay, "Critique of Violence". In that essay Benjamin presented a model of violence (or power) that was able to challenge the dialectic between law-making and law-preserving violence, a violence beyond the law. This extra-legal violence is at the heart, Agamben, claims of Schmitt's sovereign exception; the pure violence of Benjamin's essay becomes transformed into the sovereign decision that neither "makes nor preserves law, but suspends it" (*SE*, 54). In that way Schmitt wanted to take Benjamin's idea of an extra-legal violence and return it to the law. The state of exception is thus, in a familiar Agambenian formulation, "included in the law through its very exclusion" (*SE*, 54).

In *State of Exception* Agamben provides a number of **examples**, such as the "military order" given by George W. Bush in November 2011 and the suspension of articles of the Weimar constitution pertaining to civil liberties by Hitler once he had taken power. These examples help to demonstrate the ways in which an extra-legal space is intrinsic in modern political systems, a space in which the suspension of law is presented as a means of its preservation. For Agamben this paradox is due to the entwined nature of law and politics and the only way in which politics can be redeemed is to "sever the nexus between violence and law":

to show law in its non-relation to life and life in its non-relation to law means to open a space between them for human action, which once claimed the name "politics". Politics has suffered a lasting eclipse because it has been contaminated by law. (*SE*, 88)

For Agamben there needs to be a means of redeeming (see **redemption**) an idea of life, a **form-of-life** that is not captured under any **apparatus** of power, which is not divided from itself. The state of exception, like **biopolitics**, is part of the structure of the political and must be rendered **inoperative**.

STUDY

Anton Schütz

"The law, if no longer practiced, but exclusively studied: this is the gate of justice": Walter **Benjamin** (1972 II/2: 437) thus summarises **Kafka**'s short prose pieces, "The New Advocate" and "The Truth about Sancho Panza". It is precisely this notion of study that accompanies, as a second aspect if not as a synonym, Agamben's notion of the **inoperative** (*inoperosità*, *désœuvrement*, unworking). The hero of the one-page story, "The New Advocate", is a lawyer, one Dr Bucephalus. (In Kafka's Prague, "doctor" was the academic title used by a lawyer.) Now an employee in a large law firm – a "bureau", as the German text reads – where he seems to be involved in "reading and turning the pages of old law books" (Kafka 2000: 154–5), he dedicates himself (in Benjamin's reading) to the study of law rather than to the practice of it. Dr Bucephalus had earlier served as Alexander the Great's warhorse. (Alexander's miraculous and legendary horse was effectively known as Bukephalas, "the oxen-head", in Antiquity.) The horse on whose back the archetypal conqueror defeated Darius and conquered India is identified with the *law* – law *practised*, by Bucephalus, back in the times when he was an active horse, carrying his murderous rider from victory to victory. Our times, on the contrary, "know of no Alexander" (Kafka 2000: 154–5); this is, for Agamben's Benjamin's Kafka, why the unworking of the law is within reach and why its study can replace its practice.

SUBJECT

Nicholas Heron

Closely following the advances of twentieth-century linguistics, Giorgio Agamben has, on many separate occasions, more or less provocatively defined the subject as an exclusively linguistic property. It is in the immediate self-presence of the individual instance of discourse alone, that the speaker, in appropriating for itself that complex mechanism which Émile **Benveniste** termed the "formal apparatus of enunciation", expressly designates itself as subject; hence, "it is literally true", in the linguist's striking formulation, "that the foundation of subjectivity is in the exercise of language" (Benveniste 1971: 226). But while the consequences of this linguistic institution of the subject for the structure of individual languages have, according to Agamben, long been analysed, the consequences for the individual living being – which, in this very special manner, wholly commits itself to speech – remain almost entirely to be thought.

For the individual living being, in Agamben's account, the simplest act of speech constitutes a paradoxical activity in which a subjectification takes place through full desubjectification alone. In order to be able to enter language, in order to be able to speak, the individual living being – the infant – must first make itself the *subject* of language; it must say "I". And yet, as Benveniste's studies on the nature of pronouns once again have shown, unlike other signs this "I" possesses no lexical meaning but refers solely to the instance of discourse in which it is uttered. It has no extra-linguistic value but serves a purely intra-linguistic function; it enables the passage from language to actual discourse and, together with this, language's reference to its own taking place. "Enunciation thus refers", Agamben writes, "not to the *text* of the statement [*l'enunciato*], but to its *taking place*, and the individual can put language in operation only on account of identifying itself in the event itself of saying, and not in what is said in it" (*RA*, 116; trans. modified). The inference here is clear: if the appearance of a subject coincides with the event of language and not with what is said in it, then the living individual accedes to the (non)place of language only on account of fully abolishing itself as an independent reality in order to identify itself in the pure insubstantiality of the linguistic "I". For the individual living being, the trial of subjectification, its becoming a speaking being, thus runs co-extensive with an equally total desubjectification: once in language in the strictest sense it cannot speak. It is neither inside nor outside language, but constitutes *the* outside *of* language, the pure fact that language exists. In Agamben, the articulation of the sphere of subjectivity thus coincides with an unprecedented interrogation of the Aristotelian definition of the human as a *zóon logon echón*, as a living being who has language. The human being is the speaking being, the living being who has language, only because it *can*, also and at the same time, *not have language*: that is, only because it preserves the **potentiality** for speech in speech as the happening in language of a subject

It is in *Remnants of Auschwitz* that Agamben pursues his most sustained reflection on the subject. Here, decisively, he unfolds his theory of the linguistic institution of subjectivity in a distinctly biopolitical (see **biopolitics**) key. According to Agamben's striking analysis, the structure of subjectivity coincides, point for point, with that of shame. Shame – the experience of being a subject – names not only the impossibility, in the human, for the living being and the speaking being ever to coincide fully, but also and at the same time, the impossibility for them ever to be wholly prised apart. This "inseparable division", which marks our non-coincidence with ourselves, is, according to Agamben, shame. But it is this alone which makes testimony possible. Only because the living being and the speaking being can never coincide; only because there insists, between them, an irreducible gap; only because the "imagined substance" of the "I" is uniquely positioned in this gap – only for this reason can there be testimony. The witness – the subject of testimony – is what remains in the breach opened between the twin currents of subjectification and desubjectification. And testimony, in which an impossibility of speaking comes to speech and in which a subject bears witness to a desubjectification, refutes, with its every word, the ultimate aim of Nazi biopolitics: the absolute separation of the living being from the speaking being; the production, in a human body, of a mute and, so to speak, "unwitnessable" **bare life** (*RA*, 156–7).

T

TAUBES, JACOB

Jessica Whyte

Jacob Taubes (1923–87), former Professor of Jewish Studies and Hermeneutics at the Free University of Berlin, is best known for his 1987 lecture series, posthumously published as *The Political Theology of Paul* (2004). In these lectures, given to fulfil a promise to Carl **Schmitt**, with whom Taubes debated late in life, Taubes identifies that proximity between Walter **Benjamin** and St **Paul** that will play a central role in Agamben's own later attempt to reconcile the **messianism** of these two figures (see *TR*, 138–45). The latter's only reference to Taubes in that work, however, is an (uncharacteristic) defence of Theodor **Adorno**, whose imperative to "contemplate all things as they would present themselves from the standpoint of redemption" is portrayed by Taubes as an aestheticisation of the messianic (*TR*, 35).

THRESHOLD

Daniel McLoughlin

The threshold is both a textual and conceptual device in Agamben's work. As a textual device, it first appears in *The Idea of Prose*, as the title of the first essay of the work. The subject of this threshold is the idea of **potentiality**, which then frames the fragments that follow, each of which has a thematic title, such as "The Idea of Work" or "The Idea of Matter". The threshold is also crucial to the structure of *Homo Sacer*, where each of the work's three sections concludes with a threshold that recapitulates the problem that it has addressed, and then opens up a new conceptual horizon; for example, the Threshold at the end of Part I, "The Logic of Sovereignty", draws on Walter Benjamin's *Critique of Violence* to illuminate the link between sovereignty and the sacred that Agamben then takes up in Part II, "*Homo Sacer*".

Agamben first thematises the threshold in *The Coming Community*, in a fragment titled "Outside", where he describes whatever being (see **whatever singularity**) as "the event of an outside" (*CC*, 66). It is through this limit that the belonging of an entity to a set, or its identity, is determined. This limit does not, however, open on to another determinate space: "The outside is not another space that resides beyond a determinate space, but rather, it is the passage, the exteriority that gives it access" (*CC*, 66). The outside at stake in whatever being is, then, the experience of an immanent transcendence; the delimitation and determination of belonging does not imply a being or an entity that transcends belonging, only the exposure of belonging as such, "the absolute non-thing experience of a pure exteriority" (*CC*, 65). It is this pure exteriority that Agamben describes as the threshold, noting that the term for outside in many European languages is expressed by a word that means "at the door", with *thyrathen* in Greek literally meaning "at the threshold". The threshold is not, then, "another thing with respect to the limit; it is, so to speak, the experience of the limit itself" (*CC*, 66).

The limit experience of the threshold is central to *Homo Sacer*'s analysis of **sovereignty**. Agamben's analysis of Carl **Schmitt**'s *Political Theology* emphasises his description of sovereignty as a "borderline concept" that pertains "to the outermost sphere". For Agamben, what is at issue in Schmitt's definition of sovereignty is "nothing less than the limit concept of the doctrine of law and the State, in which sovereignty borders (since every limit concept is always the limit between two concepts) on the sphere of life and becomes indistinguishable from it" (*HS*, 11). At stake in sovereignty, then, is the limit between law and its outside – law and anomie, fact and law, life and law – and it is this delimitation that determines the domain of law's rule over life and hence the belonging of entities to a legal order. The space "outside" the law is not another thing with regard to the law. Rather, the sovereign decision produces the outside by suspending the law and producing a juridical void. As such, the exception is the threshold of the law, an exteriority that is immanent to it.

Agamben's analysis of the threshold in *Homo Sacer* and *State of Exception* develops his account of the outside at stake in the limit of belonging threshold. Sovereignty, however, "does not limit itself to distinguishing what is inside from what is outside but instead traces a threshold (the state of exception) between the two" (*HS*, 19). The logic of the sovereign threshold is not one of opposition, but of **abandonment,** in which the outside is included through its exclusion. This means that the threshold is a space in which inside and outside enter into a zone of **indistinction**. For example, while the state of exception creates the distinction between law and non-law, the legal status of actions within the exception is radically undecideable, an "uncertain zone in which de facto proceedings, which are in themselves extra- or anti-juridical, pass over into law, and juridical norms blur with mere fact – that is, a threshold where fact and law seem to become undecidable" (*SE*, 29).

Agamben's political thought is, then, the attempt to rethink what is at stake in the threshold of law and political belonging. In *Homo Sacer*, the life that exists on the threshold of political belonging is a **bare life**, a singularity that is stripped of political belonging. By contrast, in *The Coming Community*, Agamben argues that the threshold of political community is the very zone from which the coming politics must be thought, as whatever being (see **whatever singularity**).

TRANSMISSION

Mathew Abbott

Agamben's concept of transmission plays a key role in his critique of modernity. In *The Man Without Content*, this critique takes the form of the claim that the Kantian (see **Kant**) understanding of the artwork as an object of aesthetic contemplation is indicative of the loss of those structures of tradition through which it "transmits at every moment, without residue, the system of beliefs and notions that has found expression in it" (*MC*, 107). Indeed the very idea of "culture" as an autonomous sphere is, for the young Agamben, a symptom of an alienated process in which artistic works are accumulated in a "sort of monstrous archive" (*MC*, 108) that has no bearing on the relation between **human** beings and their **historicity**.

Transmission is also important for Agamben's philosophy of **language**. For Agamben, language is beset by a constitutive structural problem: its inability to transmit (because it must always presuppose) the *factum loquendi*. This "incurable division between the thing to be transmitted and the act of transmission" (*Po*, 60) is the metaphysical ground – or "negative foundation" (*LD*, xiii) – of the cultural **nihilism** Agamben diagnoses.

Kafka is important for Agamben because of his commitment to working through these problems of transmission. Finding in his parables a renunciation of "the truth to be transmitted" for the sake of its "transmissability" (*Po*, 153), Agamben reads Kafka both as exemplifying the problem of nihilism and as outlining the possibility of its messianic (see **messianism**) completion. Thus Agamben displays little nostalgia for "a mythical-traditional system" (*MC*, 107), finding in the destruction of tradition the potential for art's achievement of its "original project" (*MC*, 115). Using an image from **Benjamin**, he poses this in terms of whether humanity could shake the burden of the cultural treasures that have been "piled up on [its] back" in order to "get its hands on them" (quoted in *Po*, 60). This would imply a transformed relation between humanity and tradition, such that the distinction between the tradition to be transmitted and transmission itself dissolves, and culture loses its alienated autonomy to make itself available for **use**.

(THE) UNFORGETTABLE

Arne De Boever

In *The Time That Remains*, Agamben adapts the notion of the unforgettable from Walter **Benjamin**'s essay on Fyodor Dostoyevski's *The Idiot*, where it does not refer to what cannot be forgotten but to "all in individual or collective **life** that is forgotten with each instant and to the infinite mass that will be forgotten by both" (*TR*, 39). "But", Agamben writes, "the shapeless chaos of the forgotten is neither inert nor ineffective": "To the contrary, it is at work within us with a force equal to that of the mass of conscious memories, but in a different way" (*TR*, 40). What makes this forgotten unforgettable is the ways in which it acts upon memory, thus remaining active within life. The **subject**'s relation to the unforgettable is therefore neither one of memory nor one of forgetfulness, but of becoming attentive to its seemingly inert and ineffective matter that in fact shapes the subject's individual and collective life. Agamben connects this to the messianic (see **messianism**) vocation that he finds in **Paul**: the way in which subjects become part of the Pauline community as what they are not, through a being-called as what they are not. It is thus the unforgettable that is the actual site of their belonging (*TR*, 41–2).

The unforgettable is also a key term in *Remnants of Auschwitz*, where it is associated with the **Muselmann**: "He is truly the *larva* that our memory cannot succeed in burying, the unforgettable with whom we must reckon" (*RA*, 81). Agamben's essay, "Philosophical **Archaeology**", published in *Signatura Rerum*, reveals that Agamben's methodology can be described as a becoming attentive to the unforgettable: to the *archē* that, analogously to the Freudian (see **Freud**) trauma, shapes the subject's life. The notion of the unforgettable is very close to Agamben's notion of "the **contemporary**" as it is developed in *What is an Apparatus?*:

The present is nothing other than this unlived element in everything that is lived. That which impedes access to the present is precisely the mass of what for some reason (its traumatic character, its excessive nearness) we have not managed to live. The attention to this "unlived" is the life of the contemporary. (*WA*, 51)

UNSAVABLE

Sergei Prozorov

The paradox of Agamben's understanding of salvation is that its object must be unsavable. Hence salvation does not concern the recovery of what was lost and the remembering of what was forgotten. In Agamben's argument, the lost and the forgotten do not demand to be found or remembered, but to remain such as they are, in their being-thus (*O*, 82; see also *TR*, 39–41, *Pr*, 35). This paradoxical logic is applied in Agamben's theorisation of community as devoid of all identitarian predicates and appropriating its own nullity, whose model is provided by the unbaptised children in **limbo**, who know of neither God nor sin and for this reason remain beyond both perdition and salvation: "The truly unsavable life is the one, in which there is nothing to save" (*CC*, 6). Lacking any discernible features, in terms of which it could strive for salvation, this life is only graspable in its whatever being (see **whatever singularity**), the sheer **facticity** of its existence. It is to this life, whose essence is only its existence and whose form is its own formlessness, that Agamben regularly refers as **happy** (see **happiness**).

The idea of the unsavable is addressed in most detail in *The Open* (81–92), in the discussion of **Benjamin**'s figure of the "saved night" as a reconfiguration of the relation between humanity (see **human**) and animality (see **animal**). This figure is interpreted by Agamben in terms of bringing to a standstill the anthropological machine that has historically articulated humanity and animality through a reciprocal exclusion. The effect of the **deactivation** of this machine is the emergence of a "supreme and unsavable figure of life" (*O*, 87), which is no longer human in so far as it does not strive to master its own animality, and no longer animal because it is not captivated by its environment. In **Heidegger**'s terms, this life is neither open nor closed to Being, but remains wholly outside it, going beyond the ontological difference. No longer seeking salvation through either the mastery of its nature or withdrawal into it, this life is thereby saved from salvation itself.

USE

Jessica Whyte

Agamben's earliest engagement with the problem of use occurs in an important section of *Stanzas*, originally published in 1972 under the title "*Il Dandy e il feticcio*" (The Dandy and the Fetish). Here, in the context of a discussion of **Marx**, we see the first incarnation of the insight – which will become increasingly important in Agamben's later works – that "the transfiguration of the commodity into *enchanted object* is the sign that the exchange value is already beginning to eclipse the use value" (*S*, 38). While this early account identifies an erosion of the possibility of use, it is none the less oriented to overcoming nostalgia for use value, and to challenging its underlying utilitarian presuppositions. Agamben's earliest account of use is concerned to examine the possibility of a new relation to things that consists neither in a utilitarian conception of use nor in the logic of exchange.

In line with this, his later works locate this possibility within the extension of commodification, in the very destruction of natural use through the reign of exchange value. Agamben, like Guy **Debord**, Walter **Benjamin** and Theodor **Adorno**, believes that the extension of commodification ultimately empties out what Marx termed the "use value" of commodities, leaving in place empty forms, freed from the need to be useful and thus available for a new, non-utilitarian, use. As the use values of commodities are eroded, Agamben suggests, consumer society produces an absolute impossibility of using things, which face us as spectacular objects, looking out at us as if from a museum. In *Profanations*, he locates the source of the unhappiness he sees in consumer society in the fact that its inhabitants "consume objects that have incorporated within themselves their own inability to be used" (*Pr*, 83).

What does it mean to claim that things can no longer be used? In Agamben's formulation, "use" (like "meaning", "nature" and "experience") designates a supposedly originary way of life that is bound to its place by traditional authority or the forces of nature; that which is *used* is subject to a "genetic inscription within a given sphere", its use dictated by its sense and its necessary relation to an end (*Pr*, 86). The generalised impossibility of use that Agamben identifies is a product of the breakdown of any natural relation between object and function, and of a shift from a form of consumption motivated by functionality to one in which people buy things as fetish objects. If a naturalised use serves to fix things within a particular sphere, to tie them to an end, and thus to enmesh us in instrumental subject–object relations, then it is in the eclipse of use, in the emptying of substance, that Agamben believes we may locate a non-utilitarian relation to the world, in which, as Benjamin writes in "Paris, Capital of the Nineteenth Century", "things are freed from the drudgery of being useful." This, in turn, is the condition of possibility of a politics without ends. While Agamben defines sacrifice as a mechanism that "removes things, places, animals, or people from common use and transfers them to a separate sphere" (*Pr*, 74), our ability to realise the possibility of a new use relies on a particular form of *praxis* that he terms profanation, which restores things to free use.

Agamben's formulation of use signifies a rejection both of property and of right. These come together, in *The Time That Remains*, in the Franciscan order, which refused all forms of property and right in favour of what it termed a *usus pauper*, a restricted "use without right" (*TR*, 27). In such a use without legal authorisation, Agamben sees the possibility of a form of subtraction from law, rather than an open conflict with it. This recalls his debt to **Paul**, who framed the nullification of substantive vocations introduced by the messianic vocation as a form of use, exhorting the Corinthians: "Art thou called being a slave? care not for it: but if thou mayest be made free, use it rather" (I Cor. 7:17–22). "Use", Agamben suggests, is the very definition Paul gives of the messianic life that follows this nullification (*TR*, 26). While the substance of this reading of Paul is derived from Heidegger's 1921 lecture course on the "Characteristics of Early Christian Life Experience", Agamben none the less utilises the Pauline conception of use in opposition to Heidegger's "appropriation". For Agamben, the messianic subject cannot authentically seize hold of itself but is limited to making use of its nullified identity.

The mobilisation of use against right also plays an important role in Agamben's account of the new form of singularity without identity that he terms "whatever being". In *The Coming Community*, Agamben frames the non-identitarian singularity that he sees as central to a politics and a form of community that could escape the hold of the state as "a new use of the self" (*CC*, 28–9). The formulation of a singularity that "makes use" of itself, rather than being bound within a naturalised and/or politicised identity, is contrasted to a substantive identity that could be represented and granted juridical rights.

VOCATION

Yoni Molad

Vocation – more specifically, the lack of a vocation for human beings as such – is for Agamben a fundamental anthropological and ethical definition of human being, and operates as the foundation for his political philosophy. The idea is often explored through artworks and historical examples, as a leitmotif running through the different figures explored in *Stanzas*, in the repeated discussion of Klee and Dürer's paintings (*The Man Without Content*), and the end of *The Open* where we are left to contemplate the idea of the workless animal in Titian's paintings.

In *The Coming Community* Agamben explains that it is only because human beings lack a vocation that ethics is possible; otherwise ethics would be determined in advance. The idea first receives its explicit political weight in *Language and Death*, where the attempt to cover over and regulate the lack of foundation for human action is revealed as the meaning of sacrifice. The anthropological basis for Agamben's understanding of humanity becomes explicit in *The Idea of Prose*, in which lack of vocation is analysed in relation to the **infancy** in which humans dwell, and like the axolotl, are revealed as infant apes who acquired reproductive organs prior to maturation and thus remain unspecialised, remaining open to a world, by being suspended in neotenic totipotency. In the same book the contemporaneity of the idea is discussed through the concept of **nihilism** in which our epoch, as the epoch that does not wish to be an epoch, harbours an opportunity to resist epochality as such and inhabit our lack of vocation politically and aesthetically.

The fullest exposition of the term is taken up in *The Time That Remains* through a discussion of the Pauline (see **Paul**) term, *Kletos* (calling), and its subsequent taking up by Luther and Max Weber. Here Agamben defines the messianic (see **messianism**) vocation, and hence messianic life is general as a life lived under the *revocation of all vocation*, opening up a space for a free **use** of, rather than appropriation of, identities, social functions, faculties and social relations. In the essay "The Work of Man", the absence of a vocation or work for the human as such is treated through an analysis of the original inquiry undertaken by **Aristotle** and developed by Aquinas and **Dante** amongst others. In this essay the political implications become clear as Agamben attempts to think what it would mean to have a politics that "is equal to the absence of a work of man" without repeating the Aristotelian and Scholastic gestures of taking this lack of vocation as a task or a scandal to be overcome. Agamben's reflections on **potentiality** are taken up once again in a discussion of Dante, whose formulations provide a foundation for understanding community, modelled on the idea of the intellect, as the permanent articulation of potentiality and worklessness that "exposes and contains in itself the possibility of its own not existing, of its own inactivity" (Agamben 2007: 10). In this way, lack of vocation is set firmly in a place of crucial importance alongside **nihilism**, potentiality and worklessness as a fundamental political concept.

VOICE

Daniel McLoughlin

After the publication of *Infancy and History* in 1978, Agamben worked on a project titled *The Human Voice*, which asked "is there a human voice, a voice that is the voice of man as the chirp of a cricket or the bray is the voice of the donkey? And, if it exists, is this voice language?" (*IH*, 3–4). Although this work remained "stubbornly unwritten", this problem none the less appears at the centre of *Language and Death*, which casts the human voice as the model through which Western culture thinks the relation between nature and culture, the living being and language. While the term disappears in his later, explicitly political works, this is because Agamben identifies the same relation involved in **sovereignty**, and the Voice comes to be subsumed under this term.

Drawing on the grammarian Guanilo in his debate with Anselm, Agamben argues that human voice, stripped of signification (*logos*), is qualitatively different from the animal voice or *phone*. When confronted with a foreign language, we do not hear "mere meaningless sound"; while we may not understand the meaning of the sounds we hear, we are none the less aware that they have meaning. The human voice does not then indicate the immediacy of animal *phone*, but the **potentiality** for language (**communicability**), and Agamben marks this difference by capitalising it as the Voice. For the metaphysical tradition, then, to have *logos* is to have the immediacy of the voice negated and replaced by the potentiality for language; as such, while the animal voice is placed at the origin of language, "it is also true that this voice is, from the beginning, conceived of as removed" (*LD*, 39).

Language and Death is then a critique of the negativity of the Voice as the metaphysical articulation of the originary dimension of language. The distinction between *phone* and *logos* was, for the Ancient grammarians, one between the "confused voice" of animals and the "articulated" voice of the human, and it was the *gramma* or letter that effected this articulation. The letter then exists in the moat between the living being and language, but only as the negativity that divides them from one another, and in this light, Agamben criticises Jacques **Derrida**'s grammatology as returning philosophy to its originary negativity. He also links the Voice to the philosophical thematisation of human mortality. In **Hegel**'s *Jenenser Realphilosophie* I and II, the animal finds its voice in violent death, expressing itself as removed, and language, which is the voice of consciousness, is an articulated animal voice; in **Heidegger**'s *Being and Time*, Agamben argues that the Voice appears in the "call of conscience", which is a mute foundation upon which *Dasein* can authentically think death. By contrast, the stake of Agamben's linguistic thought is that the potentiality for language can be thought beyond the negative and ineffable foundation, which means thinking language without the Voice: "only if the human voice is not simply death, but has never existed . . . is it possible for man to experience a language that is not marked by negativity and death" (*LD*, 95).

WALSER, ROBERT

Jessica Whyte

"We can read much by Robert Walser, but nothing about him," Walter **Benjamin** wrote in 1929 (Benjamin 1999a: 257). Born in Switzerland, Walser (1878–1956), who was a favourite author of Franz **Kafka**, described himself as "a kind of artisan novelist . . . a writer who goes to work with a lathe" (Walser 2001: x). While he found some literary success in his lifetime, Walser lived as a wanderer and, in 1905, trained as a servant before working briefly as a butler. In 1933, after a suicide attempt saw him diagnosed (or misdiagnosed) with schizophrenia, he entered the mental asylum where he was to spend the rest of his life. When asked by a visitor why he had ceased to write, he replied: "I'm not here to write, I'm here to be mad" (Walser 2001: title page). Benjamin's short essay on Walser describes his characters as "figures who have left madness behind them" (Benjamin 1929: 259). It is this, Benjamin suggests, that gives them their "heartrending, inhuman superficiality" (Benjamin 1929: 259). Walser's characters, Benjamin writes, are like those in a fairytale, who "emerge from the madness of myth" – but whereas the characters in fairytales are "still struggling to free themselves from their sufferings", Walser begins where the fairytale ends. It is from such a perspective that Agamben approaches Walser, to whom he dedicated *The Coming Community*. In that work, Walser's characters, in their very "nullity", are cast as exemplars of that purely profane, unsaveable life that Agamben terms "simply human life" (*CC*, 7). Like the inhabitants of **limbo**, Walser's characters, he suggests, are irreparably astray in "a region that is beyond perdition and salvation" (*CC*, 6). In these lives in which there is nothing to save, Agamben sees "the most radical objection that has ever been levied against the very idea of redemption" (*CC*, 6).

WARBURG, ABY

Alex Murray

Aby Warburg (1866–1929), a German **art** historian, provides several important contexts for Agamben's work. While Warburg may not appear to hold the central place of writers such as **Benjamin** and **Heidegger**, his exploration of the image and its relationship to history was essential in Agamben's movement from his early, more conventional approach to the philosophy of art in his first book, *The Man Without Content*. In that book Agamben attempted to posit a break between modern and earlier forms of art around the figure of the artist and his relation to the work. Warburg's approach to art was far more expansive and structural, with his work attempting to diagnose what he saw as the "schizophrenic" nature of Western culture. *Stanzas* was researched partly in 1975 at the Warburg Institute in London, and later (1983) Agamben would reflect on the value that Warburg's work held: "what continues to appear as relevant in his work is the decisive gesture with which he withdraws the artwork (and also the image) from the study of the artist's conscious and unconscious structures" (*Po*, 102). For Warburg the image was able to transcend the particular historical context in which it was produced and allowed us to see a continuity, or a movement between images. In Warburg's most elaborate demonstration of this, the Mnemosyne, he would juxtapose images from across a number of historical periods to allow a trace to emerge. This method of isolating the image allowed Agamben to see a theory of art that was similar to Benjamin's understanding of history and **Benveniste**'s work on language. In doing so, Agamben's critical "**archaeological**" method developed, which was to be the basis of his work in his better-known writings.

In addition to helping Agamben formulate his method, Warburg was also important in Agamben's work on cinema. Agamben used Warburg's notion of the image as a way of tying together disparate images in order to liberate them, animating them across temporal periods in a similar fashion to cinema's liberation of the image. In effect, Warburg's theory of the image turns the history of art into one long movie reel. In "Notes on Gesture", Agamben highlights the ways in which Warburg's exploration of the image tied into the idea of **gesture**. While gesture was tied to forms of technological and biopolitical (see **biopolitics**) capture of the body, such as Tourette's attempt to measure the gait, it also marked the point at which the body became liberated from the idea of unity and uniformity. So what we see in Warburg's work on the image is an attempt to free the image, like cinema returning it to the "homeland of gesture" (*ME*, 55).

Ultimately Warburg bequeathed to Agamben the direction of what the latter would term, in an essay from the 1970s, "The Nameless Science": a method for thinking beyond the "schizophrenic" split that lay at the heart of Western culture. As Agamben stated:

the greatest lesson of Warburg's teaching may well be that the image is the place in which the subject strips itself of the mythical, psychosomatic character given to it in the presence of an equally mythical object, by a theory of knowledge that is in truth simply disguised metaphysics. (*ME*, 102)

This sense, in which the metaphysical nature of the subject is eroded, positively "desubjectivised", can be seen as analogous to Agamben's theme of inoperativity (see **inoperative**), that rendering inert of the systems and structures that underpin not just metaphysics, but also the juridical, political and ethical structures that dominate Western thought.

WHATEVER SINGULARITY

Yoni Molad

A whatever singularity is the figure the human being takes in the **coming community**, the state of the world Agamben describes as having survived **nihilism**, and realised the end of both **history** and the state. As such, whatever singularity is both a descriptive term, articulating the condition of humanity as a consequence of the deployment of spectacular capitalism on a global scale, and resembling most, of any classic social class, the contemporary planetary petty bourgeoisie, and also a prescriptive term, used to describe the ideal image of humanity. In this way, the term arguably serves as Agamben's most developed notion of the good life based on a **politics** of **language**. This conception of politics and community is developed to counteract what Agamben sees as the reactionary retreat to identity politics, or a politics based on biology, and the consequence of the exhaustion of historical revolutionary subjects which presuppose a unified substantial basis for community, be they bourgeois, post-colonial or workerist.

Agamben translates the Latin *Quodlibet ens* as *whatever being, being such that it always matters*, rather than the usual translation of *quodlibet* as "whatever, it does not matter which", thus offering a more ambiguous and reflexive conception of indifference. The indifference that pertains to the whatever singularity is its *being such that it is*, and not its being in relation to a particular predicate or property (Frenchness, homosexuality, being communist).

In mathematics, a singularity refers to a point in which a given mathematical object is not defined, or defies the expectations of an equation. For Agamben, a whatever singularity is a being that cannot be defined by one of its properties and exists in a state of ontological ambivalence in relation to predicates, in such a way that none of its predicates constitutes difference. In astronomy, a singularity refers to the point in the centre of a black hole in which gravitational forces cause matter to have infinite density and infinitesimal volume, and space and time become infinitely distorted. Like the centre of a black hole, the whatever singularity literally has no place, but rather *takes place*.

These scientific understandings of singularity are distinct from the term's more common meaning as standing out or being distinct from other things as a consequence of uniqueness. Rather than taking up this idea to develop a standard theory of individualism, Agamben emphasises the commonality of singularities, precisely due to their being "whatever, and in this way, taking after **Spinoza**, having an inessential commonality, 'a commonality that in no way concerns an essence'" (*CC*, 18): that is, precisely in their exhibiting belonging as such, and not a belonging to a particular thing, group, entity and so on. This idea is elucidated through Agamben's discussion of the **example**, the condition of being in **limbo**, and a reflection on **halos**. Most importantly, a whatever singularity offers a foundation for Agamben's understanding of **love**. A whatever singularity has no defined place, and its coming into being is not an event accomplished once and for all, but instead is understood as a perpetual *taking place*, "an infinite series of modal oscillations" (*CC*, 19). For Agamben, the whatever singularity exists in a zone of indistinction between the universal and the particular, nature and culture, proper and improper, image and thing, animal and human. It exists between potentiality and act, between having and not having, between being and not being. It is a singularity with an emptiness, an empty place that takes place as a finitude that is indeterminable according to a concept; a finitude that is not the result of wilful psychological action. A whatever singularity is a being that, like a beloved, is loved for all its properties without any of those properties constituting what it is, but only in so far as they *take place*.

In so far as it exists as a *taking place*, the whatever singularity exists as a being-in-language, exists as being-named. It is brought to life by **language**, by being called, as a **name**, without predication. The whatever singularities relate to language not as something to communicate properties or denote objects, but as an expropriating force that opens up a nihilistic space in which, like the poets Pessoa or **Caproni**, they bypass their psychological life, abandon any recognisable and identifiable figure, and enter through being in language, a realm of indistinction between human and animal, sense and nonsense, self and other, in which desubjectivation takes place. This desubjectivation is not a loss to be mourned, which would imply that the subject becomes an object in need of reappropriation, but instead, language, and the life lived within its taking place, itself becomes "the laboratory in which all known figures are undone and new, parahuman or semidivine creatures emerge" (*EP*, 64).

The whatever singularity is thus only understood, Agamben explains after discussing the paradoxes of intentionality and the aporias of linguistic being (*CC*, 74), as part of a theory of ideas. It can only be exposed as being-in-language, and can only be grasped through an anaphoric movement – the kind of anaphora that does not refer to a previous term as a presupposition but exposes the term *as such*: that is to say, it does not bring to light that which was behind, underlying or supporting, but simply demonstrates a relationship within language itself, the taking place of the term in language. The properties and qualities of whatever singularity are not qualifications of a substance, but an exposure of exteriority. Whatever singularity is determined through the totality of its possibilities but in such a way as it exists *outside of being*. This outside is not an-other place but rather a threshold or exteriority, which like a human **face** exhibits a limit or passage to a commonality and to the external world precisely because of its singularity and exemplarity (*CC*, 68). It is the outside of being, like the post-coital scenario in the Titian painting Agamben discusses – "In their fulfillment, the lovers who have lost their mystery contemplate a human nature rendered perfectly inoperative" (*O*, 87) – and thus beyond any distinction between being and beings, propriety or impropriety, at the **threshold** of a new figure of humanity.

The Latin *quodlibet*, an indefinite pronoun in English, contains a reference to will and love, *libet*, and so "whatever being has an original relationship to desire" (*CC*, 1), which Agamben refers to as the most simple and human thing (*Pr*, 53) and yet the hardest to communicate. Desire is always experienced as a will and as an image. Its existence in language becomes a problem because "to communicate one's desires to someone without images is brutal. To communicate one's images without one's desires is tedious" (*Pr*, 53); it is the communication of both together that remains the hardest. It is in the empty space between communication and image that the desire of whatever singularity finds its (non-)place. For this reason, whatever singularity, as a being of desiring images, gains political importance in the society of the **spectacle**. Being a being that exists in a direct way to its own **image**, that exists as a communication of its own image, is what Agamben calls a *special being* (*Pr*, 55–60), a being that presents and communicates itself without assuming a personal identity, that communicates its own communicability. It is only under conditions of spectacular capitalism that this communicability is expropriated (see **expropriation**), meaning it "becomes separated from itself and is constituted in an autonomous sphere: "The special is transformed into spectacle" (*Pr*, 60).

This process is what also, in characteristic fashion for Agamben, leaves open a space for its own overcoming through **profanation**. The spectacle, as seen most clearly in advertising, which awaited photography and film to fulfill its destiny, technologises the image of the **human** being, and not only its body (*CC*, 47–50). This body appears to us as a simulacrum, or as an idea: a "resemblance without an archetype". A whatever singularity is precisely, like the human face, this resemblance without archetype, which, separated from "biological destiny and individual biography", can only be grasped as an idea of a body, which like all ideas, finds its place in the empty gap between communication and imagination; the place of desire, the very same space as the taking place of **language**; the *experimentum linguae* as the foundation of an immaterial and insubstantial communicability; the experience of belonging *as such*. In this way, advertising and **pornography** reveal to us the nature of whatever singularity in an inverted spectacular form awaiting profanation.

This profanation, this bringing into being of real whatever singularities, becomes political when, rather than revealing an identity or a substantial being, whatever singularities no longer demand anything from history or the state and show themselves as belonging to a community without any identity, desiring being-in-language, something that Agamben believes occurred during the events of what he refers to as the Chinese May: the demonstrations and subsequent massacre at Tiananmen Square in 1989. What was unique to such an event, he thinks, correctly or not, was that "regardless of whether those who were in that square were actually aware of it" (*ME*, 88), what occurred was a confrontation between the state and a community that presented itself as not demanding anything, and yet appeared as a form of being in common: a being-in-common that no longer demands recognition or belonging from a state or an ossified tradition, but manifests itself as being-in-common as such (*ME*) and thus inaugurates a new era of politics; a struggle waged between the exposure of the condition of belonging as such against the inscription of belonging into a particularity or a universality, between desire and spectacle, the struggle between humanity and the state.

If the poet, by inhabiting language as a medium, is the one who, through desubjectivation, "in the word, produces life" (*EP*, 93), the whatever singularities are those who, by the same process, in politics, make the world.

WITNESSING

Jason Maxwell

Agamben's meditations on witnessing occur during *Remnants of Auschwitz*'s exploration of life in the concentration **camp**. Addressing sceptics who have called into question the very idea that mass exterminations took place there, Agamben devises an elaborate response that accounts for the existence of that which has left little or no physical evidence. Those who doubt that murders occurred within the confines of the camps base their claims on the lack of first-hand witnesses to these atrocities. Obviously, such first-hand witnesses are fundamentally impossible to locate, since only those who perished under the harsh treatment of the SS fully experienced these horrors of the camp. Meanwhile, those who survived cannot be considered "true" witnesses because they are exceptions to the rule, consisting of the small minority who were not executed. In other words, their survival disqualifies them from serving as witnesses because, unlike the *Muselmann*, they did not "touch bottom". Borrowing from the writing of camp survivor, Primo **Levi**, Agamben acknowledges that, at some level, there is an "impossibility of bearing witness" (*RA*, 34).

How does Agamben escape this seemingly unavoidable trap? For him, the witness should not be conceived of as a single individual but instead as a two-part structure comprising both *Muselmann* and survivor, which, "like the tutor and the incapable person and the creator and his material, are inseparable; their unity-difference alone constitutes testimony" (*RA*, 150). More specifically, the survivor testifies to the existence of the *Muselmann* and the fact that he constitutes the true witness who is inherently incapable of testifying directly. He attests to the impossibility of a true witness and thereby brings this impossibility into the realm of possibility: "the survivor bears witness not to the gas chambers or to Auschwitz but to the *Muselmann*" (*RA*, 164). For Agamben, this form of testimony means that the existence of Auschwitz "is absolutely and irrefutably proven", since the lack of physical evidence of the camp, rather than creating scepticism, actually strengthens his position (*RA*, 164).

WITTGENSTEIN, LUDWIG

Thanos Zartaloudis

The commentary and critique of Wittgenstein's proposition 6.44 of the *Tractatus* on the relationship between essence and existence, *quid est* and *quod est*, is the key direct reference in Agamben's work to Wittgenstein's, occurring at the end of *The Coming Community*. This is one of Agamben's most dense and important texts and it could even be said that it is an elegant summary of key elements of his thought more generally. Suffice it to suggest, here, that Agamben in a certain way responds to Wittgenstein's propositions on transcendence and **language** in a modest and yet Copernican way. In another work Agamben puts it in the following way: "Silence then is not simply a suspension of discourse, but silence of the word itself, the becoming visible of the word: the idea of language" (*IP*, 113). In this sense key concepts of Agamben's work, like the "idea of **prose**", the "taking place of language", the "**irreparable**" (the being without remedy to the way of being of things in the world), are a response to the "bitterest" proposition of the *Tractatus*: "What is properly divine is that the world does not reveal God" (*CC*: 91). References to Wittgenstein and his understanding of language and linguistics can be located in other works of Agamben's, the most crucial of which are contained in the volume *Potentialities* (*Po*: Part I).

$$\boxed{\text{Z}}$$

ZOĒ

Alex Murray

The term *zoē* is central in Agamben's formulation of **bare life** and his critique of the political (see **politics**) tradition. Turning to **Aristotle** at the beginning of *Homo Sacer*, Agamben observes that the Greeks had two terms for "life": *zoē* and *bios*. *Zoē* is defined as "the simple fact of living common all living beings (animal, men, or gods)" (*HS*, 1). If *bios* is the qualified life, the "form or way of living proper to an individual or group", then it is *zoē* against or in relation to which the political is measured. The very split or division between *zoē* and *bios* produces bare life: that is, the attempt to control or manage "life". So, for Agamben, the split between these two forms of life at the origin of the political is crucial in that politics is always the politicisation of life, the attempt to create "forms of life". Importantly, *zoē* has no plural; it is a singular idea of life before and beyond all division. The exclusion of this "simple, natural life" from the *polis* results in it appearing regularly in Agamben's work, but without greater elaboration. Agamben's work is hardly an attempt to advocate a "return" to an idea of *zoē*, but in recognising its place and the manifestation its exclusion from the *polis* has had he explores the possibility of a **form-of-life** as that which takes us beyond the divisive **apparatuses** of control and capture that still dominate both life and politics.

Bibliography

**WORKS OF GIORGIO AGAMBEN WITH
ABBREVIATIONS AS THEY APPEAR IN TEXT**

(*CC*) *The Coming Community*. Trans. Michael Hardt. Minneapolis: University of Minnesota Press, 1993.

(*EP*) *The End of the Poem: Studies in Poetics*. Trans. Daniel Heller-Roazen. Stanford: Stanford University Press, 1999.

(*HS*) *Homo Sacer: Sovereign Power and Bare Life*. Trans. Daniel Heller-Roazen. Stanford: Stanford University Press, 1998.

(*IH*) *Infancy and History: The Destruction of Experience*. Trans. Liz Heron. London: Verso, 1993.

(*IP*) *The Idea of Prose*. Trans. Michael Sullivan and Sam Whitsitt. New York: State University of New York Press, 1995.

(*LD*) *Language and Death: The Place of Negativity*. Trans. Karen Pinkus with Michael Hardt. Minneapolis: University of Minnesota Press, 1991.

(*MC*) *The Man Without Content*. Trans. Georgia Albert. Stanford: Stanford University Press, 1999.

(*ME*) *Means Without End: Notes on Politics*. Trans. Vincenzo Binetti and Cesare Casarino. Minneapolis: University of Minnesota Press, 2000.

(*O*) *The Open: Man and Animal*. Trans. Kevin Attell. Stanford: Stanford University Press, 2004.

(*Po*) *Potentialities: Collected Essays in Philosophy*. Trans. and ed. Daniel Heller-Roazen. Stanford: Stanford University Press, 1999.

(*Pr*) *Profanations*. Trans. Jeff Fort. New York: Zone, 2007.

(*RA*) *Remnants of Auschwitz: The Witness and the Archive*. Trans. Daniel Heller-Roazen. New York: Zone, 1999.

(*S*) *Stanzas: Word and Phantasm in Western Culture*. Trans. Ronald L. Martinez. Minneapolis: University of Minnesota Press, 1993.

(*SE*) *State of Exception*. Trans. Kevin Attell. Chicago: University of Chicago Press, 2005.

(*ST*) *The Signature of All Things: On Method*. Trans. Luca D'Isanto with Kevin Attell. New York: Zone, 2009.

(*TR*) *The Time That Remains: A Commentary on the Letter to the Romans.* Trans. Patricia Daly. Stanford: Stanford University Press, 2005.

(*WA*) *What is an Apparatus? And Other Essays.* Trans. David Kishik and Stefan Pedatella. Stanford: Stanford University Press, 2009.

WORKS CITED

The following is a list of all the books quoted from in the dictionary, above and beyond those that appear in the list of Agamben's major book-length publications in English, given above. They include occasional essays by Agamben and Italian versions of his work, either untranslated or translated, in the case where contributors have chosen to provide their own translation. You will also find references to works cited other than those of Agamben.

Agamben, G. (2009) *Nudità*. Rome: Nottetempo.

—(2008) *Signatura rerum. Sul metodo*. Turin: Bollati Boringhieri.

—(2008a) "K". In *The Work of Giorgio Agamben: Law, Literature, Life*. Ed. Justin Clemens, Nicholas Heron and Alex Murray. Edinburgh: Edinburgh University Press.

—(2007) *Il Regno e la gloria. Per una genealogia teologica dell'economia e del governo*. Vicenza: Neri Pozza.

—(2007a) *Ninfe*. Turin: Bollati Boringhieri.

—(2007b) "The Work of Man". Trans Kevin Attell. In *Giorgio Agamben: Sovereignty and Life*. Ed. Matthew Calarco and Steven De Caroli. Stanford: Stanford University Press.

—(2006) *Che cos'è un dispositivo?* Rome: Nottetempo.

—(2005) "Movement", seminar held in Padua at the Nomad University on the theme of war and democracy, January. Transcribed and trans. Arianna Bove. http://www.generation-online.org/p/fpagamben 3.htm.

—(2004) *Image et mémoire*. Paris: Desclée de Brouwer.

—(2004a) "Difference and Repetition: On Guy Debord's Films". In *Guy Debord and the Situationist International: Texts and Documents*. Ed. Tom McDonough. Cambridge, MA: October/MIT Press.

—(2002) *L'Aperto. L'Uomo e l'animale*. Turin: Bollati Boringhieri.

—(2001) *La Comunità che viene* (new edition with a new apostil by the author). Turin: Bollati Boringhieri.

—(1998) *Quel che resta di Auschwitz. L'Archivio e il testimone*. Turin: Bollati Boringhieri.

Arendt, H. (1973) *The Origins of Totalitarianism*. New York: Harcourt, Brace & World.

—(1958) *The Human Condition*. Chicago: University of Chicago Press.

Baugh A. C. and Cable T. (1993) *A History of the English Language*. London: Routledge.

Benjamin, W. (2003) "On the Concept of History". In *Selected Writings, Volume 4, 1938–1940*. Ed. Howard Eiland and Michael W. Jennings, trans. Harry Zohn. Cambridge, MA: Harvard University Press, 389–400.

—(2002) "Theological-Political Fragment". In *Selected Writings, Volume 3, 1935–1938*. Ed. Howard Eiland and Michael W. Jennings, trans. Edmund Jephcott. Cambridge, MA: Harvard University Press.

—(1999a) "Robert Walser". In *Walter Benjamin: Selected Writings, Volume 2*. Ed. Howard Eiland and Michael W. Jennings. Cambridge, MA: Harvard University Press.

—(1999b) "Theses on the Philosophy of History". In *Illuminations*. Ed. Hannah Arendt. London: Pimlico.

—(1986) *Reflections: Essays, Aphorisms, Autobiographical Writings*. Ed. Peter Demetz. New York: Schocken.

—(1972–) *Gesammelte Schriften*, 7 vols. Ed. Rolf Tiedemann and Hermann Schweppenhauser, with the collaboration of Theodor W. Adorno and Gershom Scholem. Frankfurt am Main: Surhrkamp.

Benveniste, E. (1971) *Problems in General Linguistics*. Trans. M. E. Meek. Florida: University of Miami Press.

Debord, G. (1995) *The Society of the Spectacle*. Trans. Donald Nicholson-Smith. New York: Zone.

Deleuze, G. (2006) *Foucault*. Trans. Sean Hand. London: Continuum.

—(1994) *Difference and Repetition*. Trans. Paul Patton. New York: Columbia.

—(1992) "What is a *Dispositif?*" In *Michel Foucault, Philosopher*. Trans. Timothy J. Armstrong. London: Harvester Wheatsheaf.

Deleuze, G. and Guattari, F. (1987) *A Thousand Plateaus: Capitalism and Schizophrenia*. Trans. Brian Massumi. Minneapolis: University of Minnesota Press.

Derrida, Jacques (2002) "Force of Law: The Mystical Foundation of Authority". In *Acts of Religion*. Ed. Gil Anidjar. New York: Routledge.

Foucault, M. (2002) *The Order of Things*. London: Routledge.

—(1978) *The Will to Knowledge. The History of Sexuality*, vol. 1. Trans. Robert Hurley. London: Penguin.

—(1976) *Histoire de la sexualité, 1: La Volonté de savoir*. Paris: Gallimard.

Freud, S. (2001) *Three Essays on the Theory of Sexuality* [1905]. In *The Complete Psychological Works of Sigmund Freud, VII*. Ed. James Strachey. London: Penguin.

Geulen, E. (2005) *Giorgio Agamben zur Einführung*. Hamburg: Junius.

Heidegger, M. (1995) *The Fundamental Concepts of Metaphysics*. Trans. William McNeill and Nicholas Walker. Bloomington: Indiana University Press.

—(1993) "Letter on Humanism" [1947]. *Basic Writings*. Ed. David Farrell Krell. San Francisco: HarperCollins.

Kafka, Franz (1980) "In the Penal Settlement". In *Metamorphosis and Other Stories*. Harmondsworth: Penguin.

—(2000) *Metamorphosis and Other Stories*. London: Penguin, pp. 154–5.

Khayati, Mustapha (2004) "Captive Words (Preface to a Situationist Dictionary)". In *Guy Debord and the Situationist International: Texts and Documents*. Ed. Tom McDonogh. Cambridge, MA: MIT Press, pp. 173–80.

Levi, Primo (1999) *The Drowned and the Saved*. Trans. Raymond Rosenthal. London: Abacus.

Lévi-Strauss, Claude (1987) *Introduction to the Work of Marcel Mauss*. Trans. Felicity Baker. London: Routledge & Kegan Paul.

Marx, Karl (1843) "On the Jewish Question". http://www.marxists. org/archive/marx/works/1844/jewish-question/.

—(1990) *Capital: A Critique of Political Economy*, vol. 1. Trans. Ben Fowkes. London: Penguin Classics.

Marx, Karl and Engels, Friedrich (1848) *The Communist Manifesto*. http://www.wsu.edu:8080/~wldciv/world_civ_reader/world_ civ_reader_2/marx.html.

Ong, W. J. (2004) *Orality and Literacy: The Technologizing of the Word*. Routledge: New York.

Pietz, W. (1993). "Fetishism and Materialism". In *Fetishism as Cultural Discourse*. Ed. E. Apter and W. Pietz. New York: Cornell University Press.

Schmitt, C. (2008) *Political Theology II: The Myth of the Closure of any Political Theology*. Trans. Michael Hoelzl and Graham Ward. Cambridge: Polity.

—(2005) *Political Theology: Four Chapters on the Concept of Sovereignty*. Chicago: University of Chicago Press.

—(1985) *Political Theology: Four Chapters on the Concept of Sovereignty* [1934]. Trans. George Schwab, Cambridge, MA: MIT Press.

Scholem, G. G. (ed.) (1992) *The Correspondence of Walter Benjamin and Gershom Scholem, 1932–1940*. Trans. Gary Smith and Andre LeFevre. Cambridge, MA: Harvard University Press.

—(1981) *Walter Benjamin: The Story of a Friendship*. Trans. Harry Zohn. New York: Schocken.

Stroumsa, G. (2005) "Moses the Lawgiver and the Idea of Civil Religion in Patristic Thought". In *Teologie politiche: Modelli a confronto*. Ed. Giovanni Filoramo. Brescia: Morcelliana.

Swift, J. (1712) "A Proposal for Correcting, Improving, and Ascertaining the English Tongue". University of Adelaide ebooks, http://ebooks.adelaide.edu.au/s/swift/jonathan/s97p/.

Walser, R. (2001) *Selected Stories*. Trans. Christopher Middleton et al. New York: New York Review of Books.

Wells, R. A. (1973) *Dictionaries and the Authoritarian Tradition*. The Hague: Mouton.

Winchester, S. (1998) *The Surgeon of Crowthorne: A Tale of Murder, Madness and the Love of Words*. New York: Viking.

Zartaloudis T. (2010) *Giorgio Agamben: Power, Law and the Uses of Criticism*. London: Routledge/Cavendish.

FURTHER READING ON AGAMBEN

This list is not to be taken as comprehensive; the secondary work on Agamben is voluminous and expanding rapidly.

Monographs

De la Durantaye, Leland. *Giorgio Agamben: A Critical Introduction*. Stanford: Stanford University Press, 2009.

Mills, Catherine. *The Philosophy of Agamben*. Stocksfield: Acumen, 2008.

Murray, Alex. *Giorgio Agamben*. London: Routledge, 2010.

Watkin, William. *The Literary Agamben: Adventures in Logopoiesis*. London: Continuum, 2010.

Zartaloudis, Thanos. *Giorgio Agamben: Power, Law and the Uses of Criticism*. London: Routledge/Cavendish, 2010.

Journal Issues (listed in date order)

Paragraph, vol. 25, no. 2, July 2002. Ed. Brian Dillon. Features articles by Cesare Casarino, Josh Cohen, Thomas Docherty, Robert Eaglestone, Marc Froment-Meurice and Daniel Heller-Roazen.

Contretemps, vol. 5, 2004. Features Agamben's essay, "Friendship", and articles by Paolo Bartoloni, Mitchell Dean, Stefano Franchi, Catherine Mills and Brett Neilson. http://www.usyd.edu.au/contretemps/contretemps5.html.

"The Agamben Effect", *South Atlantic Quarterly*, vol. 107, no. 1, 2008. Ed. Alison Ross. Features articles by Andrew Benjamin, Claire Colebrook, Jean-Philippe Deranty, Penelope Deutscher, Eleanor Kaufman, Adrian Mackenzie, Catherine Mills, Alison Ross, Lee Spinks, Ewa Płonowska Ziarek and Krzysztof Ziarek.

Law and Critique, vol. 20, no. 3, 2009. Special issue, "Giorgio Agamben: Law and Thought". Ed. Thanos Zartaloudis and Alex Murray. Features Agamben's essay, "Philosophical Archaeology", and articles by Arne De Boever, Alice Lagaay and Juliane Schiffers, Robert Eaglestone, Alysia E. Garrison, Daniel McLoughlin, Alastair Morgan, Anton Schütz and Jessica Whyte.

Theory and Event, vol. 13, no. 1, 2010. Features a symposium on Agamben, ed. Richard Bailey, Daniel McLoughlin and Jessica Whyte. Features Agamben's "Introductory Note on the Concept of Democracy" and articles by Justin Clemens, Daniel McLoughlin, Brett Neilson, Nina Power, Jessica Whyte and Ewa Płonowska Ziarek.

Edited Collections (listed in date order)

Politics, Metaphysics, and Death: Essays on Giorgio Agamben's Homo Sacer. Ed. Andrew Norris. Durham, NC: Duke University Press, 2005. Features Agamben's essay, "The State of Exception", and articles by Andrew Benjamin, Peter Fitzpatrick, Anselm Haverkamp, Paul Hegarty, Andreas Kalyvas, Rainer Maria Kiesow, Catherine Mills, Andrew Norris, Adam Thurschwell, Erik Vogt and Thomas Carl Wall.

Giorgio Agamben: Sovereignty and Life. Ed. Matthew Calarco and Steven De Caroli. Stanford: Stanford University Press, 2007. Features Agamben's essay, "The Work of Man", and essays by Matthew Calarco, Steven De Caroli, William E. Connoly, Jenny Edkins, Bruno Gulli, Dominick LaCapra, Ernesto Laclau, Catherine Mills, Antonio Negri, Paul Patton and William Rasch.

The Work of Giorgio Agamben: Law, Literature, Life. Ed. Justin Clemens, Nicholas Heron and Alex Murray. Edinburgh: Edinburgh University Press, 2008. Features Agamben's essay, "K", and essays by Justin Clemens, Arne De Boever, Alexander García Düttmann, Barbara Formis, Nicholas Heron, Deborah Levitt, Alex Murray, Anton Schütz, Jessica Whyte, Julian Wolfreys and Thanos Zartaloudis.

Articles and Book chapters not in edited collections/special issues

Attell, Kevin, "An Esoteric Dossier: Agamben and Derrida Read Saussure", *ELH*, vol. 76, no. 4, Winter 2009.

Bartoloni, Paolo, "Renunciation: Heidegger, Agamben, Blanchot, Vattimo", *Comparative Critical Studies*, vol. 6, no. 1, 2009.

— "The Threshold and the Topos of the Remnant: Giorgio Agamben", *Angelaki*, vol. 13, no. 1, April 2008.

— "The Paradox of Translation via Benjamin and Agamben", *CLCWeb*, 6.2, June 2004.

Bernstein, J. M., "Bare Life: Bearing Witness: Auschwitz and the Pornography of Horror", in *Parallax*, vol. 10, no. 1, 2004.

Bos, René ten, "Giorgio Agamben and the Community Without Identity", *Sociological Review*, vol. 53, no. 1, 2005.

De Caroli, Steven, "Visibility and History: Giorgio Agamben and the Exemplary", *Philosophy Today*, vol. 45, no. 5, 2001.

Deranty, Jean-Philippe, "Agamben's Challenge to Normative Theories of Modern Rights", *Borderlands*, vol. 3, no. 1, 2004. http://www.borderlandsjournal.adelaide.edu.au/Vol.3no1_deranty_agamben schall.htm.

Düttmann, Alexander García, "Never Before, Always Already: Notes on Agamben and the Category of Relation", *Angelaki*, vol. 6, no. 3, December 2001.

Ek, Richard (ed.), "Giorgio Agamben and the Spatialities of the Camp", *Swedish Society for Anthropology and Geography Journal Compilation*, 2006, vol. 88, no. 4.

Heins, Volker, "Giorgio Agamben and the Current State of Affairs in Humanitarian Law and Human Rights Policy", *German Law Journal*, vol. 6, no. 5, 2005.

Heller-Roazen, Daniel, "Introduction". In Giorgio Agamben, *Potentialities*. Ed. Daniel Heller-Roazen. Stanford: Stanford University Press, 1999.

Johns, Fleur, "Guantánamo Bay and the Annihilation of the Exception", *European Journal of International Law*, vol. 14, no. 4, 2005.

Kalyvas, Andreas, "The Sovereign Weaver". In *Politics, Metaphysics and Death: Essays on Giorgio Agamben's* Homo Sacer. Ed. Andrew Norris. Durham, NC: Duke University Press, 2005.

Kisner, Wendell, "Agamben, Hegel and the State of Exception", *Cosmos and History: The Journal of Natural and Social Philosophy*, vol. 3, nos 2–3, 2007.

Marion, Esther, "The Nazi Genocide and the Writing of the Holocaust Aporia: Ethics and Remnants of Auschwitz", *MLN*, vol. 121, no. 4, 2006.

Neilson, Brett, "Cultural Studies and Giorgio Agamben", *New Cultural Studies: Adventures in Theory*. Ed. Gary Hall and Clare Birchall. Edinburgh: Edinburgh University Press, 2006.

Prozorov, Sergei, "Why Giorgio Agamben is an Optimist", *Philosophy and Social Criticism*, vol. 36, no. 7, 2010.

— "The Appropriation of Abandonment: Giorgio Agamben on the State of Nature and the Political", *Continental Philosophy Review*, vol. 42, no. 3, 2009.

— "Giorgio Agamben and the End of History: Inoperative Praxis and the Interruption of the Dialectic", *European Journal of Social Theory*, vol. 12, no. 4, 2009.

Schütz, Anton, "Thinking the Law With and Against Luhmann, Legendre and Agamben", *Law and Critique*, vol. 11, 2000.

Sharpe, Matthew, "'Thinking of the Extreme Situation . . . '. On the New Anti-Terrorism Laws, or Against a Recent (Theoretical and Legal) Return to Carl Schmitt", *Australian Feminist Law Journal*, vol. 24, 2006.

Sinnerbrink, Robert, "From *Machenschaft* to Biopolitics: A Genealogical Critique of Biopower", *Critical Horizons*, vol. 6, no. 1, 2005.

Thurschwell, Adam, "Spectres of Nietzsche: Potential Futures for the Concept of the Political in Agamben and Derrida". www.law.csuohio. edu/faculty/thurschwell/nietzsche.pdf.

Watkin, William, "The Idea of Prose in Contemporary Poetry: Lyn Hejinian's My Life Project and the Work of Giorgio Agamben", *Textual Practice*, forthcoming 2011.

— "Projective Recursion: The Structure of Ron Silliman's Tjanting", *Jacket*, vol. 39, 2010.

— "The Materialization of Prose: Poiesis versus Dianoia in the work of Godzich & Kittay, Schklovsky, Silliman and Agamben", *Paragraph*, vol. 31, no. 3, 2008, pp. 344–64.

— "'Though We Keep Company with Cats and Dogs': Onomatopoeia, Glossolalia and Happiness in the work of Lyn Hejinian and Giorgio Agamben", *Jacket*, vol. 36, 2008.

Whyte, Jessica, "Particular Rights and Absolute Wrongs: Giorgio Agamben on Life and Politics", *Law and Critique*, vol. 20, 2009, pp. 147–61.

Zartaloudis, Thanos, "The Case of the Hypocritical", *Law and Critique*, vol. 16, 2005.

— "Without Negative Origins and Absolute Ends: A Jurisprudence of the Singular", *Law and Critique*, vol. 13, 2002.

Notes on Contributors

Mathew Abbott is a PhD candidate in Philosophy at the University of Sydney. His thesis is concerned with political ontology, particularly in relation to the philosophies of Heidegger and Agamben. His research interests include contemporary and twentieth-century European philosophy, aesthetics, philosophy and literature, and phenomenology.

Kevin Attell is Assistant Professor of English at Cornell University. He is the translator of Agamben's *The Open: Man and Animal* and *State of Exception*, and co-translator of *The Signature of All Things*.

Paolo Bartoloni is Established Professor of Italian at the National University of Ireland, Galway. He is the author of *On the Cultures of Exile, Translation, and Writing* (Purdue University Press, 2008) and *Interstitial Writing: Calvino, Caproni, Sereni, and Svevo* (Troubador, 2003). He has edited the volumes *Re-Claiming Diversity: Essays on Comparative Literature* (La Trobe University, 1996) and, together with Shane Kendal and Karen Lynch, *Intellectuals and Publics: Essays on Cultural Theory and Practice* (La Trobe University, 1997).

Justin Clemens has co-edited many books on contemporary European thinkers, such as *The Work of Giorgio Agamben* (Edinburgh University Press, 2008), *The Praxis of Alain Badiou* (Re.Press, 2006) and *Jacques Lacan and the Other Side of Psychoanalysis* (Duke, 2006). He teaches in the School of Culture and Communication at the University of Melbourne.

Claire Colebrook is Professor of English at Pennsylvania State University. She is the author of many books, including *Irony: The New Critical Idiom* (Routledge, 2003), *Gender* (Palgrave, 2004), *Deleuze: A Guide for the Perplexed* (Continuum, 2006), *Milton, Evil and Literary History* (Continuum, 2008) and *Deleuze and the Meaning of Life* (Continuum, 2009).

Arne De Boever did his doctoral studies at Columbia University in New York and teaches American Studies in the School of Critical Studies and the MA Program in Aesthetics and Politics at the California Institute of the Arts. He has published articles on literature, film and critical theory, and is one of the editors of *Parrhesia: A Journal of Critical Philosophy*. His current research focuses on biopolitics and the novel.

Steven DeCaroli is Associate Professor of Philosophy at Goucher College in Baltimore. He has published numerous articles and book chapters on political philosophy and philosophical aesthetics, and is the co-editor, with Matthew Calarco, of *Giorgio Agamben: Sovereignty and Life* (Stanford University Press, 2007).

Alysia Garrison is a PhD candidate in English at the University of California, Davis. Her dissertation is a study of colonialism and modernity in the history of the novel. She has published articles on the work of Giorgio Agamben in *Law and Critique* (2009) and on the novel trilogy of Samuel Beckett in *Samuel Beckett: History, Memory, Archive* (Palgrave, 2009).

Nicholas Heron is a doctoral candidate in the School of Culture and Communication at the University of Melbourne. He is the editor, together with Justin Clemens and Alex Murray, of *The Work of Giorgio Agamben: Law, Literature, Life* (Edinburgh, 2008).

Deborah Levitt is Assistant Professor of Culture and Media Studies at Eugene Lang College, The New School. Recent publications include essays in *The Work of Giorgio Agamben: Law, Literature, Life* (Edinburgh University Press, 2008), *The Year's Work in Critical and Cultural Theory* (Oxford University Press, forthcoming 2010) and *Inflexions* (forthcoming 2011). She is also completing a book manuscript entitled *The Animatic Apparatus: Media, Biopolitics, Spectral Life*.

Jason Maxwell is a PhD student at the Pennsylvania State University, whose research focuses on the intersections between theory and rhetoric. He is currently at work with Claire Colebrook on an introductory volume on Agamben.

Daniel McLoughlin is a doctoral candidate in Philosophy at the University of New South Wales, working on the political philosophy of Giorgio Agamben. He has written on problems in Agamben's work, including nihilism, the relationship between law and language, and the sacred for *Law and Critique* and *Theory and Event*. He has also published on Carl Schmitt, modernity and crisis for the *Australian Feminist*

Law Journal. He is co-editor of a symposium on *Homo Sacer* for *Theory and Event* entitled "Form-of-Life: Giorgio Agamben, Ontology and Politics".

Catherine Mills is Sesqui Lecturer in Bioethics at the University of Sydney. Her main research interests lie in the areas of biopolitics, especially the work of Foucault and Agamben, and the ethics and politics of human reproduction. She is particularly interested in ideas of subjectivity, normalcy and responsibility. She has previously published *The Philosophy of Agamben* (Acumen, 2008) and is currently completing a manuscript on reproductive ethics. She has also published numerous articles in feminist theory, bioethics and political theory.

Claudio Minca is currently Professor and Head of the Socio-Spatial Analysis chair group at Wageningen University and Professor of Geography at Royal Holloway, University of London. He has written widely on geographical theory, tourism and travel, and biopolitics. His most recent books are *Travels in Paradox* (Rowman & Littlefield, 2006, with Tim Oakes), *Social Capital and Urban Networks of Trust* (Ashgate, 2009, with Jouni Hakli) and *Real Tourism* (Routledge, 2011, with Tim Oakes).

Yoni Molad is an independent scholar and has taught across the social sciences in various Australian universities. His research focuses on intersections between philosophy and political economy. He is currently working on a critical theory of entrepreneurialism.

Alex Murray is a Lecturer in Twentieth-Century Literature at the University of Exeter. He is the author of *Giorgio Agamben* (Routledge, 2010) and *Recalling London* (Continuum, 2007). With Justin Clemens and Nick Heron he edited *The Work of Giorgio Agamben: Law, Literature, Life* (Edinburgh 2008) and, with Philip Tew, *The Modernism Handbook* (Continuum, 2009).

Connal Parsley teaches Critical Jurisprudence and Ethics in the Melbourne Law School, University of Melbourne. He is currently completing a doctoral thesis which examines the nexus between concepts of image and law in the work of Giorgio Agamben.

Sergei Prozorov is Academy of Finland Research Fellow at the Department of Political and Economic Studies, University of Helsinki. He is the author of four monographs, the most recent being *The Ethics* *of Postcommunism* (Palgrave, 2009). He has also published articles on political philosophy and international relations in *Philosophy and Social Criticism, Continental Philosophy Review, Political Geography, Review of International Studies, European Journal of Social Theory, International Theory* and other journals.

Carlo Salzani is Adjunct Research Associate in the Centre for Comparative Literature and Cultural Studies at Monash University, and Alexander von Humboldt Postdoctoral Research Fellow at the Rheinische Friedrich-Wilhelms-Universität Bonn. He has published *Constellations of Reading: Walter Benjamin in Figures of Actuality* (Peter Lang, 2009) and *Crisi e possibilità: Robert Musil e il tramonto dell'Occidente* (Peter Lang, 2010), and has edited, with Barbara Dalle Pezze, *Essays on Boredom and Modernity* (Rodopi, 2009).

Andrew Schaap is a Lecturer in Politics at the University of Exeter. He is author of *Political Reconciliation* (Routledge, 2005) and editor of *Law and Agonistic Politics* (Ashgate, 2009). He is currently writing a book on *Human Rights and the Political* (Glasshouse, forthcoming).

Anton Schütz is a Senior Lecturer in Law at Birkbeck College, University of London. He has published widely in the fields of continental philosophy, jurisprudence, the history of religion and secularisation, and the evolution of scientific methodology.

Robert Sinnerbrink is Lecturer in Philosophy at Macquarie University, Sydney. He is the author of *New Philosophies of Film: Thinking Images* (Continuum, 2011) and *Understanding Hegelianism* (Acumen, 2007); and co-editor of *Critique Today* (Brill, 2006) and *Work, Recognition, Politics: New Directions in French Critical Theory* (Brill, 2007). He has published numerous articles on contemporary European philosophy, critical theory, aesthetics, and philosophy of film, including studies of the relations between Agamben, Heidegger, Derrida and Benjamin.

William Watkin is Professor of Contemporary Literature and Philosophy at Brunel University, West London. He is the author of *In the Process of Poetry: The New York School and the Avant-Garde* (Bucknell, 2001), *On Mourning: Theories of Loss in Modern Literature* (Edinburgh University Press, 2004) and *The Literary Agamben: Adventures in Logopoiesis* (Continuum, 2010). He has just completed his fourth monograph, *Agamben and the Aesthetics of Indifference*.

Jessica Whyte completed her doctorate on the political thought of Giorgio Agamben in the Centre for Comparative Literature and Cultural Studies, Monash University, in 2010. She has published articles on Giorgio Agamben, Jacques Rancière, Walter Benjamin, Immigration Control and Guantanamo Bay in *Theory and Event*, *Law and Critique*, *Australian Feminist Law Journal*, *Arena Journal*, *Conflitti Globali* and *Ephemera*, and has published chapters in the collections *The Work of Giorgio Agamben: Law, Literature, Life* (Edinburgh University Press, 2008) and *Trauma, History, Philosophy* (CSP, 2008). She is a co-editor of the *Theory and Event* Symposium, "Form of Life: Giorgio Agamben, Ontology, Politics" (2010).

Thanos Zartaloudis is Lecturer in Law at Birkbeck College, University of London. He is the author of *Giorgio Agamben: Power, Law and the Uses of Criticism* (Routledge/Cavendish, 2010) and has published widely on continental philosophy and law. He is also the Greek translator of Agamben's *Coming Community*.